Tourism and African development

African Studies Centre
Research Series
14/1999

Tourism and African development

Change and challenge of tourism in Kenya

Isaac Sindiga

Routledge
Taylor & Francis Group

LONDON AND NEW YORK

First published 1999 by Ashgate Publishing

Reissued 2018 by Routledge
2 Park Square, Milton Park, Abingdon, Oxon, OX14 4RN
52 Vanderbilt Avenue, New York, NY 10017

Routledge is an imprint of the Taylor & Francis Group, an informa business

Copyright © African Studies Centre, Leiden, 1999

All rights reserved. No part of this book may be reprinted or reproduced or utilised in any form or by any electronic, mechanical, or other means, now known or hereafter invented, including photocopying and recording, or in any information storage or retrieval system, without permission in writing from the publishers.

Notice:
Product or corporate names may be trademarks or registered trademarks, and are used only for identification and explanation without intent to infringe.

Publisher's Note
The publisher has gone to great lengths to ensure the quality of this reprint but points out that some imperfections in the original copies may be apparent.

Disclaimer
The publisher has made every effort to trace copyright holders and welcomes correspondence from those they have been unable to contact.

A Library of Congress record exists under LC control number: **362969**

Cover photo: Samburu girl, Kenya (photo: Dick Foeken)

ISBN 13: 978-1-138-36526-1 (hbk)
ISBN 13: 978-1-138-36527-8 (pbk)
ISBN 13: 978-0-429-43082-4 (ebk)

Printed in the United Kingdom
by Henry Ling Limited

Preface

Before the publication of this book the shocking news of Isaac Sindiga's sudden death in May 1999 reached us at the African Studies Centre. He stayed at the Centre as a visiting fellow during the first half of 1997. At his arrival he was the Head of the Department of Tourism at Moi University in Eldoret, Kenya. When he left, he had meanwhile been promoted to the function of Principal at Kisii Campus, Egerton University. During his stay at the Centre, we had learned to know him as a very friendly person, as a real gentleman, as a man of great wisdom and a broad interest, and last but not least as a devoted and very productive scholar.

As far as the latter is concerned, the main activity during his stay concerned the writing of the first draft of this book. The book analyses the contribution of tourism to African development, using Kenya as a country case. It weaves together ideas gleaned from a myriad of documentary sources. The study also forms a synthesis of African field experience, personal observations and many years' participation in tourism research and education. Isaac Sindiga also gave two seminars at the Centre. At the first, the framework for his study on tourism and African development was discussed. The second was entitled The Maasai Enigma and the Construction of Tourist Images. Finally, during the last month of his stay, he wrote the chapter on Tourism for the Kenya Coast Handbook.

It is tragic and hard to grasp that he has never seen the main product of his work in Leiden.

Dick Foeken, July 1999

Contents

List of Tables *ix*
List of Figures *x*
List of Boxes *x*
List of Appendices *x*
Abbreviations and acronyms *xi*
Foreword *xiv*

1. **International tourism and Africa** *1*
   Patterns of global tourism *2*
   Patterns of tourism in Africa *3*
   Western culture and tourism *8*
   Tourism's externalities *8*
   The concept of tourism *9*
   Tourism and recreation *11*
   Types of tourism and tourists *11*
   Conceptual and methodological considerations *14*
   Choice of Kenya as a country case *16*
   Organization *17*

2. **Tourism and development in Africa** *19*
   Africa's development crisis *19*
   Implications of shifting development paradigms to tourism *21*
   Tourism and African development *23*
   Tourism and regional development *31*
   Effects of tourism development without planning *32*
   Summary and conclusion *33*

3. **Kenya's biophysical and social environment** *35*
   Location *35*
   Biophysical environment *37*
   Government and history *40*
   Population *46*
   Economic situation *49*
   Social situation *51*
   Infrastructure development *51*
   Summary and conclusion *57*

4. Tourism in Kenya 59
Basic characteristics *59*
Development of tourism *68*
Management of tourism-led conservation *74*
Tourism and the economy *76*
Summary and conclusion *84*

5. The structure of Kenya's tourism industry 86
Investment in the tourism industry *87*
Tourism promotion and marketing *89*
Structure and ownership of tourism enterprises *92*
Summary and conclusion *99*

6. Change and challenge of unplanned tourism development 101
Critical issues in Kenya's tourism *102*
Breakdown of the infrastructure *103*
Environmental change *104*
Wildlife-human conflicts *105*
Socio-cultural changes *112*
Uneven distribution of tourism benefits *117*
Competitiveness *117*
Domestic tourism *119*
Regional development *123*
Political violence *123*
Summary and conclusion *124*

7. Alternative tourism and sustainable development 126
Definitions *127*
Interest in ecotourism *128*
Ecotourism in Kenya *131*
Local communities and ecotourism in Kenya *136*
Incentives for conservation *140*
Community initiatives in wildlife-based tourism *142*
Framework for community-based tourism development *143*
Summary and conclusion *145*

8. Regional cooperation in tourism 146
Basis for regional cooperation in tourism *146*
Regional cooperation in Africa *149*
Examples of regional cooperation *150*
Regional cooperation in tourism in East Africa *153*
Prospects for regional cooperation *158*
Intra-Africa tourism *159*
Summary and conclusion *161*

9. Tourism and African development: Conclusion 162

Appendices *167*

References *199*

List of tables

1.1	International tourist arrivals and receipts worldwide, 1988-1997	2
1.2	International tourist arrivals and percentage share by region, 1988-1997	4
1.3	International tourism receipts, percentage share by region and percentage change, 1988-1997	5
1.4	Tourism trends in Africa by sub-regions, 1996-1997	7
1.5	Leading tourism destinations in Africa by international arrivals, 1996	7
1.6	Frequency of types of tourists and their adaptations to local norms	13
2.1	Changing development paradigms and implications for tourism, 1960-1965	24
2.2	Estimates of jobs per hotel bed	29
3.1	Kenya's major ethnic groups	48
3.2	Kenya's population characteristics	48
3.3	Number of urban centres by size of population, 1948-1989	49
3.4	Kenya's sectoral shares in the real gross domestic product, 1964-1995	50
3.5	Kenya: Sources of employment and employment growth	50
3.6	Earnings from road and rail traffic, 1989-1993	54
4.1	Targets for Kenya's tourism development, 1997-2001	61
4.2	Kenya tourism trends, selected years 1972-1997	62
4.3	Tourist attractions in Kenya	63
4.4	Hotel bed-nights occupied by country of residence, 1997	64
4.5	Number of visitors to national parks and game reserves, 1990-1997	65
4.6	Departing visitors by country of residence and purpose of visit, 1996-1997	66
4.7	Tourism's contribution to Kenya's total export earnings	77
4.8	Average expenditure of international tourists to Kenya	78
4.9	Direct employment in tourism in Kenya	81
5.1	KTDC investments and loans as at 30 June 1994	90
5.2	KTDC commercial fund loan from inception up to 31.03.93 by province	91
5.3	Number of beds of classified hotels and lodges by tourism region	94
5.4	Distribution of tour operators by region, 1997	96
6.1	Problem wild animals in Kenya by district	107
6.2	Hotel bed-nights occupied by Kenyan residents, by region, 1995-97	121
8.1	East-African tourism, international arrivals and receipts	156
8.2	Origin of tourists to Africa, 1995	160
8.3	Origin of tourist for selected African countries, 1995	160
A.5.1	Tourism courses at Kenya Utalii College	181

List of figures

2.1 Leakages from gross receipts from international tourism *28*
3.1 Kenya reference map *36*
4.1 Kenya – Protected areas *71*
6.1 Kenya – Wildlife-human conflict *106*

List of boxes

3.1 Political history of independent Kenya: a chronology *42*
A.1 Moi University B.Sc. tourism degree objectives *178*

List of appendices

1. Sub-Saharan African countries: basic indicators *168*
2. Kenya population 1979 and 1989 by province and district *170*
3. Kenya national and marine parks and reserves *172*
4. Tourism education in Kenya *174*
5. Public sector organisations in Kenya's tourism industry *180*
6. Private sector bodies in Kenya tourism *183*
7. Criteria for hotel classification in Kenya *186*
8. Tourism and commercial sex in Kenya *189*

Abbreviations and acronyms

ACTS	African Centre for Technology Studies
AIDS	Acquired Immune Deficiency Syndrome
APP	African Peoples Party
ASC	African Safari Club
AT&H	African Tours and Hotels
AWF	African Wildlife Foundation
CAMPFIRE	Communal Area Management Programme for Indigenous Resources
CEEAC	Communauté Economique des Etats de l'Afrique Centrale (Economic Community of Central African States)
CEAO	Communauté Economique de l'Afrique de l'Ouest (West African Economic Community)
CIDA	Canadian International Development Agency
CLT	Catering Levy Trustees
COMESA	Common Market for Eastern and Southern Africa
CVTE	Continuing Vocational Training and Education
DFCK	Development Finance Company of Kenya
DTC	Domestic Tourism Council
EAA	Ecotourism Association of Australia
EAC	East African Community
EACSO	East African Common Services Organization
EAHC	East African High Commission
EAPA	East African Publicity Association
EASA	East African Safari Air
EATTA	East African Tourist Travel Association
ECCAS	Economic Community of Central African States
ECOWAS	Economic Community of West African States
EIU	Economist Intelligence Unit
ESK	Ecotourism Society of Kenya
GDP	Gross Domestic Product
GNP	Gross National Product
GLEC	Great Lakes Economic Community
GNP	Gross National Product
HIV	Human Immune Deficiency Virus
IBRD	International Bank for Reconstruction and Development
IGADD	Inter-governmental Authority on Drought and Development
ILO	International Labour Office

IUCN	International Union for the Conservation of Nature
JICA	Japan International Cooperation Agency
KA	Kenya Airways
KADU	Kenya African Democratic Union
KAHC	Kenya Association of Hotelkeepers and Caterers
KANU	Kenya African National Union
KATA	Kenya Association of Travel Agents
KATO	Kenya Association of Tour Operators
KBHA	Kenya Budget Hotels Association
KFA	Kenya Flamingo Airways
KHRC	Kenya Human Rights Commission
KLM	Koninklijke Luchtvaart Maatschappij (Royal Dutch Airlines)
KPU	Kenya Peoples Union
KTB	Kenya Tourism Board
KTDC	Kenya Tourist Development Corporation
KWS	Kenya Wildlife Service
LPA	Lagos Plan of Action
Ltd.	Limited
MCHA	Mombasa and Coast Hotelkeepers Association
MTW	Ministry of Tourism and Wildlife
MUDOT	Moi University Department of Tourism
MW	megawatt
NCCK	National Christian Council of Kenya
n.d.	no date
NEMU	National Election Monitoring Unit
PTA	Preferential Trade Area for Eastern and Southern Africa
P.A.	Public Address
SAPs	Structural Adjustment Programmes
STDs	Sexually transmitted diseases
SADCC	Southern African Development Coordination Conference
TCCP	Tsavo Community Conservation Project
TUI	Touristic Union International
UC	Kenya Utalii College
UDEAC	Union Douanière et Economique de l'Afrique Centrale (Central African Customs and Economic Union)
UK	United Kingdom
UNDP	United Nations Development Programme
UNECA	United Nations Economic Commission for Africa
UNESCO	United Nations Educational Scientific and Cultural Organization
USA	United States of America
USAID	United States Aid for International Development

UTC	United Touring Company
VFR	Visiting Friends and Relatives
WCI	Wildlife Conservation International
WCK	Wildlife Clubs of Kenya
WCMD	Wildlife Conservation and Management Department
WDF	Wildlife Development Fund
WTO	World Tourism Organization

Currency
K.Sh.	Kenya Shilling
K£	Kenya Pound (one pound = 20 shillings)
US$	United States dollar (one US$ = Kshs.60 at 1998 exchange rate)

Measures
km.	kilometre
sq. km.	square kilometre
m.	metre
sq. m.	square metre

Foreword

This book analyses the contribution of tourism to African development using the Kenya country case. Although tourism has made a significant contribution to the economies of various countries in terms of GDP, foreign exchange earnings, employment, government revenues, and regional development. It was not until the late 1980s that the service industry in general and tourism in particular was recognized as such. Indeed, tourism tends to be ignored both in development theory and international trade ostensibly because it does not produce goods.

Tourism development builds on existent overseas demand. At a time of serious economic decline in sub-Saharan Africa, tourism could provide substantial resources to kickstart and/or maintain the development process. Besides, tourism activity generates much change and challenge in the destination areas. Africa has not been spared the environmental, social and cultural impacts which are associated with tourism in general and mass tourism in particular. Such changes are both positive and negative; however, existing knowledge tends to be generalized. It is clear that understanding the nature of tourism impacts requires detailed data on typologies of tourists and tourism and guest-host interactions.

This study is a contribution to the debate on tourism and Third World development. Although there are many sceptics who consider tourism as fickle business overly dependent on politico-economic factors in geographically distant lands (Lea, 1981; 1993), any such charges should be informed by knowledge on what is taking place at the grassroots. This work weaves together ideas gleaned form a myriad documentary sources many of which are published in highly specialized international journals generally unavailable to policy makers, the social science community, regional planners, resource managers, and students of tourism in Africa. In addition, this study is a synthesis of African field experience, personal observations and many years' participation in tourism research and education. In fact, the idea of this study was triggered by the general lack of source materials which could be used to teach the new undergraduate tourism programme founded at Moi University, Kenya in the early 1990s.

Although my views on this subject have been stimulated by many contributions in the global tourism academy and beyond its disciplinary boundaries, I would like to acknowledge a number of individuals who have laboured for our better understanding of tourism in Kenya. Frank Mitchell (1970) is an economist who made and early contribution to the literature through his detailed study on the economic role of tourism in East Africa. While pointing to tourism's economic benefits, Mitchell drew attention to the complexity of calculating net gains from tourism. And so did Walter Elkan (1975) in his study of the economics of tourism in Kenya and Tanzania. In particular, Elkan pointed to the highly variable net benefits that could result from different tourism policies. Elkan cautioned against wide generalizations on the value of tourism. Joseph Ouma (1970) is a geographer whose monograph on the evolution of tourism in East Africa provides much detail on the history of tourism in Kenya and East Africa as a whole during the colonial period. Another early study was done by Vojislav Popovic (1972) who provided an outline picture of tourism in the entire Eastern Africa region during the 1960s. His work is concerned with documenting the status of tourism development in his chosen region by country. Philipp Bachmann (1988), another geographer, documented the role of tourism in development in Kenya in the early 1980s. His field focus is Malindi, the well known tourism destination at the Kenya coast. Rosemary Jommo (1987) studied the participation of indigenous people in Kenya's tourism economy. Her detailed analysis within the framework of the underdevelopment theory demonstrates the dominance of foreign capital and the marginalization of indigenous African entrepreneurs in tourism business. M.T. Sinclair (1990; 1992), a British economist, had the opportunity, by virtue of a World Bank consultancy, to study the structure, organization and management of Kenya's tourism industry. Her contribution to the subject adds useful insights and empirical data (see also Sinclair, Alizadeh and Onunga, 1992). Peter Dieke's (1991; 1994; 1995) work spurred my interest in tourism policy issues and the political economy of tourism in Africa. Peter's contribution to the development of the Department of Tourism at Moi University is very much appreciated. Daniel Nyeki's (1992) contribution is restricted to ecological material rather than tourism per se. His detailed catalogue of Kenya's protected areas and their ecosystems provides a handy source material on the subject. As early as 1984, G. Wesley Burnett's research and interest in tourism and national parks drew my attention to the problems of tourism and natural resource management in Africa. I am grateful to him for a long and productive association since the mid-1980s.

I would like to thank people and institutions in three continents for supporting me in various ways to allow this work to be executed. In the Netherlands, I am indebted to the African Studies Centre, Leiden for appointing me a visiting research fellow for the first half of 1997. Specifically, I wish to thank Dr. Gerti Hesseling, the Centre director for many kindnesses; Dr. Dick Foeken and his family for their support; Dr. Deborah Fahy Bryceson for allowing me into her home at the historic Dutch city of Delft on several occasions; and Joop Nijssen for making my transition between Africa and Europe quite smooth. Dr. Tjalling Dijkstra welcomed me into the Netherlands at Schiphol on that cold wintry day in early January 1997 and became a true friend indeed. Tjalling assisted me to tour and gaze at the city of Amsterdam and kept me informed of the Kenya news throughout my residence at Leiden. The same can be said about Marieke van Winden who showed me Leiden's culture at the Stadsgehoorzaal, guided me on a tour of the world class port of Rotterdam and assisted me in countless ways. The African Studies Centre staff attended my initial seminar where the framework for this study was formulated. I would like to thank the participants and in particular Dr. Laurens van der Laan for their comments and interest in the study.

Documentary resources were provided by the African Studies Centre library and I would like to thank Ella Verkaik-Steenvoorden and Sjaan van Marrewijk for accessing literature in the library and through the interlibrary loan facility. At Wageningen Agricultural University, Rene van der Duim arranged my use of the tourism literature as did Klaas Speelman at the Christelijke Hogeschool Noord Nederland, Leeuwarden.

I spent one week in Canada at the University of Guelph and used the library. Dr. Donald G. Reid hosted me during that period and we continue to have very productive collaboration in the tourism field.

In Kenya, Moi University granted me sabbatical leave so that this work may be done. Dr. John S. Akama relieved me of my duties as Head of the Department of Tourism. When I was appointed Principal, Kisii College Campus within Egerton University in May 1997, the Vice-Chancellor, Prof. J. C. Kiptoon allowed me to stay at Leiden for another five weeks so that an initial draft of this work could be completed.

A complete draft of this work which was done at Leiden was reviewed by Dr. Dick Foeken of the African Studies Centre and Prof. Marc Wuyts of the Institute of Social Studies at The Hague. Their constructive criticisms led to major revision of the work. They are, however, not responsible for the mistakes which remain in the final product.

This book was initially word processed by Nancy van Loenen, assisted by Mieke Zwart-Brouwer and Ria van Hal. I would like to thank them for the many hours they laboured so as to put order to my massive handwritten script. Subsequent work and computer assistance were provided by Jemimah Nyamweya, Joyce Ombego and Robert Omari Otieno at Kisii College Campus. I am much grateful for their patience and diligence in executing numerous tasks.

Finally, Mary Kanunah, wife and colleague, allowed me to spend six months in Europe to conduct research for this book in the face of complicated family responsibilities. I would like to thank her for her unselfish support, love and dedication. This contribution is for Mary.

Isaac Sindiga,
Kisii, Kenya.

1

International tourism and Africa

The intent of this study is to examine the contribution of tourism in African development using the example of Kenya. A number of activities are intertwined in the study as follows: (1) to assess the contribution of tourism in development; (2) to document the development of tourism in Kenya; (3) to examine the outcomes of international tourism on the environment and society in Kenya; (4) to examine the response of Kenyan communities to international tourism; and (5) to make recommendations for alternative tourism strategies with applicability to other African countries. The general goal of this study is to assess whether tourism is a viable development strategy for Africa.

By inquiring into the role of tourism in development it is not intended to narrow the discussion to reflect merely tourism's economic contribution to Africa. This is the fashion of most assessments — to touch only on the macro-economic characteristics; in a word, the business of tourism. Such studies focus on the transnational companies which do the tourism business and the national governments which invite them. Seldom are questions asked on how tourism affects social structures or contributes to development at the local level.

Development is not merely a rise in the per capita incomes. It subsumes "reduction of poverty and greater equity to progress in education, health and nutrition, and to the *protection of the environment*" (World Bank, 1991: 4). Only environmental protection through effective resource management strategies can assure sustainable development. Tourism within the context of African development must contribute towards the problem of poverty alleviation and the overall economic progress of the continent. Perhaps a mix of strategies including agricultural transformation, industrialization, and tourism development is required to mobilize sub-Saharan Africa's production forces by making optimal use of the existing natural resources. Carefully planned tourism development could provide crucial resources for Africa's economic transformation. In choosing to conduct this study therefore, I wish to emphasize that African tourism should have a developmental role in tune with the aspirations of the peoples of the continent.

This study takes advantage of the literature which has been accumulating over the years on the role of tourism in development. In doing this, I am acutely aware of Elkan's (1975) plea more than two decades ago that any assessment of the role of tourism should be eclectic and that each country case should be considered separately because "the balance of advantage is greatly dependent upon the policies pursued with regard to the particular form of hotel and tourist development" (p. 123). Yet, lessons from tourism development elsewhere in the world can be brought to bear on a particular case in order to see the common threads which run through them.

This chapter discusses the magnitude and patterns of global and African tourism. It then traces the basis of international tourism to modern western culture. This is the backdrop of examining the externalities of tourism. The second part of the chapter examines the concepts of tourism and recreation, provides a topology of tourism and tourists, and discusses the conceptual and methodological approaches to analysing tourism and development. This is followed by a justification of using Kenya as a country case study for tourism and African development. Ultimately, the chapter sketches the organization of the book. Overall this introductory chapter encapsulates the issues discussed in the rest of the study.

Patterns of global tourism

Tourism and travel are the world's largest industry in terms of the numbers of people participating, the amount of resources generated, and employment capacity. International tourist arrivals have been increasing steadily from 394 million people in 1988 to 458 million in 1990 to 518 million in 1993, 595 million in 1996 and 612 million in 1997 (Table 1.1). During the 1988-1997 decade, international tourist arrivals grew by an average rate of 5.4 percent.

Table 1.1
International tourist arrivals and receipts world-wide, 1988-1997
(millions of arrivals; receipts in thousands of millions and percentage change)

	1988	1989	1990	1991	1992	1993	1994	1995	1996	1997	Average 10-year growth
Arrivals (m)	394	426	458	463	502	518	549	563	595	612	
% annual growth	8.5	8.0	7.4	1.2	8.4	3.1	6.1	2.5	5.6	2.9	5.4
Receipts (US$ b)	204	221	268	277	313	321	353	401	434	443	
% annual growth	15.6	8.3	21.5	3.2	13.3	2.4	9.8	13.8	8.2	2.2	9.8

Source: WTO, Personal communication, June 1st, 1998.

Should the trends of the past decade persist, the WTO projects that global tourism will reach 700 million international arrivals by 2000 and 937 million by 2010. Similarly, the resources generated by tourism are considerable. In the mid-1990s, tourism accounted for more than 10 percent of the world total gross domestic product. International tourism receipts (excluding international transport) increased from US$ 204 billion in 1988, US$ 268 billion in 1990 and US$ 401 billion in 1995 to US$ 443 billion in 1997 (Table 1.1). The rate of growth of receipts from international tourism in the 1988-97 decade was much higher than that of the tourist arrivals (Table 1.1.). Indeed, tourism's receipts grew at a higher annual average rate over the 1980s (9.6%) than either exports of merchandise (5.5%) or commercial services (7.5%) (Dieke, 1998: 32). It is projected that receipts from tourism will increase to US$ 600 billion by the year 2000. In terms of global capital investments in infrastructure, facilities and equipment, and employment generation, tourism is a giant industry. One estimate indicates that one out of sixteen people in the world work in tourism (Richter, 1992). Without considering details as to the quality of employment, this figure points to the significance of tourism in the global economy.

The geographical patterns of world tourism show great differences both in international arrivals and receipts. Also, the regions that generate the greatest numbers of tourists are Europe, the Americas and Japan. Table 1.2 shows international tourist arrivals by region and year using the classification of the WTO. For the 10-year period represented by these data, Europe received 60 percent of the arrivals, followed by the Americas (20 percent), East Asia/Pacific (13 percent), Africa (3.5 percent), the Middle East (2 percent) and South Asia with 0.7 percent. The tourism receipts appear to follow a similar pattern (Table 1.3). As Table 1.3 indicates, Europe was the leading world tourism region with 52 percent of the receipts during the period, followed by the Americas (27 percent), and East Asia/Pacific with 16 percent. At the bottom of the ranking was Africa (2 percent), the Middle East (1.7 percent), and South Asia with only 0.9 percent of the receipts.

These aggregate figures provide the big picture about the patterns of tourism at the global scale. They do, however, conceal the relatively large differences within any one region. There are large variations and some countries are better endowed than others in tourism activity. Also, there is a large domestic tourism activity within individual countries especially in the developed world. The data for such internal travel which generates much revenue and employment are not reflected in this discussion.

Patterns of tourism in Africa

Africa's share of the world tourism market appears rather small for the geographical size of the continent and its population. International tourist arrivals increased from about 13 million in 1988 to 15 million in 1990, 19 million in 1993, 20 million in 1995 and 23 million in 1997 (Table 1.2). International tourism receipts (excluding international transport), which was US$ 5 billion in 1988, stagnated at that level until 1992 (6 billion)

Table 1.2
International tourist arrivals and percentage share by region, 1988-1997 (millions of arrivals)

Region	1988	1989	1990	1991	1992	1993	1994	1995	1996	1997	Average growth, 1988-1997
World	394	426	458	463	502	518	549	563	595	612	
% share	100.0	100.0	100.0	100.0	100.0	100.0	100.0	100.0	100.0	100.0	
Africa	13	14	15	16	18	19	19	20	22	23	3.5
% share	3.3	3.3	3.3	3.5	3.6	3.6	3.5	3.5	3.7	3.8	
America	83	87	94	97	104	104	106	110	117	119	20.1
% share	21.0	20.4	20.5	20.9	20.7	20.0	19.3	19.5	19.7	19.4	
East Asia/ Pacific	47	48	55	56	64	71	77	81	89	89	13.2
% share	11.9	11.3	12.0	12.1	12.7	13.7	14.0	14.4	15.0	14.5	
Europe	240	266	282	282	302	310	331	334	349	361	60.3
% share	61.0	62.4	61.6	60.9	60.2	59.8	60.3	59.3	58.6	59.0	
Middle East	8	9	9	8	11	11	13	14	14	15	2.2
% share	2.0	2.1	2.0	1.7	2.2	2.1	2.4	2.5	2.4	2.5	
South Asia	3	3	3	3	4	4	4	4	4	5	0.7
% share	0.8	0.7	0.7	0.6	0.8	0.8	0.7	0.7	0.7	0.8	

Source: WTO, Personal communication, June 1, 1998.

Table 1.3
International tourism receipts (excluding international transport), **percentage share by region and percentage change, 1988-1997**

Region	1988	1989	1990	1991	1992	1993	1994	1995	1996	1997
World (US$ billions)	204	221	268	277	313	321	353	401	434	443
% share	100.0	100.0	100.0	100.0	100.0	100.0	100.0	100.0	100.0	100.0
% annual growth	15.6	8.3	21.5	3.2	13.3	2.4	9.8	13.8	8.2	2.2
Africa (US$ b.)	5	5	5	5	6	6	7	7	8	9
% share	2.5	2.3	1.9	1.8	1.9	1.9	2.0	1.7	1.8	2.0
% annual growth	20.1	-1.7	18.0	-6.3	23.7	2.0	8.5	6.4	15.0	3.1
Americas (US$ b.)	51	60	70	78	85	91	95	103	113	120
% share	25.0	27.1	26.1	28.2	27.2	28.3	26.9	25.7	26.0	27.0
% annual growth	19.3	17.3	16.5	11.1	9.8	6.7	4.6	7.9	9.7	6.8
East Asia/Pacific (US$ b.)	30	34	39	40	47	53	63	74	81	83
% share	14.7	15.4	14.6	14.4	15.0	16.5	17.8	18.5	18.7	18.7
% annual growth	32.6	12.3	14.4	3.2	17.2	11.0	19.5	17.6	10.1	2.2
Europe (US$ b.)	111	115	147	148	167	163	178	207	220	218
% share	54.4	52.0	54.9	53.4	53.4	50.8	50.4	51.6	50.7	49.2
% annual growth	11.1	3.7	27.7	0.06	13.1	-2.4	9.6	15.8	6.4	-0.8
Middle East (US$ b.)	4	4	4	4	5	5	6	7	8	9
% share	2.0	1.8	1.5	1.4	1.6	1.6	1.7	1.7	1.8	2.0
% annual growth	-4.7	3.5	-2.4	-14.4	33.4	12.2	12.0	17.1	18.8	14.7
South Asia (US$ b.)	2	2	2	2	3	3	3	3	4	4
% share	1.0	0.9	0.7	0.7	1.0	0.9	0.8	0.7	1.1	0.9
% annual growth	1.6	6.3	2.4	14.9	19.0	-3.3	14.4	13.8	13.1	5.9

Source: WTO, Personal communication, June 1, 1998.

despite relative growth in the number of tourist arrivals (Tables 1.2 and 1.3). The receipts increased slowly to US$ 7 billion in 1994 and only US$ 9 billion in 1997 (Table 1.3). When these figures are viewed within the perspective of world tourism in general, they are comparatively low. The arrivals as a proportion of the world total made up only 2.5 percent in 1980, 2.9 percent in 1985, 3.3 percent in 1990, 3.6 percent in 1993 and 3.8 percent in 1997 (Table 1.2; Dieke, 1995). Although the average growth of tourist arrivals in Africa for the period 1988-1997 was 3.5 percent, the average earnings grew much more slowly (Table 1.3). In fact, there was relative decline in receipts from 1985 to the late 1990s. Africa's share of receipts from international tourism declined from 2.5 percent in 1980, to 2.2 percent in 1985 to 2 percent in 1990, 1.9 percent in 1993 and 1.8 percent in 1996 (Table 1.3; Dieke, 1995). In 1997, the figure was just under 2 percent. These figures show a priori that the absolute numbers of tourist arrivals are not necessarily reflected in foreign exchange earnings. Perhaps many of the tourists to Africa spend little money for reasons which are discussed in Chapter 2. Overall these figures show that Africa as a region for world tourism is rather poorly developed and that the impact of tourism in development is relatively small.

Within Africa, there is great variation in terms of the numbers of tourist arrivals and foreign exchange earnings (Table 1.4). Most tourists go to North Africa, southern Africa and eastern Africa. For example, of the 23 million international tourist arrivals in 1997, 34.7 percent went to North Africa[1], 30.5 percent to South Africa[2], 23.6 percent to eastern Africa, 9.8 percent to western Africa and 1.4 percent to middle Africa. Table 1.4 shows that tourist arrivals declined in 1997 over the previous year for middle and western Africa subregions. In the same period receipts declined for middle Africa and North Africa. The latter may have lost its market share to southern Africa.

Over the African continent, tourism appears to be well developed in only a few countries. These are Tunisia, South Africa, Morocco, Zimbabwe, Kenya, Botswana, Mauritius and Namibia (Table 1.5). Indeed, the sub-regions of the continent are at varying levels of tourism development. As Dieke (1997) notes, North Africa is a mature destination which is close to the European market. The sub-Saharan Africa sub-region, though dynamic, suffers from lack of joint and coherent promotion and marketing policies (Dieke, 1997).

---

[1] Inexplicably, the WTO excludes Egypt and Libya from the North Africa tourism sub-region. These figures therefore do not reflect tourism activity in those two countries, both of which are included in the Middle East.

[2] South Africa should rightly be called southern Africa to reflect the geographical location but the WTO does not appear to follow that convention. The countries represented are Botswana, Lesotho, Namibia, South Africa, and Swaziland. It may be noted also that the majority of the tourists in southern Africa appear to represent movements within the region rather than from outside the African continent. Such tourists appear to spend less money than those from outside Africa. This is probably accounting for the relatively low receipts for South Africa, Zimbabwe and Botswana in relation to the numbers of arrivals as shown on Table 1.5. See Chapter 8 for an analysis of these trends.

Table 1.4
Tourism trends in Africa by sub-regions, 1996-1997

Sub-region	Tourist arrivals (000s) 1997	% change over 1996	Tourism receipts (US$ million) 1997	% change 1996	% of Total Africa 1996	% of Total Africa 1997
Eastern	5,491	7.1	2,243	0.2	26.8	26.0
Middle	328	-3.5	78	-7.1	1.0	0.9
North	8,077	11.4	2,768	-3.4	34.3	32.1
South	7,102	9.6	2,745	12.7	29.2	31.9
Western	2,272	-3.5	778	6.9	8.7	9.0

Countries of the African Tourism Region
Eastern Africa: Burundi, Comoros, Djibouti, Ethiopia, Kenya, Madagascar, Malawi, Mauritius, Reunion, Rwanda, Seychelles, Somalia, Tanzania, Uganda, Zambia and Zimbabwe
Middle Africa: Angola, Cameroon, Central African Republic, Chad, Congo (Brazzaville), Congo (Kinshasa), Gabon, and Sao Tome and Principe
North Africa: Algeria, Morocco, Sudan, Tunisia (The WTO counts Egypt and Libya in Middle East)
South Africa: Botswana, Lesotho, Namibia, South Africa and Swaziland
Western Africa: Benin, Burkina Faso, Cape Verde, Cote d'Ivoire, The Gambia, Ghana, Guinea, Mali, Niger, Nigeria, Senegal, Sierra Leone and Togo

Source: WTO, Personal communication, June 1, 1998

Table 1.5
Leading tourism destinations in Africa by international arrivals, 1996

	Arrivals (thousands)	Receipts (US$ million)
South Africa	4640	1738
Tunisia	3885	1436
Morocco	2693	1292
Zimbabwe	1743	219
Kenya	907	493
Botswana	660	178
Mauritius	435	473
Namibia	405	265
Reunion	339	---
Tanzania	326	322

Source: WTO, Personal communication, 2 April 1997

In general, there are relatively fewer tourists in West Africa where the major attractions are the cultural heritage of the area especially for African-Americans, and medieval empires (Williams, 1976). The spectacular scenery such as the East African Rift Valley system, volcanic mountains and national parks are missing in West Africa.

Having sketched the trends in global and African tourism, I now turn to a discussion on the origins of international tourism. This is followed by an analysis of the impacts of tourism and the conceptual foundations of tourism.

Western culture and tourism

Tourism is rooted in modern Western culture. In Western Europe and North America, there is the widespread perception that tourism is essential to life; that "getting away" is a symbol of socio-economic status, and that it is healthy (Shaw and Williams, 1994). Indeed,

> A majority of Americans and Europeans see life as properly consisting of alternations of these two modes of existence: living at home and working for longish periods followed by taking vacations away from home for shorter periods (Graburn, 1977: 18).

This perception has led to the desire of the citizens of those countries to aspire to go for holidays at least once a year. This has been encouraged not only by the increase in incomes, mobility and leisure time but also by the extraordinary transformation of society by automation and technology. People are able to work faster thereby leaving them with a large amount of discretionary time for leisure (Nelson and Butler, 1974; Pearce, 1989; Reid, 1995). Also, employers recognize that periodic getting away from work in pursuit of leisure and recreation activity enhances productivity. For this reason, some employers pay for holidays for some of their workers as part of their employment package. These benefits have popularized travel with the consequence that tourism has turned into mass tourism.

Most of the European, American and Canadian tourists travel within their own countries. Increasingly, developing countries are receiving the overspill from the tourism in developed countries. Africa is one of the destinations in this international tourism.

Tourism's externalities

International tourism has led to profound economic and socio-cultural impacts. These impacts or what has been termed tourism's externalities are particularly serious in Africa. Given these consequences, questions are increasingly being asked on whether international tourism is sustainable over the longer term.

Tourism's externalities may be positive or negative. On the positive side, these externalities bring attention to a place as a tourist attraction. In fact, attractions are at the very core of tourism. And these attractions are created on the basis of natural endowments (scenic landscapes, wildlife, coastal beaches etc.), historical significance, culture, arts, crafts, dance, and a myriad cultural attributes. Also, the fact that an attraction exists makes it possible for potential tourists to plan to visit at a later date; conversely, the place preserves their option to visit although they may never actually do so (Johnson and Thomas, 1992). But the attraction or resource must be carefully husbanded in order to maintain, enhance and preserve its integrity. Only this way will the attraction continue to meet visitor satisfaction, attract more visitors, and remain as a viable option for those who may visit in the future.

On the negative side, tourism does impose costs on others who may not be fully compensated by what tourists pay.

> The presence of such externalities means inter alia that, even in a competitive market, buyers of tourism services do not always pay a price that reflects the true cost of the provision of those services — because suppliers do not have to meet all the costs incurred by their activity — and that as a result "the market" generates a socially inefficient level of tourism activity (Johnson and Thomas, 1992: 3).

The effect of tourism's negative externalities is best indicated by the deterioration of both the physical and the human or socio-cultural environments (Dietvorst and Ashworth, 1995). Perhaps in no other area are tourism's externalities in Africa better exemplified than at the interface of tourism and the local people. Tourism may threaten the property rights of local communities (Chapter 6). Disputes on resource allocation have been reported between such communities, various stakeholders and the tourists themselves (Sindiga, 1995).

In Africa, wildlife-based tourism is conducted in exclusive conservation habitats or protected areas. Such habitats were carved out of areas used for farming by local communities thereby destabilizing traditional livelihood systems (Sindiga, 1984; Kiss, 1990). Consequently, wildlife — human conflicts over pastures and waters enclosed in protected areas have ensued (Chapter 6). It will be seen therefore that, at least in theory, the way property rights are allocated will greatly influence the distribution of incomes and losses from tourism (Johnson and Thomas, 1992).

Unless the effects of negative externalities are mitigated in a sensitive and creative way, the basis of tourism could be undermined. Throughout Africa, there are virtually no guidelines on the environmental impacts of tourism development. Many of the developers and operators in the industry (usually multinational corporations) are interested in maximizing incomes and enhancing their profit margins. They do this by taking advantage of weak government control of their activities. As a result, tourism generates little development among host communities. Worse, there appears to be little concern for sense of place despite advertisements about natural unspoilt environments but which hardly mention people.

The concept of tourism

Despite the frequent use of the term "tourism", it does not have a precise definition. The word means different things to different people (Morley, 1990). Jafar Jafari (1990) notes that different groups of people perceive tourism in disparate ways. To governments, tourism means economic activities, revenues, employment, per capita expenditure, and perhaps regional development. To industry, it means promotion, arrivals, departures, length of stay, receipts and so on. To religious groups, tourism evokes a sense of pilgrimage, spiritual search, universal brotherhood, unacceptable forms of tourism practices. To host destinations it may arouse the idea of intrusion, European tourists, British tourists, American tourists, Canadian tourists, Japanese tourists. And to the tourists themselves it means an escape from daily routines, indulgence in leisure pursuits, rest and relaxation, education, wilderness, experiencing other cultures and so on. Conservationists see tourism as a reason for preserving natural and cultural environments, as an important source of funding for conservation, reviving traditions of the past and promoting cultural events. To the academic community, tourism is a giant global industry which caters for millions of tourists every day. As such, research must be conducted on the industry's costs and benefits, its structure, form, stability, functioning and how it changes over time and the impacts of the phenomenon of tourism at local, regional, national and international levels (Jafari, 1990).

All these views show the many facets of tourism depending on who is looking at it. However, a scholar who is working on tourism must obtain an operational definition for his/her enterprise. Also, it is important to have a precise definition for the purpose of keeping statistics; and for estimating the size of the sector (Prentice, 1993).

Some authors see tourism as including all travel except commuting (Gunn, 1988) whereas others take tourism to be travelling away from home for leisure purposes. But in this latter case, there is no agreement on the physical distance that one must travel before qualifying to be called a tourist. It is now widely accepted that tourism includes all travel that involves a stay of at least one night but less than one year, away from home. Travel which is done within 24 hours is generally considered as an excursion. The purpose may be pleasure (holiday, culture, sports, visiting friends and relatives etc.), professional (meeting, business, religious function) or some other motive such as studies, health and so on (Inskeep, 1991). Yet, others take tourism to be simply "leisured mobility" undertaken by an individual (Smith, 1977). Tourism may also be defined by pointing out what it is not. Smith (1993), for example, notes that the following categories of people, entering another country do not qualify as tourists: those wanting to emigrate or seek employment, those visiting as diplomats or military personnel, refugees, nomads, border workers or those staying for more than a year. The rest are defined as tourists with the condition that they must stay for at least one night.

Whatever definition is adopted, it is clear that tourism comprises a number of things namely, travelling and visiting for leisure and even business. Also, tourism takes place only occasionally, during holiday or vacation; and, it involves travel over a considerable distance and/or time (Mitchell and Smith, 1989: 388). And as noted above, tourism is primarily travel for pleasure or leisure. It is therefore an alternate to work (Smith, 1977).

Tourism and recreation

Tourism is closely related to recreation. The essential distinction is that recreation can be done after work during the week and weekends; also, it frequently occurs close to a person's home (Mitchell and Smith, 1989). Recreation provides an opportunity for a person to recover from physical or mental fatigue (rest), to recover from tension (relax), and to recover from boredom (entertainment) (Pearce, 1989: 115, citing Leiper, 1984).

Recreation areas can be located close by or away from population centres. To visit places away from the centres of population requires travel and overnight accommodation or several days. Those areas located in urban or peri-urban areas include playgrounds, school grounds, swimming pools, theatres, drive-in cinemas, gymnasia and so on. On the other hand, national parks located at a distance from home offer numerous opportunities for tourism and recreation for example picnicking, camping, fishing, hiking, photographing, canoeing, backpacking and other activities (Nelson and Butler, 1974). Some have argued that tourists using a park seek its extrinsic facilities, whereas recreationists go for its intrinsic values (McKercher, 1996). But whether a person thinks that he or she is engaging in tourism or recreation is a question of attitude (McKercher, 1996). This is partly because tourism is an imprecise term. Recreation and tourism appear to "differ more in degree than in kind"; both activities are pursued for pleasure and both require planning, travel to the experience, participation in the activity itself, travel back home, and recall of the experience (Mitchell and Smith, 1989).

Types of tourism and tourists

Tourism

Tourism is very difficult to classify. No single typology can accommodate the many possible cases that exist in reality. But how is classification to proceed in view of the infinite possibilities for dichotomies? Tourism may be rural or national; nature-based or cultural. A classification could proceed along themes such as architectural tourism; theme park; sun-sand-sex; religious pilgrimage and so on. There indeed are many possibilities. For example a kind of religious tourism has developed in Harlem, New York in the United States. European tourists especially Swedes and Germans flock to African-American churches on Sunday mornings. They are attracted by the unique African-American way of worship in which gospel singing in the tradition of Negro spirituals of a past generation plays a prominent role. The tourists pay a fee and also donate money to the churches. This allows the churches to make extra income for their development projects.

Most studies focus on one or more of the following dimensions: characteristics of the tourist (income, lifestyle, education); characteristics of the tour (duration, number of countries or places visited); mode of organisation (individual or all-inclusive package); type of facilities used (mode of transport and type of accommodation); and motivation for the journey (for example visiting friends and relatives, business, holiday, conference) (de Kadt, 1979). Valene Smith (1977) has offered a typology of tourism which picks on any number of these dimensions. In addition, her categorization draws attention to the impact of tourism on society and environment in a host destination.

Smith's five types of tourism are as follows: ethnic, cultural, historical, environmental, and recreational. In *ethnic tourism*, the tourists visit native villages and watch dances and traditional ceremonies. They also purchase arts and crafts. The interest of the tourists is in the culture of indigenous people. However, the term ethnic tourism is now also used to refer to people who are visiting their original homelands or places of their ancestral origins (Inskeep, 1994: 20). This is especially so for overseas migrants who choose to visit their original homelands or those of their ancestors. For example, Dutch Canadians may pay homage to the Netherlands, the Anglo Saxons to England, the Irish Canadians to Ireland and so on. Africans in the American diaspora are increasingly visiting Ghana and Senegal, both countries believed to have been entrepots for slaves being taken to the Americas several centuries ago (Asmah, 1997; Perrault, 1990; Williams, 1976). Such visits which are intended to discover the ancestral roots of a people have spiritual and emotional value. As the African-American middle class group expands in the United States it is expected that more tourists will go to Africa in the future (Perrault, 1990). *Cultural tourism* involves observing peasant communities as objects of study. The tourists seek to see whatever is remaining of a vanishing culture. The visitors are entertained in costumed festivals and other performances. Those interested in *historical tourism* seek to explore the wonders of the past (Gamble, 1989) such as historical monuments, archaeological sites and so on. Such visits are usually education-oriented and often guided. In *environmental tourism*, the journey is to remote areas or places of environmental interest. Finally, *recreational tourism* is for people who want to relax and be close to nature. It includes sports activities, sunbathing, curative spas, good food and entertainment. Recreation tourism is seen as the "sand, sea, sex" tourism which allows "away-from-home freedom to indulge in the new morality" (Smith, 1977: 3).

Tourists

Smith (1977) also provides a typology of tourists. A slightly modified version of her typology is summarized in Table 1.6. It is instructive to note the numbers of tourists in each category and to glean their adaptations to local conditions at destination areas. The type of tourists, their background, values, purpose for visiting, and expectations on host communities will greatly influence their impact on the environment and society at destination areas. In the classification of tourists, drifters, explorers and elite travellers, generally cause little disruption because they travel in small numbers. Their presence may not even be noticed. Similarly, off-beat and unusual tourists are not disruptive of local areas. They are comfortable using local hotels and public transport just like the residents.

The mass tourists or institutionalised tourists, so called because of their dependence on others (travel agents and tour operators) to make all the arrangements for their journey including travel, transport, insurance, and accommodation (Gamble, 1989: 4), have the greatest impact on the local areas they visit. In character, form and impact, mass tourism is different from other forms of tourism.

Table 1.6.
Frequency of types of tourists and their adaptations to local norms

Type of tourist	Number of tourists	Adaptations to local norms
1. Drifter	very small	accepts fully
2. Explorer	very limited	accepted fully
3. Elite	barely seen	adapts fully
4. Off-beat	uncommon but seen	adapts fully
5. Unusual	occasional	adapts somewhat
Institutionalized tourists		
6. Incipient mass	steady flow	seeks western amenities
7. Mass	continuous influx	expects western amenities
8. Charter	massive arrivals	demands western amenities

Sources: Smith, 1977; Gamble, 1989: 3-4

Based on Western middle class behaviour and values, mass tourists fill up hotels of every category, pensions, and hostels but as a common denominator, they expect a trained, multi-lingual hotel and tourist staff to be alert and solicitous to their wants as well as to their needs (Smith, 1977: 10).

Smith further notes that they have a "you get what you pay for attitude". In other words, "the mass tourist really wants to be confirmed in his prejudices and to be left alone in a milieu as similar as possible to his own familiar background" (de Kadt, 1979: 52). An African country wishing to attract this type of international tourist must invest heavily in infrastructure including world-class accommodation, restaurant, communication and transport facilities and high quality services in order to meet its needs and demands.

Mass tourism became possible after the Second World War with the rise of large passenger aircraft and with increasing incomes in Western countries. As noted earlier, several other factors provided the impetus for mass tourism. These included smaller family sizes, higher general education, increase in mobility because of automobiles and greater urbanization and confinement which made people want to go away for a period (Bachmann, 1988).

The major characteristics of mass tourism include the following (Shaw and Williams, 1994):
- Large numbers; the tourism product is offered under conditions of mass production.
- Increasing expenditure on consumer goods associated with tourism. Such include skin creams for a summer holiday; skis and skiing accessories for the winter holiday; and tents and camping gear for a holiday in natural areas.
- Only a few producers dominate particular markets e.g. Disney for theme parks and a small number of tour and travel companies for all-inclusive package holidays.
- Producers develop new attractions, for example, by opening up new mass destination areas, e.g. Thailand, The Gambia, South Africa, Zimbabwe.
- Mass tourism products are little differentiated e.g. the Mediterranean beach holiday offers the same mix of architecture, facilities, food, drink and so on, wherever it is

located (Shaw and Williams, 1996). The Club Mediterranée group, for example, owns or controls 261 properties with over 127,000 beds world wide (Harris and Walshaw, 1995: 89). Its core business is its 106 resort villages in 35 countries; and an assortment of related businesses (conference centres, incentive and corporate travel, cruising and so on) (Harris and Walshaw, 1995). Their product is standardized for all their locations.

Finally, there are the charter tourists. These really are mass tourists who arrive at a destination in large numbers, usually using chartered aircraft. The charter tourists wear name tags, are assigned numbered buses, counted on board, travel together in a convoy of vehicles to their hotels and demand Western standards of food and accommodation (Smith, 1977: 10). Charter tourism is alluring. Usually the tour would be organized by a travel agent who is able to obtain very low prices in an all inclusive package covering air travel, insurance, accommodation, and local transport at the destination. The tourists themselves may pay for a few extras, although they need not do this. For the destination areas in Africa or elsewhere in the Third World, mass tourists in all-inclusive packages cause great problems. In terms of foreign exchange income, there is significant loss to a host country. Although the travel agents are paid in hard currency, they negotiate prices in local currencies which may depreciate thereby getting less revenue. Also, a large proportion of the money paid abroad never reaches the African country which nevertheless has to apply resources to the satisfaction of the visitor (Sinclair, 1990; Sindiga, 1994; Chapters 2, 4, and 5, this volume).

Conceptual and methodological considerations

One of the challenges of studying the contribution of tourism to development is to identify theoretical and methodological tools for analysis. Are the data available? Are the data synchronic or diachronic? Are they comparable? At what scale is tourism to be studied — global, continental, national, regional or local? These and other questions may appear mundane; however, they are critical for tourism as a newly emerging discipline without firm theoretical and methodological structures. Some background to tourism as a research discipline would place this matter in context.

Tourism as a research discipline
Tourism is a cross-disciplinary field which has been the subject of research for several decades. Early tourism studies were economic in nature and were intended to work out the monetary flows and benefits from the tourism activity (Jafari, 1990). This was followed by a wave of studies which focused on the socio-cultural impact of tourism. This way the benefits of tourism were brought into sharp focus. Following this, scholarly attention went to alternative forms of tourism development with a view to minimizing the negative impacts thereby making tourism sustainable (Jafari, 1990). These developments have led to a scientific body of knowledge on tourism to which the social sciences make a substantial contribution. The tourism research is finding expression in numerous professional journals and also in the cognate areas of hospitality

and leisure studies (Sheldon, 1990). But, like every new discipline, tourism's literature is scattered through other literatures (Dartnall and Store, 1990). And more importantly, tourism studies are still conducted in several other disciplines including anthropology, economics, geography, history, leisure, recreation, management, political science, psychology, regional planning and sociology. This, indeed, is a multidisciplinary field which is a strength for tourism studies. But it can also be a disability. Different scholars in different fields tend to utilize their disciplinary structures when working on a tourism problem. This causes communication difficulties.

The conceptual and methodological debates
The tourism literature shows that there are two approaches to the analysis of tourism and development, namely the political economy and the functional approaches (Lea, 1993). Below, I discuss each of these approaches.

Also known as the core-periphery model (Dieke, 1994), the proponents of the political economy approach argue that tourism, just like any form of economic activity, is governed by the political and economic structures which regulate world trade. This is because tourism is a global phenomenon which transcends national frontiers. It should therefore be analysed as such. The political economy approach recognises that the contemporary patterns of international tourism follow the economic structures established during the colonial period. The argument follows the underdevelopment/dependency school and world system scholarship which hold that the world economy (read capitalist economy) shapes all societies notwithstanding their geographic location (Bradshaw, Kaiser and Ndegwa, 1995). For Africa, the most influential argument by the dependency school was put forward by Colin Leys (1975) in his study of underdevelopment in Kenya. The nature of tourism as a luxury export, Lea (1981: 30) argues, creates structural dependency on external demand leading to alien developments to which the local people cannot relate to. The sustenance of these tourist developments must depend on external support.

The political economy approach tends to be qualitative in nature (Dieke, 1994) and focuses on the organization, structure, and cost-benefit analysis of tourism in the Third World (Lea, 1993). Practitioners of this approach recognize that international tourism is inequitable between the developed and developing countries and that the inequity is here to stay unless there is a dramatic change in the power relations between the North and the South (Lea, 1993). Perhaps to provide a middle ground, Green (1979) believes that a developing country should make firm negotiated agreements based on careful planning and knowledge and skills, costs and benefits with its transnational company partners in tourism development. Only this way can small African economies reduce the leakages from international tourism and obtain equitable returns to their share of investment.

The functional approach was developed by Mathieson and Wall (1982) and attempts to classify tourism in terms of its functional parts while ignoring the historical experience of development (Lea, 1993). The functional model recognises three basic elements of tourism as follows: (1) dynamic element: movement to and from a destination; (2) static element which comprises of the stay at the destination; and (3) the consequential element consisting of a study of the major economic, social and physical impacts of tourism (Mathieson and Wall, 1982: 14-34). The dynamic element essentially is the demand component of tourism and the factor which motivates people to seek outdoor recreation. The static element comprises of characteristics of the tourist and those of the destination. These heavily influence the impacts of tourism which form the consequential element.

The proponents of this approach claim that it is an analytical tool which steers clear of polemics. The idea is to project a view of tourism in which problems are sorted out through management and appropriate policy instruments (Lea, 1993). The functional approach emphasizes the economic contributions of tourism. The argument is that economic indicators can be quantified (Dieke, 1994: 617; Green, 1979). These economic indicators are seen as tourism's performance criteria. The most common are foreign exchange, revenues, employment and contribution to GNP. The approach is silent on causal relationships and ignores political structures and the wider societal and development issues (Dieke, 1994; Lea, 1993). Apart from this criticism most studies which follow this approach usually focus on the nation-state thereby ignoring both the international and local factors and the interactions taking place at these different levels (Bradshaw, Kaiser and Ndegwa, 1995).

This study uses a combination of the political economy and functional approaches; in some cases only a selection of the main features of the two approaches can provide the framework for a detailed case study. Proceeding with this way of analysis requires further justification. Tourism is a very international affair. Its impact ripples through to the national and local levels. The tourists must interact with many spaces in the course of their journey. They cross a national border or fly to an airport which is a national facility. The tourists then use the infrastructure, for example roads which are financed from the national treasury. They go to local areas to enjoy resources which are maintained at the cost and goodwill of the local people. Ultimately, they use accommodation facilities put up with national and/or international finance.

Viewed this way, meaningful analysis must proceed at the three levels identified. For this reason, both the political economy and functional approaches can be used for a clearer understanding of tourism and development. As Lea (1993) notes, the political economy approach appears better suited for tourism analysis in the destination areas in the developing countries whereas the functional approach can describe the structure and organization of tourism in the source areas.

Choice of Kenya as a country case

The choice of Kenya as a country case study of tourism and African development is somewhat expedient because I live and work in that country. This provides me with the unique advantage of first hand experience of tourism issues in Kenya. Besides, Kenya is one of the most developed tourism destinations in sub-Saharan Africa (Chapter 4). With over three decades of tourism development experience, Kenya combines beach tourism along the Indian Ocean coast and safari tourism developed in an extensive network of about five dozen national parks and reserves dispersed widely across the country. Kenya was one of the first countries in the world to conserve marine resources through a system of marine parks and reserves.

Kenya is also believed to have the first university degree programme in the sub-Saharan African region (Sindiga, 1994; 1996c). The Department of Tourism at Moi University which I had the privilege to found and lead for some five years started a B.Sc programme in tourism in 1991/92. This department was a response to Kenya's needs in high level manpower for the tourism industry. This, it is hoped, would redress the balance of expatriate employment especially at the supervisory and management levels. These graduates will also provide badly needed knowledge and skills in negotiating agreements with transnational companies in tourism for the benefit of Kenya. Also, the tourism graduates will be better placed to start small scale indigenous enterprises in tourism and to promote the country's tourism industry. Only increased ownership of tourism enterprises by local people can assure greater retention of the foreign exchange earned from tourism.

It was while introducing undergraduate students to the role of tourism in development that it became clear that there was a dearth of local literature on this subject. How would tourism and development be analyzed? What are the experiences of other African countries in tourism and development? What theoretical structures and methodological tools are available for the task? Other questions which came out of our students included the negative environmental impacts of tourism on Kenya's national parks and the beaches, the human-wildlife conflicts in protected areas, and the socio-cultural malaise associated with tourism. Would tourism-led development be sustainable?

To these and many other questions, this book is a modest contribution. It is hoped that policymakers, social scientists, regional planners, resource managers and students will find this analysis illuminating. The observations and conclusions made herein will be applicable to other African countries.

Organization

Chapter 2 examines the contribution of tourism in African development by focusing on tourism's record on foreign exchange earnings, employment, government revenues and regional development. One of the issues which comes out is that tourism's contribution to the African economy is rather small. However, there are serious environmental and socio-cultural impacts on the resources base. These negative impacts are exacerbated because Africa's tourism development has proceeded without planning. The goal of this chapter is to provide a framework for analysis for application to the detailed Kenya country case. In Chapter 3, I discuss Kenya's historical, biophysical and social environments. This provides the basic locational, environmental, governmental, historical, biophysical, social and economic characteristics of the country as a background to tourism development. The second section of Chapter 3 focuses on the status of Kenya's infrastructure development. Such infrastructure facilities as transportation networks, electricity and communications and basic services including water and sanitation are essential for general economic growth and tourism development.

Chapter 4 examines the basic characteristics of Kenya's tourism, how it developed, the management of tourism-led conservation, and tourism's role in the Kenyan economy. Empirical data are used to examine the detailed contribution of tourism to foreign exchange earnings, employment and government revenues. The final section of this chapter examines proposals for increasing foreign exchange earnings and their retention within the country and employment opportunities. Then in Chapter 5 the analysis proceeds with a discussion of the structure of the tourist industry in the country. The first part deals with indigenous Kenyan investment in the tourism industry followed by marketing and tourism promotion. Ultimately, the chapter discusses the structure and ownership of tourism enterprises. This is because the pattern of ownership reflecting both domestic and foreign interests has implications for the retention of foreign exchange earnings, the employment generated in tourism, and hence the development capacity of tourism in the country.

In Chapter 6 I consider the change and challenge of unplanned tourism development in the country. The Chapter focuses on the critical issues which began to rear their head in the 1990s following three decades of ad hoc tourism expansion without the benefit of a plan. These critical issues of Kenya's tourism include breakdown of infrastructure, environmental impacts, wildlife-human conflicts, socio-cultural impacts, uneven distribution of tourism benefits, uncompetitiveness, a relatively small domestic tourism sector, limited regional development and political violence.

Chapter 7 examines the case for alternative tourism and sustainable development in Kenya, whereas Chapter 8 considers the prospects for regional cooperation in tourism in Africa and the status of intra-African tourism. The central feature of the latter are the potentials and limitations of increasing intra-Africa tourism. The final chapter provides a summary and draws conclusions covering the entire study.

2

Tourism and development in Africa

This chapter examines the contribution of tourism in African development. The goal is to assess whether tourism is a viable development strategy for the continent. The analysis focuses on the performance indicators of tourism, namely foreign exchange receipts, employment, government revenues and regional development. The chapter shows that it is difficult to make a definitive assessment of tourism in Africa because the industry has developed on the continent in an unplanned manner. Consequently, there are no explicit criteria by which general performance can be measured. First, the chapter discusses the development crisis in Africa and examines the failed development strategies. This is the background of discussing tourism and African development.

Although the value of tourism in development has long been recognised (Mitchell, 1970; Popovic, 1972), international attention to the role of tourism in development in the developing countries was spurred by a UNESCO-World Bank seminar held in Washington DC in 1976 (de Kadt, 1979). Since then the subject has been taken up in an increasing volume of literature focusing on the Third World in general (e.g. Britton, 1982; Cater, 1987; Harrison, 1992a; Lea, 1993; Brohman, 1996) and Africa in particular (Gamble, 1989; Dieke 1993a; 1995; Poirier and Wright, 1993; Curry, 1990; Wright and Poirier, 1991; Summary, 1987; Harrell-Bond and Harrell-Bond, 1979). The role of tourism in development has become especially urgent because of Africa's declining economic fortunes.

Africa's development crisis

Sub-Saharan Africa appears to have three development options: expanding and increasing the range of its primary exports from agriculture and mining; focusing on industrialization as a strategy for achieving quick and sustained economic growth; and promoting tourism because of the existence of an overseas demand for it (Gamble, 1989). The first two options have been tried out in the past without encouraging results for the majority of the people of Africa. In the contemporary period, Africa suffers from endemic economic stagnation leading to chronic poverty. So serious is the problem that the continent has a burden of international debts, fiscal deficits, rising inflation levels, and declining economic growth (World Bank, 1991). Other problems are agricultural stagnation, declining agricultural yields, declining per capita food production and poor export record (Killick, 1992). In several countries, debt servicing obligations exceed entire export earnings (Taylor, 1992). Poverty has increased and the majority of the population cannot meet their basic needs (see Appendix 1).

The manifestations of the African crisis destroy productive capacities and infrastructure for development. Clearly, post-independence development strategies have not worked for Africa. First, there was the encouragement of the newly independent countries to produce more and more primary raw materials for export to metropolitan countries. It was expected that income from these raw materials would be remitted back to Africa to become the basis of development. The producers of the raw materials had no say in the prices that their products fetched in the markets in the developed world. This was partly because there was never mutual dependence between Africa and Europe (Zwanenberg and King, 1975: xxii). Africa's exports were only a small portion of the global supply of the same commodities. Consequently, African countries could not influence the prices in the metropolitan centres where the products were sold.

Moreover, in Africa the infrastructure created for exporting the raw materials was not suited to the development needs of the resident populations. A dialectical relationship nonetheless emerged wherein Africa was incorporated into the international system thereby creating the historical relationships between the metropole and the satellite, the centre and the periphery. History students note that this relationships which was started in the colonial period carried forth to the postcolonial era (Rodney, 1974). As suppliers of raw materials, African countries became "underdeveloped"; conversely, Europe and North America" developed" (de Souza and Porter, 1974; Rodney, 1974; Leys, 1975).

Second, import substitution industrialization strategy was introduced. The emphasis shifted to establishing industries in developing countries for basic manufactured goods required for development. A few of the raw materials could be semi-processed in Africa before export; also, assembly plants were established with completely knocked down kits and spare parts coming from abroad. It was argued that such industrialization would create jobs for Africans and save on foreign exchange and lead to faster development. For it to function as expected, import substitution required regulation and protection against direct imports. It soon became clear that employment was not expanding as fast as had been initially projected. And goods thus produced tended to be more expensive than comparable goods from abroad because of lack of economies of scale of the industries. Rweyemamu (1973) who examined the industrialization process in Tanzania found that dependency relations and unequal exchange gave rise to what he termed "perverse capitalist industrial development". The production structure inherited from the colonial period persisted and was perpetuated by a neo-colonial pattern of investment. The industrialization efforts of the 1960s in sub-Saharan Africa failed to remove surplus labour from agriculture according to the postulates of neo-classical economic theory. This led to a shift from industrialization to agriculture in the 1970s and 1980s. Development thinkers wished to halt the migration streams of unemployed people from the rural areas to the urban areas where long-anticipated expansion of the modern urban wage sector economy failed to take place. Increasing urban unemployment, the development of expansive slum settlements in Africa's large cities led to a back-to-the-land policy in many countries. This focus on rural development was intended to initiate agriculture-related economic activities thereby stemming the tide of the rural-urban migration stream.

In a world structured in an either-or fashion, that is, either agriculture or industry and vice versa, there was no opportunity to include the contribution of services (including tourism) to economic development (Sinclair, Alizadeh and Onunga, 1992). In fact, the general recognition of the role of the service sector in employment was not done until the late 1980s. As such tourism has been neglected not just in development literature but also in international trade theory, where the focus is on the exchange of goods and not services (Sinclair, et al., 1992: 49). Without explicit recognition in the literature, the place of tourism in development can only be deciphered from empirical examples. The following discussion reviews the shifting development paradigms and points out the implications of each of them to tourism development. With a caveat that tourism was never really considered in development thought, the following discussion is somewhat speculative.

Implications of shifting development paradigms to tourism

Since the colonial period, there have been shifting paradigms in the analysis of African development. The modernization theory was formulated during Africa's independence decade of the 1960s (Soja, 1968). Partly a product of colonialism, the modernization theory's basic premise was that Western culture is world culture. As such western science and technology would diffuse to Africa and the rest of the world and induce psychological, social and cultural change to produce a modern society from a traditional one. According to Soja's (1968) geography of modernization, the nation-state would be the central form of organization. The centre initiates, disseminates and perpetuates modern ways. Unless it was directed properly, a country's modernization map could become very uneven.

This way of thinking had implications for tourism. It would view tourism, both domestic and international, as a modernizing force through which the new ways could diffuse. As such, the proponents of modernization theory would support tourism as an agent of change. Until the early 1960s, African tourism had been undertaken by a few rich people from Western Europe and North America, many of whom were interested in sport fishing, sport hunting, and the collection of trophies. These early tourists travelled by ship and a few by aircraft. Some kind of incipient tourism had started. The coming of large jet aircraft and the commencement of charter safaris from the mid-1960s accompanied by greater attention to the welfare of workers in Western Europe led to many more travellers, not just the affluent class. The all-inclusive package tour was relatively inexpensive for the long-haul trips to Africa and became a boon to tourism (Lamprey, 1969: 143). Within a short time, incipient tourism would turn into mass tourism.

In the 1970s there was a paradigm change to dependency theory which was also known as the development of underdevelopment or world system theory (Leys, 1975; Rweyemamu, 1973; Rodney, 1974; Brett, 1973; Cooper, 1981). The dependency theory was informed by neo-Marxian thought and rejected status quo economic arrangements whereby African economies have a permanent unequal relationship with the capitalist economy. In this sense therefore trade could not be expected to be the engine of development in the peripheral economies of Africa and the Third World (Cooper, 1981: 9).

Under the dependency theory, international tourism would be seen as an "export" of peripheral economies. The organization, sourcing of tourists, international transportation and management of international tourism, would be done from Western Europe and North America. The ground management, local transportation, accommodation and tour guiding at destination areas would essentially be handled by transnational companies or their local subsidiaries. These companies kept monopolistic control of the tourism industry in the peripheral economies. Like the case of primary raw material exports, peripheral economies were unable to take full advantage of tourism development. Many such economies attempted to marshal government resources to invest in tourism enterprises especially in accommodation. This proved difficult as multinational corporations with their large resources held much clout in negotiations and pricing of tourist services to the disadvantage of the peripheral economy.

The development fashion changed in the 1980s when donor-led international development emphasized social welfare and basic needs for the peoples of the peripheral economies. The implications for tourism were that local people were encouraged to participate in tourism-related economic activities. Usually, such participation did not go to the core of the tourism business but secondary aspects such as arts and crafts in the informal sector.

The structural adjustment reforms era of the 1990s with its emphasis on economic liberalization and removal of trade restrictions appears to open up the peripheral economies for imports from the developed world. Structural adjustment programmes (SAPs) were introduced in the 1980s but never really became an important part of the economic management of African countries until the early 1990s. As policy tools for economic management, SAPs aim at increasing efficiency in all sectors of the economy thereby raising the rate of growth. For Kenya, for example, SAPs are aimed at reducing government spending, restructuring the public service with a view to having a smaller workforce, divesting from economic activities which could best be done by the private sector, and providing incentives to investors (Kenya, 1997:46-47). Other areas of reform are rationalising public expenditure, cost-sharing on all market-oriented public services, and liberalization of prices and marketing systems.

Massive privatisation of public corporations is going on in Africa leading to government divestiture from businesses. Publicly-owned tourism enterprises will likely go into the hands of the local elite and/or foreign interests. Due to the recognition of the heavy leakages and the serious socio-cultural and environmental impacts of mass tourism, alternative tourism is in vogue (Chapter 7). Although much has been written about eco-friendly tourism which is expected to provide higher returns for the African economy, there has been little assessment on what this means on the ground. Is ecotourism, for example, a business gimmick by the tour operator or is it a reality changing the face of international mass tourism? In what ways will the local communities in destination areas benefit from tourism?

Table 2.1 provides a schema representing the changing development paradigms and the implications for tourism covering about four decades. The table summarizes this discussion but provides as well the main vocabulary used in the development literature over time. Despite the shifts in development thought, African development remains problematic.

In the wake of Africa's development crisis, some scholars have suggested that tourism could become the catalyst or basis for broad-based development thereby solving Africa's development challenge (de Kadt, 1979; Green, 1979; Dieke, 1994). Others have given tourism only qualified support (Lea, 1993). A growing literature argues for tourism as a means of export diversification so as to decrease the instability of exports although these objectives have not been met (Sinclair and Tsegaye, 1990). Yet, a few scholars think that tourism can be beneficial to only a few countries with the majority having little opportunity to create a competitive and viable large scale tourism industry (Poirier and Wright, 1993: 162; Teye, 1991).

Many countries, however, acknowledge the crucial role of tourism in development (Tosun and Jenkins, 1996). In Namibia, for example, tourism generates about 6 percent of the GDP which is the same share as agriculture (Namibia, nd.: 223) whereas in Kenya, tourism's contribution to GDP is 11 percent (Chapter 4). Yet, development planners wishing to include tourism receipts in a country's books of accounts must be wary of their work. Tourism is an unstable luxury export. It is dependent on external demand which is in turn affected by a myriad factors beyond the control of the planners. Under the circumstances, what contribution can tourism make to development in Africa?

Tourism and African development

The case for tourism and development is somewhat different from other sectors of the economy. Because it does not produce goods, tourism's contribution to development is indirect through generating revenues (Green, 1979: 81-82). It involves the creation of an infrastructure of attractions, accommodation facilities, travel and transport, and communications which allow visitors to go to the source of an attraction. Those who think in economic terms and look at tourism as an "export" industry will say that there is no actual transference of goods. The consumer of the export must go to its source thereby requiring that certain arrangements be made. Such preparations include packaging the tourism product, and arranging accommodation, travel and local transportation. Because of the investment demands of tourism, the industry is well developed in only a few countries.

Table 2.1
Changing development paradigms and implications for tourism, 1960-1965

Development paradigm	Main components	Major concepts/vocabulary	Implications for tourism
1. Modernization (1960s)	diffusion of innovations; western culture is world culture; centre initiates, disseminates and perpetuates modern ways	diffusion, change, top-down, centre-periphery, nation-building, integration, "modernized" elite and masses, top-down, growth pole, growth centre	Tourism is a modernizing force; supports tourism as agent of change; incipient tourism development
2. Underdevelopment/ dependency (1970s)	neo-colonialism; structural dependency; metropole-periphery; international capital	historical experience; neo-dependency marxists, core-periphery, top-down	Tourism is an "export" in international trade and is subject to same rules; domination of multi-national companies, mass tourism
3. Donor-led international development (1980s)	rural development, basic needs, development from below, development from within	bottom-up, participatory, preferential trade	Mass tourism as a source of foreign exchange, participation of host communities
4. Structural adjustment (1990s)	liberalization	exchange controls; removal of trade restrictions; privatisation; sustainable development; enabling environment.	Effects of mass tourism felt, alternative tourism; eco-friendly tourism; participation of host populations in tourism.

For most of Africa, however, tourism development has elicited much critical commentary:

> Tourism in most sub-Saharan African countries is hardly an industry since the tourism infrastructure is weak, tourism organization is poor, and net revenue is meagre. Almost all tourist arrivals consist of African nationals resident abroad returning to visit friends and relatives, business visitors, and those visiting expatriate residents. The primary vacation or leisure tourism sector is undeveloped (Teye, 1991: 288).

Although Nigeria, for example, traditionally has not given much priority to tourism (Lea, 1981: 30) leading Nigerian novelist Chinua Achebe (1984) adjudges that the country does not meet the requirements of international tourism:

> Nigeria is one of the most disorderly nations in the world. It is one of the most corrupt, insensitive, inefficient places under the sun. It is one of the most expensive countries and one of those that give least value for money. It is dirty, callous, noisy, ostentatious, dishonest and vulgar (Achebe, 1984: 10).

Despite his angry tone, Achebe emphasizes a number of elements which may discourage tourism — reputation of a destination, attitudes and behaviour of the hosts, the pricing of the tourism product, and political stability. Speaking directly to the problem of developing a vibrant tourism industry in Nigeria, Achebe complains that

> It is a measure of our self-delusion that we can talk about developing tourism in Nigeria. Only a masochist with an exuberant taste for self-violence will pick Nigeria for a holiday; only a character (...) seeking to know punishment and poverty at first hand! No, Nigeria may be a paradise for adventurers and pirates but not tourists (Achebe, 1984: 10).

It is a well appreciated fact that tourists are highly sensitive to political instability which could threaten their personal safety and security (Sharpley, Sharpley and Adams, 1996; Teye, 1991; 1986; 1988). So, apart from developing the physical tourism infrastructure, political stability must be cultivated as an important factor in influencing tourism. Also in the very near future, the issue of human rights and internal governance of countries which seek to attract tourists especially from the West will come under scrutiny. Already, politically-motivated travel advice from Western governments appears to have a profound effect on would-be tourists with many cancelling their planned trips (see for example Sharpley, Sharpley and Adams, 1996). Only countries which practise democratic ideals, adhere to the rule of law, and respect human rights will maintain political stability essential for tourism development.[1]

But the African continent of the late 20th century is replete with examples of political violence. From Somalia and Sudan in the east to Rwanda, Burundi, Congo Brazzaville, Congo Kinshasa, Uganda and Chad in the centre, Angola in the south, Liberia, Sierra Leone, Guinea and Senegal in the west and Western Sahara and Algeria in the north, Africa is in turmoil. Africa's continuing poor performance in tourist arrivals is

---

[1] The new alternative development movement seeks to empower local groups in decision-making and it asserts universal human rights for the majority. See Friedmann (1992).

blamed on safety fears. This may affect South Africa and most of North Africa save perhaps Morocco. There is more to attracting tourism than merely investing in the infrastructure.

The argument for tourism as a development strategy is primarily economic although esoteric ideals such as bringing increased understanding among peoples and cultures are invoked. Among the economic factors for developing tourism are generating foreign exchange, employment and government revenues through taxes. Tourism also aids in regional development. Each of these is considered below.

Foreign exchange

Tourism may appear to bring into a country a large amount of hard currency. Most assessments use gross foreign exchange earnings as a basis for their conclusions (de Kadt, 1979; Elkan, 1975). But this is only half the picture as the net tourism receipts may be relatively small. Also, tourism has many hidden costs.

A more meaningful measure of foreign exchange receipts discounts the leakages from the gross receipts and arrives at a figure of net receipts from tourism. Many tourism enterprises in the Third World are owned and managed by foreign companies usually multinational corporations. In the case of Botswana and Lesotho, South African companies invested large sums of money in hotel development in the years following independence (Crush and Wellings, 1983: 677). These companies which monopolize the organization of international mass tourism (Brohman, 1996: 54) earn handsome profits by charging management fees, making limited direct investment, and through various licensing, franchise and service agreements (Lea, 1993). This keeps the parent company in a controlling position thereby allowing it to repatriate most of the foreign exchange.

The leakages from gross tourism receipts include money used in tourism promotion through advertising and maintaining overseas offices, international air travel and local transport, interest payments, profits and remittances of wages abroad by expatriate staff (Figure 2.1). In addition, part of the foreign exchange must pay for direct purchases of food and drink from overseas, construction and maintenance of hotels, restaurants, roads and communications. A large proportion of foreign exchange reserves may be lost due to massive investments in infrastructure (Curry, 1982; Lea 1981). The construction of an airport, for example, can consume investible surplus from tourism and other governmental resources thereby minimizing the value of tourism to a country. Also, vehicles and spares are usually imported. It may be noted, however, that the quantity of imports such as food and drink will vary from one country to another. Whereas West African countries may import most of the food for tourists, this is not the case in East Africa. Here, 80 to 90 percent of the food is locally procured (Green, 1979). Even within East Africa, there are internal country differences. In Tanzania most of the food is imported whereas Kenya produces all the food consumed by tourists in the country (Elkan, 1975: 129). If less food is imported, there is less foreign exchange used on this count.

Relatively large amounts of foreign exchange are lost to the developed world because of the structural dependency created through widespread foreign ownership, control and management of tourism enterprises in the Third World. The magnitude of the leakage varies from country to country. One estimate from the 1970s for Swaziland put the leakage at about 60 percent (Crush and Wellings, 1983: 689). Estimates are thus highly variable and range from 20 to 80 percent (Lea, 1981: 28).

These large outflows put into question the profitability of tourism to a country. It has been argued that small, less diversified economies such as that of The Gambia suffer the greatest leakages and therefore obtain the least benefits from tourism (Green, 1979; Gamble, 1989). This reduces tourism's potential for generating broad-based development through economic growth (Brohman, 1996). In contrast, a country with a large diversified economy will reduce the imports and retain most of the foreign exchange. Kenya is frequently cited as one such example (Dieke, 1995).[2]

Contrary to the impression created in the literature, net tourism receipts or net foreign exchange earnings of tourism (see Figure 2.1) does not measure the net impact of tourism on gross national product. Domestic resources, that is labour, capital, skills and land are used to supply tourist goods and services. These resources could be put to alternative use if they were not applied to tourism (Mitchell, 1970): 2; Hazlewood, 1979: 106). The value of these host country inputs must be discounted from tourism's net foreign exchange earnings before a measure of the "net tourism impact on (marginal contribution to) GNP" (Mitchell, 1970: 2) can be established. This imbroglio shows the difficulty of measuring costs and benefits of tourism to the economy leading some scholars to remark that benefits are often exaggerated (Lea, 1981: 25).

A further caveat can be made about generalizations made on net foreign exchange earnings from tourism. Elkan (1975) has cautioned about applying generalizations of costs and benefits of tourism from one country context to another. His plea is for separate policies which a country pursues and whether it goes for large or small-sized hotel projects. Elkan gives the example of Tanzania's development of beach hotels some distance from Dar es Salaam as a way of minimizing the socio-cultural impact of tourists on a socialist citizenry.[3] In this case, locations closer to the capital would have been more economical and could allow tourists time in Dar es Salaam in the evenings where they

---

[2]   This might be true in a relative sense. Kenya, however, experiences serious leakages with packaged all-inclusive beach tourism involving little or no local travel within the country (Kenya; 1991a; Sindiga, 1994). Also, there are heavy leakages in international air travel because most tourists go in chartered and scheduled foreign airlines (Sinclair, 1990; Sindiga, 1996a; Chapter 5).

[3]   A vigorous debate on the role of tourism in Tanzania's socialist development was conducted through that country's national print media in 1970. The interested reader can consult Shijvi (1975). Here, it can only be noted that under the Arusha declaration of 1967 by which the country moved to the left, Tanzania saw tourism as being incompatible with its socialist ideology. In particular, the country appeared to protest the presence of rich visitors, a perception which would dramatize inequality between guests and hosts thereby exposing Tanzanians to capitalist forms of consumption. It would also undermine cultural life and allegedly destroy wildlife (Kahama, 1995). In addition, Tanzania's tourist industry was put under the direction of an inefficient public sector which did not see the importance of facility development and maintenance. Then there were the huge bureaucratic procedures at airports and other entry points, and even at state banks where it took two hours to obtain bank change. An overvalued local currency made tourism too expensive. By 1973, investments in tourism had virtually ceased. Further, in 1977, Tanzania closed its border with Kenya and this decision was not reversed until 1983. Under the circumstances, tourists to East Africa started and completed their holidays in Kenya. See the rendering of these issues in Kahama (1995: 154-158). It may be pointed out that the inflexibility of the heavily centralized state bureaucracies in socialist systems makes it difficult to do the business of international tourism (Hall, 1992).

Figure 2.1
Leakages from gross receipts from international tourism
(Gross tourism receipts - leakages = net tourism receipts)

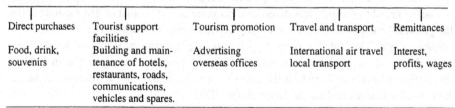

Source: Slightly modified from Gamble, 1989: 10.

could spend additional money. Elkan (1975: 129) persuasively concludes that policies chosen to promote tourism will have a strong bearing on the costs and benefits of tourism.

Employment

Tourism is labour-intensive. People must serve in the various sub-sectors of the industry including tour guiding, nature and cultural interpretation, game viewing, travel and transport services, promotion, sport, and in the area of food, beverage and alcohol service, and accommodation. Other tourism-related employment is in entertainment, the arts and hand-crafted curios. Indirectly, tourism creates employment in agriculture for the food requirements of the visitors. Also, infrastructure development such as road construction and hotel construction may provide many short term jobs. Tourism also supports other areas such as money and banking. It may also be mentioned that tourism attracts a number of activities in the informal sector. These include male and female prostitution, hawking of various merchandise, professional friendships, begging or simply following the tourists. There is also the issue of tourism and child prostitution in such countries as Sri Lanka, Thailand and the Philippines; in Africa it is reported to be on the increase in Kenya (Christian Aid, 1995). These linkages, through employment, tend to spread the benefits of tourism in a local area.

A number of estimates have been put forward on the level of employment created per hotel bed (Table 2.2). Although these data are for different years and are not strictly comparable, they do provide some indication as to the level of employment. In a strict sense, however, not all tourism requires hotel beds. Some tourists prefer outdoor camping using simple sleeping bags but their number may be small. The hotel bed employment ratio makes sense when considering the upmarket and mass tourists and is easily applied in many different contexts.

It has been argued that tourism creates greater employment than other forms of investment such as manufacturing (Elkan, 1975). This is then used as a justification for enormous investment in tourism. But many scholars (Gamble, 1989; Elkan, 1975; Green, 1979; Lea, 1981) have recognised that it is generally more expensive to create a job in a hotel than in manufacturing. Tourism has a relatively "high ratio of capital to

Table 2.2
Estimates of jobs per hotel bed

Country/Region	Jobs per bed (Direct employment)	Source
Tunisia	0.88-1.12	Poirer and Wright, 1993: 158
North Africa	2 - 3	Green, 1979: 84
East Africa	2 - 3	Green, 1979: 84
Tanzania	0.80	Elkan, 1975: 125
Kenya	0.84	Elkan, 1975: 125

labour" (Green, 1979: 87). In fact the net benefit of tourism investment could be considerably reduced if a country chooses to construct large-sized hotels and other prestige projects. Elkan (1975: 126-7) found that the larger Kenyan hotels were more expensive to build and had greater costs per bed. He concluded that small-sized hotels would maximize on hotel employment. Another factor which influences tourism's capacity to generate employment is the amount of imports (including food and drink) which must be brought in on account of tourism. The greater the size of the imports the less the number of jobs resulting from tourism activity.

Direct employment in tourism has been criticized on two grounds: most of it is unskilled and its availability is highly seasonal. Lack of skills and seasonality are very intricately intertwined. Some estimates indicate that 75 percent of workers in tourism have no skills or training for the jobs that they do (Gamble, 1989). This is a problem in as far as it affects the level of wages, security of tenure and the ability to influence better working terms. Also, the quality of productivity is affected by lack of training.

International tourism in Africa tends to be highly seasonal in a temporal sense. The majority of the West European and North American tourists visit during the northern hemisphere winter. The numbers begin to dry up in April; the annual cycle commences again in August/September or October. The problem of seasonality affects all tourism destinations especially those that promote the beach holiday from Tunisia to the Gambia and Kenya.

During the low season many employees lose their jobs. In the Gambia, for example, 50 percent of the hotel workers are laid off as the hotels close down between April and October for lack of patronage (Dieke, 1993b). In Kenya, residents are encouraged to utilize the hotels at special rates adjusted downwards (Sindiga, 1996a; Chapter 6). It is more cost-effective having guests who pay less than keeping beds unoccupied. However, many hotels, especially at the coast close down for renovations and a number of workers are inevitably kept out of the payroll. Gamble (1989: 15) provides an overall figure of low-season redundancies for all Africa of 25 percent of the workers. But whether the figure is 25% or 50% is not really the issue; a large number of people is involved.

Because of the uncertainty of their employment, the bargaining clout for better terms and conditions of service is considerably reduced. In Kenya, persons on casual terms of employment have no medical cover, no house allowance; and cannot join a trade union. Many tourism workers tend to be trapped in a cycle of hopelessness.

For semi-skilled, supervisory and management positions, tourism enterprises may not employ people from the local areas. Tourism businesses which are competing to meet international standards to attract the institutionalized tourism market may look for readily trained people. Such people may not necessarily come from the locality in which a tourism enterprise is established thereby generating conflicts with the indigenous people (Eastman, 1995). In the local eyes, it is another instance of outsiders exploiting local resources for profit while giving back virtually nothing. This denies tourism the goodwill of local communities. It does not speak well for an industry which is notoriously foreign dominated in its management and ownership ranks.

Questions have been raised about the quality of jobs available for the local people in the tourism industry. Charges have been made and rightly so, that the jobs are menial and tend to be servile (Bachmann, 1988; Sindiga, 1994). This has led to negative comments about tourism as "a final form of colonialism" where indigenous people are exploited by outsiders (Middleton, 1992: 53). Such jobs include working as porters, labourers, gardeners, drivers, waiters, and so on. In contrast, jobs requiring skills and professional training tend to be held by expatriates. In the Gambia, all tourist hotels are operated by European staff and Gambians work merely as waiters, bartenders, receptionists, cleaners and such like (Campbell, 1990: 42). Beyond this, hotel workers in particular, are expected to conform to alien attitudes and practices, sometimes against their own cultural values and norms (Bachmann, 1988). But what are the merits of these criticisms?

Whatever jobs are available should be open to those who wish to take them up. What, however, is at issue is that supervisory and management positions should be equally open for competition among the residents who possess the required skills. It is important to point this out because key positions in hotels and other tourism enterprises are not filled by expatriates because there are no local people to do so. Rather, it is because of the mistaken belief that the expatriates would raise the standard of service (Dieke, 1994: 62; Harrell-Bond and Harrell-Bond, 1979). However, in countries such as Namibia, basic tourism personnel including hotel managers, cooks and waiters are in short supply because of lack of training facilities (Namibia, n.d.: 222).

In the Gambia, a World Bank/United Nations Development Programme plan of 1973 provided for a progressive increase of expatriates in the development of Gambian tourism on the assumption that they would provide the expertise which local people "ostensibly lacked" (Harrell-Bond and Harrell-Bond, 1979). Such a plan was based on wrong notions about Africa and Africans. It is the idea of pushing in as many expatriates on the assumption that Africans cannot do it themselves. Over the longer term, such plans which exclude local people are not sustainable. As for the conflict of cultures between hotel workers and tourists, this is an inevitable consequence of choosing to work in tourism. Tourists come from varied backgrounds, hold divergent views, and visit for many different reasons. Their encounters with local people are somewhat like business rather than mutual personal meetings. But the contact can become smoother through sensitizing both the guests and hosts about mutual respectability.

There is also the question of employment and gender in the tourism industry. Most of the workers in various sub-sectors of the industry tend to be men (Elkan, 1975). If this is true, it is a matter which merits further inquiry to discover the underlying reasons. Although among Muslims, culture and tradition may preclude women from serving in tourism (Sindiga, 1996b), the apparent preference for men waiters in African hotels, bars and restaurants requires further research.

Finally, Dieke (1997) has noted that tourism employment remains a relatively new opportunity in Africa. Most people, especially in remote villages, do not even understand the concept of tourism. Consequently, many Africans hold misconceptions about tourism employment. Such cultural barriers, however, can be reduced through a programme of education (Dieke, 1997: 9).

Government revenue
Perhaps the greatest net gain from the resources generated by tourism accrues as government revenue. This is collected from licensing fees levied on tourism enterprises, and income tax both from the businesses and the individuals who work there. Government also obtains excise and customs duty on various tourism-related imports such as capital equipment, vehicles, and drinks. There is also sales tax on the purchase of domestic goods.

Another net gain from tourism income is the wages and salaries paid to local staff. These personal emoluments are net gains from the foreign exchange brought in by tourism. Finally, a country may draw a share of surpluses generated by tourism. The domestic share of gross operating surplus will however depend on such factors as ownership of the facility, rate of interest on loans, infrastructure costs, tax rates and management fees (Green, 1979).

Tourism and regional development

The spatial or regional dimension of development is a way of assessing the impact of a phenomenon on people in a locale at various scales. The regional approach is useful for gauging the level of development using specific indicators. Ultimately a pattern emerges which shows the differential impact of development across the landscape. This can then be used to make effective interventions at the local, regional or national level.

In virtually all the countries of Africa, tourism is spatially concentrated. Deliberately or unwittingly tourism tends to be developed in enclaves separated from local communities. In these enclaves the tourists lead their own lives in self-contained entities with hotels, bars, discotheques, swimming pools, massage parlours, indoor sports and other conveniences. Sometimes the tourists' contact with local people is only through the attendants. In short, some kind of Western ghetto is created to meet the requirements of the mass or institutional tourist who would like to enjoy his/her holiday without being disturbed. This way, tourism in Africa has developed without the participation of the local people. As Poirier and Wright (1993: 162) have noted, the tourism enclave phenomenon makes contact between tourists and indigenous culture to be "packaged rather than spontaneous, contrived rather than original, whether in terms of organized exhibitions or mass-produced artifacts".

In Tunisia, the tourist enclaves are located along the Mediterranean coast. The majority of the hotels are developed around Tunis; along the beaches of Hammamet-Nabeul; the 'Sahel' and Djerba-Gabes islands (Poirier and Wright, 1993). In Egypt, tourism is centred on Luxor, a place of outstanding archaeological ruins on the River Nile; Cairo, Aswan, Abu Simbel, Alexandria, Suez, Sinai and Hurghada (Gamble, 1989). For the Gambia, tourism is restricted to the Atlantic ocean beaches near Banjul. And in Kenya, tourism is concentrated along the coast especially at Mombasa and Malindi; Nairobi; and upcountry national parks and reserves.

The spatial concentration of tourism leads to a similar pattern in the distribution of the available jobs. And because of the seasonal nature of the employment, only people who are close by are able to benefit from it. However, this need not be so, especially in a country such as Kenya with intensive mobility and circulation of people across the national economic space.

Tourism has sometimes opened up remote places through providing infrastructural facilities such as roads, piped water, electricity, communication lines and through the development of accommodation facilities; however, these may not always be articulated to serve local population centres (Sindiga, 1996b). Malindi and Lamu on the Kenya coast, which had declined for several centuries, were revived by a thriving tourist industry over the past four decades (Middleton, 1992; Sindiga, 1996b; Bachmann, 1988).

Effects of tourism development without planning

Except perhaps for Tunisia (Gant and Smith, 1992; Poirier and Wright, 1993) there has been no serious sectoral planning of tourism in any African country (Lea, 1993; Green 1979). Even Kenya with a relatively strong tourist industry, the assessment made about two decades ago is still largely true.

> Kenya's sectoral planning for tourism is weak, in marked contrast to its negotiating ability which is good and its strategic ambitions for the sector which are high (Green, 1979: 97).

And because sectoral planning is weak "no rational evaluation of a tourism strategy can be made without knowledge of the goals it is intended to further and alternative ways of furthering them" (Green, 1979: 99).

Very frequently, national plans show lists of "hoped for outcomes" in the tourism sector rather than agenda for implementation (Lea, 1993: 74). The Kenya government statements, for example, for many years called for one million tourists in the year 1990 but never went beyond that to say what would be done once that number was attained. Also, they do not specify how the desired tourist arrivals relate to national development objectives (Chapter 6). Planning for tourism serves a number of other purposes: minimizing potential conflicts with competing land uses; developing desired tourism; and projecting its impact on environment and society now and in the future (Lea, 1993). In order for tourism to be sustainable, its planning must be based on local capacities and community perspectives without which it cannot succeed (Murphy, 1985).

Planning requires baseline information about the tourism sector, its history, its functioning, how it has been changing over time, its performance potential for further development and how optimal benefits can be obtained (Lea, 1993; Green, 1979). Only this way can the positive and negative contributions of tourism be pinpointed with a view to formulating policies and projects which could enhance the positive role and ameliorate the negative consequences.

Also, regions of tourism concentration experience certain negative socio-cultural consequences. The enclave nature of African tourism development takes Western culture to remote communities which may have unviable livelihood systems. Soon, the indigenous people are encouraged to enter into some kind of patron-client relationship either to make money or to escape from their objective material circumstances. Migot-Adholla *et al.* (1982: 88-89) have noted that such relationship may range from begging, posing for photographs or performing dance routines for a fee and casual or organised sex.

Among the tourists, such behaviour as scant dressing, open affection between the sexes, kissing in public and so on, may go against local tradition and culture leading to local opposition of the tourism industry. In this case, tourists become purveyors of the negative aspects of Western culture. In stead of regional development, tourism could lead to regional resentment. These problems could be minimized or mitigated with careful planning and management (Inskeep, 1991).

But tourism planning must be done on a continuous basis. Such planning which is practical and action-oriented, combines planning with implementation as a single process (Gunn, 1988). Although tourism planning and development has to be long range (10 to 20 years), combining this with implementation resolves immediate issues (Inskeep, 1994: 9). The nature of tourism demands that plans be oriented towards rapidly changing situations which may not be anticipated in periodic conventional planning. This is what is called strategic planning and is focused, selective and concerned with handling unexpected events (Gunn, 1988; Inskeep, 1994).

Summary and conclusion

This chapter has provided the argument and structure for a detailed study of tourism on development for any African country. It has shown the complexity of assessing the impact of tourism on a continental scale. Both the levels of returns from and the impact of tourism on the society and the environment are heavily influenced by government policies and type of tourism. Foreign exchange receipts and employment opportunities, for example, diminish considerably with large-scale developments in the tourism industry which lead to a large volume of imports. The impacts of tourism on space over time and among social groups are highly variegated.

Development is about change — behavioural, attitudinal, social, cultural, economic and even political. Every development effort must bring about change. Although much has been written about the impacts of tourism among host communities, most of the literature is cast in a negative mode frequently depicting Third World people as static and must therefore be protected from tourism. Moreover, most of the existing knowledge on the impacts of tourism tends to be generalized. In order to understand tourism's many impacts, detailed typologies of tourism and tourists and the nature of guest-host interactions must be delineated (Wall, 1996), along the lines suggested by Valene Smith (1977). Only then can a meaningful analysis be done on the impact of tourism in Africa.

Tourism's contribution to the African economy appears to be frequently overestimated. The structure, organization and management of international tourism favours multinational corporations from the developed world. This assures a very large outflow of the resources generated by tourism in the continent. When the leakages of foreign exchange are discounted, plus the local resources invested in tourism, the net impact is rather small. This situation could be ameliorated by strict sectoral planning of tourism development. However, planning alone is not sufficient; there must be a political will on the part of African bureaucrats to implement the provisions of tourism planning so as to assure that their countries obtain maximum benefits from tourism. But such an arrangement that guarantees African countries an equitable share of tourism's revenues could discourage rather than encourage trans-national corporations from investing in tourism in Africa. That is the challenge. Tourism employment has generated a lot of interest because only subordinate jobs tend to go to the local people with the supervisory and management positions being filled by expatriates. The popular but erroneous explanation for this arrangement is that Africans have not been trained to take up senior ranks in tourism. The problem, however, is that there are usually no plans to reverse the matter. Transnational companies keep a large expatriate management staff component as part of their agreement to work in Africa (Chapter 5). And as they usually control the tourism enterprises this cannot be reversed. The answer to the problem would be a structural change of the ownership and control of tourism businesses in Africa to allow the progressive entry of local people into the management arena of this industry. In a number of African countries, notably Kenya, a cadre of university-trained professionals in tourism now exists (Sindiga, 1996c). These people should be given the opportunity to manage Africa's tourism industry.

3

Kenya's biophysical and social environment

This chapter has three purposes — to outline the historical and political framework within which tourism is conducted in Kenya; to discuss the biophysical, social and economic characteristics of the country; and to examine certain key infrastructural services including transport, access to clean water, sanitation, electricity, and communications. Whereas the purpose of the first objective is to highlight the historical and political tensions and especially the role of ethnicity in the politics of the country as this may affect tourism, the second discusses the physical potential and social background upon which the tourism industry has been developed. The third objective is predicated on the notion that infrastructural services are central to economic growth in general and the business of tourism in particular. This background is necessary for understanding the analysis of Kenya's tourism and especially its potentials and constraints in the proceeding chapters.

Location

Kenya is located in eastern Africa and has a territorial area of 582,646 square kilometres. The country is about the size of Texas or 2.4 times as large as Great Britain. About 11,000 square kilometres or two percent of Kenya is covered by the water of the Indian Ocean, Lake Victoria and several inland lakes especially in the Rift Valley (Figure 3.1). The country lies across the equator between 4° 21' North and 4° 28' South latitudes and 34° and 42° East longitudes. Kenya is bordered by the Republic of Somalia and the Indian Ocean to the east, Uganda to the west, Ethiopia and Sudan to the north and northwest, and Tanzania to the south.

Figure 3.1

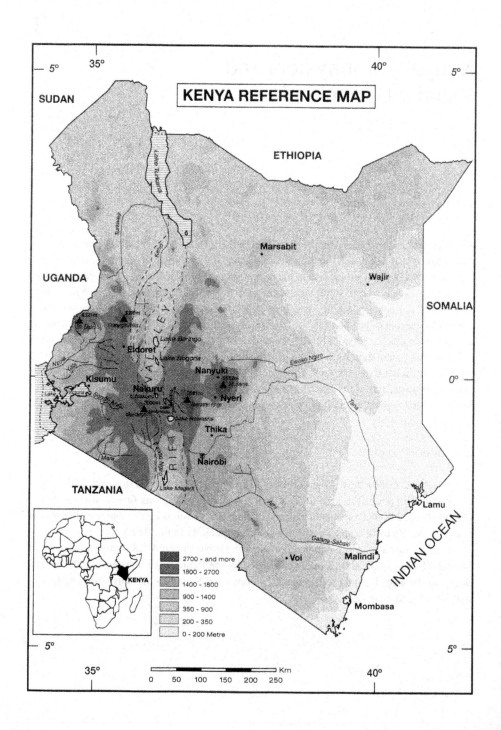

Biophysical environment

This section describes the country's physical environments which form the foundations for the development of tourist activities. This forms the basis for discussing Kenya's human environment in subsequent sections.

Relief

Kenya's relief is quite varied and ranges from sea level at the Indian Ocean coast to over 5000m in altitude (Figure 3.1). The land rises from the coastal plain (0-600m) to the highlands (2000 to 3000m) and to several volcanic peaks, the highest of which is Mount Kenya (5199m). Other peaks are Mount Elgon (4310m) at the Kenya-Uganda border, Aberdare range (3999m) at the eastern edge of the Rift Valley, the Cherangani range (3370m), and the Mau escarpment (3098m). Cherangani range is the highest non-volcanic mountain in Kenya (Krhoda, 1994a). Despite the presence of a mountainous topography, mountain climbing and hiking is an underdeveloped activity in Kenya (Chapter 4).

Kenya possesses almost every landform and landscape type from equatorial, tropical, savannah, aeolian, glacial, volcanic and tectonic (Ojany and Ogendo, 1973: 38). This great diversity of physical landscapes provides both variety and beauty. The great African Rift system, for example, is best delineated in Kenya and there are breath-taking viewpoints of this geological phenomenon. On the floor of the Rift Valley are several volcanic cones such as Longonot (2776m), Menengai (2279m), Silali (2355m), Suswa (2355m) and Shombole (1564m) (Ojany and Ogendo, 1973). In a number of cases the peaks of the cones have been blown off to create craters; however, the Menengai one is sufficiently large to be called a caldera. These varied landforms further provide the potential for hiking and camping.

Drainage

Kenya's drainage system is heavily influenced by relief. Rivers flow from the highlands to various depressions. The main problem with Kenya's rivers is the seasonal fluctuation of the volume of water. This is probably caused by "hydrometeorological problems" (Ojany, 1971: 138). The lack of water at certain times of the year affects water users including disrupting hydro-electric power generation.

Lake Victoria forms a large depression which was probably formed by forces of downwarping. In the Kenya Rift Valley are several lakes which occupy the lowest parts of the floor. These lakes which are highly variable in size, include Turkana (6405 sq. km.), Baringo (129 sq. km.), Bogoria (34 sq. km.), Nakuru (52 sq.km., although it has a history of fluctuating between 5 and 52 sq. km. over the past several decades), Elmenteita (21 sq. km.), Magadi (104 sq. km.), and Naivasha (210 sq. km.) (Kenya, 1994d: 4; Ojany and Ogendo, 1973: 53-55). Lake Amboseli is seasonal and dries up when there is a shortage of rain water whereas Lake Nakuru's size is highly variable depending on the supply of water.

The Rift Valley lakes provide an important tourist attraction. Lake Nakuru National Park is known as a bird sanctuary with one to two million lesser flamingoes and a large number of other birds. When the water level goes down these birds migrate seasonally to other lakes especially Bogoria and Natron (in northern Tanzania). Lakes Naivasha (1890m above sea level) and Baringo, both fresh water lakes, have numerous species of birds. At Lake Naivasha, over 340 bird species have been spotted in one visit whereas 400 species have been identified at Lake Baringo (Nyeki, 1992: 76, 83).

Lake Bogoria has geysers and hot springs and a sampling of wildlife. Lakes Turkana, Baringo and Naivasha are also known for fresh water fish. They support a thriving fishing industry. Lake Turkana is situated in the desert and has rich bird life and crocodiles. For sporting fishermen, the lake offers the huge Nile perch and tiger fish (Nyeki, 1992: 82).

Forests form an important element in a country's drainage system and can at the same time have touristic value. For instance, the tropical rainforest remnants at Kakamega and Arabuko-Sokoke have great species diversity. Kakamega forest has indigenous tree species such as Elgon teak, red stinkwood and African satinwood (Nyeki, 1992). Also, it has unique butterflies, birds, reptiles and animals. Arabuko-Sokoke at the coast has a significant proportion of *Mbambakofi (Afzelia quanzenzis)* and *Brachystegia speciformis* (Wass, 1994). In addition, the forest has a number of endangered and rare animal species such as Golden rumped elephant shrew (*Rhynchocyon chrysopygus*), the Sokoke bushy-tailed mongoose (*Bdeogale crassicauda omnivora*) and Ader's duiker (*Cephalophus adersi*) (Virani, 1995). Its rare birds include the Sokoke scops owl (*Otus ireneae*) and Clarke's weaver (*Ploceus golandi*) (Virani, 1995).

Indian Ocean coast
Kenya's Indian Ocean coast measures about 640 km long and borders the Republic of Somalia to the north and the United Republic of Tanzania to the south. Most of the region rises from sea level to about 200 m in altitude; and to well over 1500 m in the Taita hills in the interior. The coastline has fringing coral reef running continuously at a distance varying from 0.5 km to 2 km off-shore. This reef is broken at the mouths of the River Sabaki just to the north of Malindi, the River Tana and several smaller rivers entering the Indian Ocean. In particular, the enormous silt discharged by the Sabaki river, estimated at 2 million tons of sediment annually (Ongwenyi, 1983 cited in Krhoda, 1994a), has hindered coral formation in Malindi to the north of Vasco da Gama pillar. As a result, it is impossible to develop beach tourist facilities in this area. The coral reef acts as a barrier to strong sea waves and in this way it protects the coastline from erosion. The white sand beaches of the Kenya coastline are due to the reef.

A narrow belt of land with a width of 3 km in the south and more than 50 km near the mouth of the River Tana forms the coastal plain which is the most significant portion of the coast for tourism activity. This area has a mean temperature of 22° C and is hot and humid; however, temperature rises to more than 30° C. The soil consists of corals, sands and alluvium. Coral soil and beach sand overlay the raised coastal reef. The land is suitable for cultivation and livestock rearing as rainfall allows. The main crops grown are coconut palm trees, mangoes, citrus fruits, bananas, maize and sugar cane.

Kenya's large number of natural beaches is a major tourist attraction. The coral reefs off the beach have spectacular colours. The lagoons behind the coral reef are good grounds for such recreation activities as swimming, goggling, surfing and sailing. The coral reef keeps away dangerous sea animals including sharks (Visser and Koyo, 1992). Coral fishes come in a myriad shapes, sizes, and colour and form an excellent seascape.

The Kenya coast is a *ria* or drowned coastline which experienced a rise in sea level during the Pleistocene period. This rise in sea level led to the drowning of river mouths thereby creating several tidal creeks, sheltered bays and deep water inlets. These allow a range of opportunities for safe sport fishing (Ouma, 1970). Malindi in particular is world famous for big game fishing including marlin, tunny, sailfish, kingfish, barracuda, dolphin, giant rock cod and big sharks (Kenya, 1971a; Ouma, 1970).

Lamu's sheltered waters offer potential for cruising and yachting by providing several places to visit and safe anchorages (Kenya, 1971a). The area to the east of Lamu is quite rich in marine life and can attract diving, goggling, shark fishing and game fishing. Boating can also safely be done at Kilifi creek, Mtwapa and Tudor with opportunities for open sea cruising and sport fishing. Other areas for such boating activities are Vanga, Wasini Channel, Funzi Bay and Ganzi.

The estuarine parts of the coast where fresh water and sea water mix are excellent habitats for mangrove forests, and cover an area of 64,990 hectares (Visser and Koyo, 1992; Mutua-Kihu, 1984). The forests yield fuelwood and timber; and the mangrove ecosystem is a rich ground for fish, crabs, prawns and oysters (Visser and Njuguna, 1992; Visser and Koyo, 1992). Save for the Mida creek which has been developed for sight-seeing and bird watching, mangrove forest areas have remained unexploited for tourism (Visser and Koyo, 1992: 67).

Climate and ecological habitats
As noted above, Kenya's latitudinal location, its varied relief and landforms combine to give the country a range of climatic possibilities from equatorial to hot desert to temperate. The ecological habitats vary as well spanning the spectrum from mangroves and swamps along the coast to bushland and woodland, grassland types and barren desert in the interior, dense rain forest, bamboo forest, mountain heath and moorland, and permanent ice on top of Mount Kenya (Sindiga and Burnett, 1988). Overall, rainfall is the most important climatic factor. The amount of rainfall influences the type of farming undertaken in various parts of the country.

Rainfall can be used as an indicator of ecological potential (Sombroek, Braun and van der Pouw, 1982). Based on average annual rainfall and the average annual evaporation, various zones of moisture availability exist in Kenya, ranging from humid to very arid. When combined with temperature, this classification can provide a good picture of the variations in ecological potential as was done to produce detailed maps of agroclimatic or agro-ecological zones for Kenya (Sombroek, *et al.*, 1982; Jaetzold and Schmidt, 1982; 1983a, 1983b).

Despite its size, Kenya is short of good agricultural land. Given current farming practices and technology, potentially cultivable land is limited to 17.7 percent of the total land area. As will be shown below, this is the land in the highlands, around Lake Victoria and along the Indian Ocean coast, in which 75 percent of Kenya's population live. The marginal semi-arid, arid, and very arid zones make up the remaining 82.3 percent of the country and accounts for about 25 percent of the country's population, and 50 percent of the total livestock (Kenya, 1997: 49). This is also the area which carries most of the wildlife, the basis of Kenya's tourism industry.

The carrying capacities of some of the rangelands has long been exceeded because of population pressure exerted by humans, livestock and wildlife (Sindiga, 1984; Rajotte, 1983). Although the inhabitants of these areas survive mainly through herding, there appears to be a symbiotic relationship between pastoral peoples and herbivorous wild animals. Wild animals are more likely to survive very dry periods than livestock and they sometimes bridge the protein shortage gap (Croze and Mbuvi, 1981). This relationship perhaps provides partial explanation for the conservation of rich wildlife resources on the East African rangelands. Kenya's network of national parks and reserves has mainly been developed in the arid and semi-arid parts of the country.

Government and history

Administration
Administratively, Kenya is divided into eight provinces, each of which is further divided into several districts. Each district in turn has divisions, locations and sublocations. The latter are the smallest administrative units. Superimposed on this central government divisions are local government authorities. Essentially, each district is also a county council. The urban areas are run either as city, municipal council, town council or urban council in order of size, significance or political expediency (see Table 3.6). Nairobi is the only urban area with city status.

In the colonial period, provincial and district boundaries were drawn along ethnic lines. A single ethnic group was usually bound in an administrative area. Although some provinces and districts were cosmopolitan, this official divide-and-rule policy tended to emphasize ethnic exclusiveness and this carried forth to independent Kenya. As will be seen below, the administrative structure had potential to threaten the new nation-state.

Colonial period
Kenya was a British protectorate between 1895 and 1920 when it was declared as a colony. Initially known as the East Africa protectorate and administered from Zanzibar, the British regarded the land as of great strategic significance in their scheme to control Uganda and secure the Nile valley. During the first half of the twentieth century, the Kenya colony was dominated by a small group of European settlers who came primarily from Britain and South Africa; in addition, small groups arrived from Australia, New Zealand and Canada (Ogot, 1974). These settler farmers were quite wealthy and controlled the colonial government. Below this group in colonial Kenya's socio-economic hierarchy were Indians who worked as shopkeepers and traders. Some Africans, initially the Waswahili, Somalis and Sudanese served as policemen, porters and soldiers. At the bottom of the hierarchy were the majority of the Africans. This latter group suffered the brunt of British colonialism in Kenya. They lost the fertile land in the highlands which was expropriated to give way to the European settlers.

The establishment of *Pax Brittanica* led to the rigid partitioning and classification of the colony's rural space into "scheduled", that is, land exclusively alienated for European settlement; and "reserve" or land set aside for exclusive African habitation. The few Indians in the colony were kept out of agriculture by law. Consequently, distinct systems of socio-economic arrangement derived from the land classification. Africans lost both economic and political power and were prevented from owning land in the scheduled areas. However, Europeans gained access to the resources of African areas, especially labour but the reverse process was ruled out. In addition, the colonial government imposed a hut tax on all African households. This measure was intended to raise revenue for the government. In another sense it was intended to force Africans to work for Europeans in order to raise the money to pay the annual tax.

In general, the distribution of the beneficial side effects of colonialism, such as improved health and nutrition, modern educational facilities, better farming techniques, and easier transport and communications primarily served the interests of the British rather than indigenously expressed demands and local development (Soja, 1979). This colonial arrangement provided a class of people with the resources for starting domestic tourism in Kenya. As will be shown in Chapter 4, this wealthy class of European farmers could afford the time and the resources to create the demand for, and undertake internal tourism activities. Settler colonialism pushed for the creation of national parks and reserves after an initial period of carefree hunting. The purpose of protecting wildlife was to regulate sport hunting and the collection of trophies. In time, the European settlers felt the need to create accommodation facilities, camping grounds and tourism infrastructure which would become the basis of a thriving tourism industry in independent Kenya. The settlers took time off especially during Christmas and Easter vacations to go to the Indian Ocean coast and the parks for a holiday.

Post-Independence period
Box 3.1 provides a chronology of independent Kenya's political history. The country regained its independence in 1963 and became a republic in 1964 under an executive president. Since independence, Kenya has had elected governments after every five years. Except for a brief period between 1966 and 1969, Kenya developed as a *de facto* one-party state, a status which was legalised in June 1982 with the Kenya African National Union (KANU) monopolizing political power. The status quo was maintained until 1992 when a multi-party parliamentary democracy was established.

Under one-party rule, certain basic freedoms such as speech and public assembly were circumscribed. The electronic media (radio and television) were government-owned and controlled. Although the mass circulation newspapers were foreign-owned, they tended to exercise self-censorship so as to stay in tune with government requirements.[1]

---

[1] The exception to this was when Kenyan newspaper editor, George Githii attacked the practice of detaining people without trial *(The Standard,* July 20, 1982, p. 4). It is instructive that the editor's views were widely discussed and criticized in parliament. The board of directors of *The Standard* newspapers quickly relieved the editor of his duties because of his opinions thereby assuaging the political establishment (Nyamora, 1982: 6). This case confirmed widely-held views at the time that newspaper editors could publish certain things at their own peril. There were, indeed, instances where editors were humiliated in public if they did not toe the establishment line *(The Standard,* July 20, 1982, p. 4).

BOX 3.1: Political history of independent Kenya: a chronology

1963: Kenya regains independence from the United Kingdom. The first parliament comprised of KANU which the forms the government and opposition members from KADU and APP.

1964: Kenya becomes a republic with an executive president; and a de facto one party state following voluntary dissolution of the opposition parties thereby leaving KANU with a monopoly of political power (Ojwang, 1990).

1966: A number of radicals break away from KANU and form KPU. Parliament has two political parties.

1969: The government bans KPU and parliament reverts to one party status.

1971: Reports of an attempted coup d'etat against the KANU government surface and several people are tried and imprisoned for treason.

1978: Jomo Kenyatta, the founding president of Kenya, dies on August 22 and is succeeded by Daniel arap Moi, his vice-president in a peaceful political transition.

1982: Attempted coup by members of the Kenya Air Force; Kenya is declared a de jure one party state and all dissent is thereafter suppressed. Extensive use of preventive detention law to silence critics of the government and the one party system.

1992: Law prohibiting multi-party political participation repealed. Multi-party parliamentary and civic elections conducted in December.

1997: Clamour for constitutional reform reaches its height and an inter-parties parliamentary group introduces a limited legal, administrative and constitutional reform package aimed at providing a level playing ground for the second multi-party elections in that year. Second multi-party general elections for presidential, parliamentary and civic candidates held on December 27. KANU retains power for another five years.

Matters came to a head in 1982 when Kenya was declared a single party state by law. This action was followed by the detention without trial of a number of politicians and academics thereby creating a very tense political environment (*The Standard,* 1982: 4). To many people, the legalization of the one-party state meant the criminalization of free speech, freedom of association, and political dissent. The ensuing political tension led to a coup attempt against the government by junior officers of the Kenya Air Force on August 1st 1982, almost two months after Kenya became a *de jure* one-party state. Although the coup attempt was suppressed by loyalist forces, the government clamped down on all dissent leading to the intensification of political suspicions.[2] Besides, dissenting voices went underground only to break out again from 1990 onwards when the movement for multiparty democracy began to gather momentum. This led to liberalization of the political space and a multiparty general election in 1992.

Despite the country's political problems in the period up to 1990, Kenya's economy remained reasonably sound. There was also a perception of political stability, at least in comparison to many countries in the sub-Saharan Africa region. Unlike many African countries which experienced political instability resulting from military dictatorships in the first three decades of political independence, Kenya remained relatively stable and peaceful under civilian rule. Also, in the era of the Cold War, Kenya always was a supporter of the West in a region characterized by socialist and marxist expansion.

Tanzania, the southern neighbour had long embraced *Ujamaa,* African socialism as its political ideology; Ethiopia which at the beginning had an absolute monarchy passed into the hands of a communist dictatorship under Mengistu Haile Mariam. Somalia became a military autocracy. And Uganda went through a period of experimentation with socialism under Milton Obote (1962-1971) before entering a decade of military dictatorship and murder under Idi Amin Dada (1971-79). It was this background which made Kenya a favourite country for Western governments. This Western support and the country's relatively well developed tourism infrastructure led many international visitors to the country. Kenya's relative success, especially in the first two decades of independence, has been attributed to a number of reasons. Among these is the fact that at independence the country retained white-settlers who had technical management skills thereby maintaining production and capital formation (Lamb, 1982). Consequently, "Kenya operates far more efficiently than most African countries, and foreign investment and tourists from the West have poured into the country, providing greater economic stimulus" (Lamb, 1982: 64). Other reasons for Kenya's success included giving top priority to the agricultural sector; developing the social infrastructure, especially hospitals and schools; keeping defence spending low; and maintaining a capitalist model of development with a monetary reward system for initiative (Lamb, 1982: 64). In brief, Kenya was doing the right things in the Western mind. This assisted in attracting foreign investment capital, a substantial part of which went into tourism development, through hotel development and tour operations business (Langdon, 1980: 151).

---

[2] A number of publications document the crackdown on political dissent in Kenya in the 1970s and 1980s. These include Thiong'o (1981); Kinyatti (1996); Africa Watch (1991); and Kihoro (1998).

The political situation from 1990

Since 1990, Kenya's tourism numbers began to decline (Chapters 4 and 6). One estimate puts the decline of Kenya's tourism industry at 40 percent in 1992 alone partly because of political violence and insecurity (National Election Monitoring Unit, 1993: 3). Although many other factors account for the decline, it is clear that local insecurity generated by political violence was largely to blame. As happens in similar situations, international tour operators and travel agents swiftly blacklisted Kenya as a politically unstable destination. The context of Kenya's political violence requires to be discussed.

Goran Hyden (1996) noted that donors and international financial organisations have, since 1990, added political democratization to the array of policy prescriptions for Africa. As a result of this conditionality, international bodies joined local demands for the liberalization of Kenya's politics through increasing participation in the political process. Many saw multi-party democracy as the basic ingredient to achieving the goal of a plural political system. It may, however, be recalled that the country's experimentation with multipartyism before the mid-1960s was a failure. Drawing from that experience, the KANU leadership argued that the major dynamics of the initial multipartyism, namely ethnic competition and rivalry, tribal and racial divisions, and contradictions between the proponents of plural politics and those in favour of unitary state policies (Ojwang, 1990: 45), would begin to rear their ugly head again and tear the nation-state apart. As Ojwang (1990: 45) further notes:

> The brief experience with the multi-party system hardly revealed the constructive constitutional functioning of a parliamentary opposition. The spectacle of a fully accepted opposition, keeping the government on its toes and alternating with it in holding the reins of power, was certainly not the mark of Kenya's first experience with a multi-party system.

Many KANU politicians, particularly the Kalenjin and Maasai, opposed multipartyism by fronting for a political philosophy of regionalism which sought to create a government of semi-autonomous regions *(majimbo)*. Such views were represented by KADU in the independence constitution before the party dissolved itself voluntarily and merged with KANU which stood for a unitary government. Essentially, the Kalenjin politicians saw the clamour for democratization from a rather narrow perspective. To them, it was a conspiracy by the major ethnic groups in the country, notably the Kikuyu, Luo and Luhya, to snatch political power from President Daniel arap Moi. Herein was the justification for attempting to remove the Kikuyu, Luhya, Gusii and other groups who had been resettled in the Rift Valley province by the Kenyatta government. The multiparty debate degenerated into ethnic competition for power. Even with these apprehensions among KANU's leadership, the tide for democratization was too strong. On December 10, 1991 the government reluctantly accepted to open up democratic space by repealing the legislation which made Kenya a single party state.

As if to fulfill the prophecy, ethnic clashes broke out in the country towards the end of 1991 in the former "White Highlands", where many ethnic communities had been resettled after independence. In subsequent years, the clashes sporadically flared up in one part of the country or other thereby seriously affecting social and economic life and tourism activities. While recognising the causes of the clashes were multi-dimensional and complex (for example, Kenya, 1992), a consultant for the UNDP was nevertheless able to conclude that the principal causes of the clashes

> are directly and unequivocally related to the ongoing democratization in Kenya and where traditional ethnic rivalries and competition over land, which had been effectively kept dormant throughout most of the post-colonial period, have now been re-ignited by opposing political forces. A consequence of this is that various ethnic groups, who for the past decades had been living in harmony and mutual interdependence, have been brought into violent conflict with each other (Rogge, 1993).

Earlier, a parliamentary select committee identified the root causes of the 1991/92 clashes to be political and that they had been fuelled by some government officers (Kenya, 1992: 82). Indeed, it was widely believed that ethnic clashes were part of a KANU-sponsored plan to undermine the political democratization process thereby providing a reconfigured political space which would allow the party to recapture majority seats in parliament (for example, KHRC, 1997). Another reason for the clashes was the misconception that some ethnic communities could displace others and acquire their land (Kenya, 1992: 82). Those to be expelled were seen to be against the political status quo in the country. By 1993, the clashes had displaced one percent of the country's population from their homes (Rogge, 1993). The displacements occurred in many provinces, namely: Rift Valley — Nakuru, Trans Nzoia, West Pokot, Turkana, Elgeyo-Marakwet, Kericho, Nandi, Uasin Gishu, Laikipia, Bomet and Narok districts; Western — Bungoma, Busia, Kakamega and Mount Elgon districts; Nyanza — Kisumu, Kisii and Nyamira districts; Eastern — Kitui, Meru, Marsabit and Isiolo districts; Coast — Tana River and Lamu districts; and North Eastern province — Mandera, Garissa, and Wajir districts (Kenya, 1992). However, the clashes in Eastern, Coast and North Eastern provinces appear to be perennial. There is general insecurity and rampant cattle rustling in the specified districts within these provinces.

The clashes created a large internally displaced population and a deterioration in ethnic relations in the country. The United States Committee for Refugees estimated that Kenya had 210,000 internally displaced persons by 1995 (Gardner and Blackburn, 1996: 7). In a sense, the ethnic clashes are a sign of the failure of the country's political institutions to hold the country together. Although there were no direct attacks on tourists, the general insecurity created a poor environment for conducting the tourism business.

Violence at the Coast, 1997
In August 1997 ethnic violence erupted in the Coast tourism region covering Kwale, Mombasa and Kilifi districts. The violence subsided in November 1997 by which time hundreds of people were dead or injured, thousands displaced from their homes, hundreds of kiosks, some selling tourist arts and crafts, and residential buildings destroyed by fire and the tourist economy severely undermined (KHRC, 1997). The clashes were ignited by an attack on Likoni police station by a gang of more than 100 armed people. This area is settled by a relatively large mix of up-country Kenyans (20 percent of the population) comprising mainly of the Kamba, Luo, Kikuyu and Luhya. In time, isolated incidents of violence and arson took place in Mombasa and Malindi.

Although Kenya's national press claimed that the Coast violence was initiated by coastal peoples against up-country immigrants who mainly work in tourism establishments, the motivation and causes of the violence appear to be much more complex. It is still an open question whether the violence of 1997 was initiated by coastal people or whether it was organised up-country. Those who subscribe to the latter view argue that as part of their election plan, the ruling elite instigated the clashes in time for the second multiparty general election in order to displace up-country people suspected to favour opposition parties (KHRC, 1997). However, there are internal factors which may partly explain the violence. Coast people are frustrated by lack of employment opportunities and problems relating to land ownership. Whereas up-country people may be perceived to take jobs which the local people could do, it may be noted that the majority of the local Muslims would not work in tourism establishments because they regard the menial jobs offered as some kind of slavery (Sindiga, 1996b). On land ownership, most coastal peoples are squatters, that is, they do not have legal rights on the land which they occupy (Martin, 1973). The land is classified as either trustland, that is land not yet allocated on title but whose management is vested in local governments, or belongs to individual landlords.

In the 1997 Coast violence, not a single tourist or tourist hotel or big business was targeted by the raiders. However, there was a drastic fall in tourist numbers and tourism income. The KTB estimated a loss of about US$ 280 million in tourist earnings between mid-1997 and mid-1998 because of the Coast violence and the insecurity associated with the 1997 general elections (*East African Standard,* January 6, 1998, p. 7). Bed occupancy at the Coast fell to as low as 24 percent in April 1998 compared to 52 percent in the previous year (*Daily Nation,* May 15, 1998, p. 5). Many tourist hotels drastically reduced their tariff whereas others closed down for renovations. In the process, many people lost their employment. The efforts of individual tourism establishments to revive tourism could, however, not bear fruit until political violence, ethnic tensions and general insecurity are addressed satisfactorily by the political establishment.

In general, Kenya's transformation from a single-party to a multi-party parliamentary system did not come with peace and tranquility. As elsewhere in sub-Saharan Africa, real democratic change has eluded many countries which have introduced multiparty politics. For example, democratization appears to have led to anarchy in Niger, turmoil in Zambia, and political impasse in Mali (Gaye, 1998: 2). Multiparty general elections without comprehensive legal, administrative and constitutional reforms do not lead to the expansion of democratic space for the population. Without such reforms, ethnic rivalry and the monopoly of power by the winners cannot be assuaged. For this reason, Kenya began a major constitutional review process in 1998 aimed at providing certain guarantees for various freedoms before the next multiparty general election scheduled for 2002.

Population

Kenya is a multi-ethnic and multi-racial country. The country has over 40 different ethnic communities which are defined as linguistic groups. There are also Europeans, Asians and Arabs in Kenya's cultural mix. These communities represent cultural groups with a multiplicity of cultural practices and traditions. Kenya's ethnic mix is particularly significant because of the variation in the sizes of the individual groups.

The most dominant group is the Kikuyu with over 20 percent of the population. Table 3.1 shows the twelve main ethnic groups in Kenya using the 1989 national census data. These groups form about 92 percent of the population. The Bantu-speaking peoples (Kikuyu, Luhya, Kamba, Gusii, Meru, Mijikenda, Embu and Taita) form the main segment of Kenya's population. The Luo who are River-lake Nilotes and the Kalenjin (Highland Nilotes) follow as individual groups. Kenya has numerous minority ethnic communities. This ethnic pluralism, although a challenge, can be an asset to the creative energy of a modern nation-state. The African examples of Somalia and Rwanda demonstrate that it is simplistic to conclude that ethnic pluralism causes civil strife. The creative talents of a plural society can be channelled to greater social, economic and cultural development.

Kenya has a youthful population which grew from 15 million people in 1979 to 21 million in 1989 (Appendix 2). The population was estimated to be 27.5 million in 1995 and is projected to increase to 31.9 million in the year 2001 (Table 3.2). This rapid population growth presents serious difficulties in economic development. The relatively young population leads to a high dependency ratio and inflates the bill for providing health care, education and social services. Although the total fertility rate appears to be declining, the population momentum already created by a large youthful population will push the numbers up steadily before it starts to stabilize after many years.

Kenya's population densities are highly variable across districts (Appendix 2). They range form over 517 and 411 persons per square kilometre in the high potential districts of Kisii and Kakamega, respectively, to as low as 2 to 3 persons in Wajir and Tana River which are low potential districts. This highly variable population distribution poses difficult challenges in providing services in different environments. Besides, population pressure from the high potential areas has, for decades, forced people down the ecological gradient to the semi-arid and arid areas. Their attempts to eke out a living from cultivation has increased the probability of drought and repeated crop failure. By cultivating portions of the rangelands, traditional pastoral economies are destabilized. This leads to overpopulation and dramatically contributes to resource abuse.

Also, Table 3.2 shows that the country is rapidly urbanizing. This is having serious impacts on urban development and infrastructure. As a proportion of the total population, the urban population grew from 14 percent in 1979 to 16.8 percent 1989 (Table 3.2). The numbers of urban centres, considering a lower population limit of 2000 (Kenya, 1994e; Obudho and Aduwo, 1990) have been increasing as well (Table 3.3). Unfortunately, most of these urban centres are restricted to the high potential area in the highlands and the coast. This reflects the history of urbanization in Kenya. Urban centres sprung up along the Kenya-Uganda railway, that colonial project which opened up Kenya for European settlement in the highlands, connecting Mombasa and Kisumu; others emerged from administrative outposts of the colonial government. Also, the distribution

Table 3.1
Kenya's major ethnic groups

Ethnic group	Number (1989)	Percent of total
1. Kikuyu	4,455,865	20.76
2. Luhya	3,083,273	14.38
3. Luo	2,653,932	12.38
4. Kalenjin[1]	2,458,123	11.46
5. Kamba	2,448,302	11.42
6. Gusii	1,318,409	6.15
7. Meru	1,087,778	5.07
8. Mijikenda[2]	1,007,371	4.70
9. Maasai	377,089	1.76
10. Turkana	283,750	1.32
11. Embu	256,623	1.20
12. Taita	203,389	0.95
TOTAL	19,633,904	91.55

NOTES:
1. This was the first time that the Kalenjin appeared as one ethnic group in the Kenya census. The Kalenjin are classified linguistically as Highland Nilotes and speak several related languages as follows:

Nandi	-	once called Chemwal;
Kipsigis	-	("Lumbwa");
Nyangori	-	(Terik);
Keiyo	-	(Elgeyo);
Tugen	-	("Kamasya");
Marakwet	-	(including Endo);
Pokot	-	("Suk");
Kony	-	wrongly termed Elgon Maasai, together with the Pok and Bungomek (collectively called "Sabaot");
Sebei	-	Live in Uganda; and Okiek or Dorobo (Sutton, 1976: 22-23; Ogot, 1981: 84). In the 1989 census report, the Okiek were listed as a separate ethnic group. The word "Kalenjin" means "I tell you" and was adopted in the 1940s (Ogot, 1981: 84).

2. The Mijikenda are Bantu-speaking peoples of the Kenya coast who traditionally occupied nine separate villages each of which became a sub-tribe within the Mijikenda community. These groups speak separate but related languages. They are the Wagiriama, Wadigo, Wakauma, Wajibana, Waribe, Warabai, Wakambe, Wachonyi and Waduruma.

Source: Kenya, 1994a: 6-2

Table 3.2
Kenya's population characteristics

	1979	1989	1995 (estimate)	2001 (projected)
Total population (million)	16.2	23.2	27.5	31.9
Growth rate (percent per year)	3.9	3.4	2.9	2.5
Density (persons per sq.km.)	26	37	43	49.9
Urban population (million)	2.3	3.9	5.3	7.4
Total fertility rate	7.8	6.7	5.4	4.8

Source: Kenya, 1997: 131

of population shows that Nairobi and Mombasa are primate cities monopolizing most central place functions. In 1989, Nairobi's population of 1,324,570 people was about 2.9 times as large as Mombasa, the second ranking urban centre. Both Nairobi and Mombasa accounted for 46 percent of the urban population. Along the coast, Mombasa is about 13.6 times larger than Malindi, the second ranking urban centre in population in the province. Urban primacy can have the effect of stifling the growth of secondary towns thereby perpetuating regional inequality.

The urban population was estimated to be 19.3 percent in 1995 and is expected to form 23.2 percent of the total population in the year 2001. With this level of urbanization the country must learn new ways of meeting the basic requirements of large urban populations including housing, water, electricity, roads, refuse and sewage disposal, health and education facilities and such like.

Table 3.3
Number of urban centres by size of population, 1948-1989

Size of population	1948	1962	1969	1979	1989
100,000+	1	2	2	3	6
20,000 - 99,999	1	2	2	13	24
10,000 - 19,999	2	3	7	11	192
5,000 - 9,999	3	11	11	22	322
2,000 - 4,999	10	16	25	42	61
Total	17	34	47	91	139

Sources: Obudho and Aduwo, 1990: 54; Kenya, 1994e: 9-17.

Economic situation

Kenya is an agicultural country. Agriculture's contribution to real GDP growth has been higher than any other sector of the economy. The agricultural sector contributed 36.6 percent of GDP between 1964 and 1974, 33.2 percent from 1974 to 1979, 29.8 percent between 1980 and 1989, and 26 percent in the period 1990-95 (Kenya, 1997: 50; Table 3.4). It can be noted from these figures that agriculture's relative contribution to the GDP has been declining. However, without any significant mineral resources, agriculture remains one of the most important sectors of the Kenyan economy both in terms of economic growth and employment generation. By far the preponderant number of Kenyans lives and works in the rural areas either directly in agriculture or in agriculture related activities (Table 3.5). But given the diminishing contribution of agriculture to the GDP, its role in generating greater employment will be seriously affected. Also, it may be noted that wage employment grew by about 3.6 percent per year from 1964 to 1973. This improved to 4.2 percent from 1974 to 1979 but declined to 3.5 percent in the 1980s and a dismal 1.9 percent per year in the early 1990s (Kenya, 1997). One of the reason for this decline is that the growth of the Kenyan economy has never kept pace with the population growth. In the 1960s, the country's population growth rate was about 3 percent per year.

Table 3.4
Kenya's sectoral shares in the real gross domestic product, 1964-1995

Sector	1964-73	1974-79	1980-89	1990-95
Agriculture	36.6	33.2	29.8	26.2
Manufacturing	10.0	11.8	12.8	13.6
Services	53.4	55.0	57.4	60.2
Total	100.0	100.0	100.0	100.0

Source: Kenya, 1997:6

This peaked at 4 percent per year in the 1970s and 1980s essentially because of a high fertility rate and declining mortality. Fortuitously, the growth rate has been reduced to 3.5 percent in the 1990s because of a declining fertility rate (Kenya, 1994a; 1997; see also Table 3.2).

The country relies heavily on coffee, tea, and horticulture for foreign exchange earnings. In 1990, tea accounted for 25.5 percent of the total value of exports, coffee took 17.9 per cent and horticulture about 13 percent. By 1995, the figures were 19.3 percent, 15.5 percent and 11.4 percent for tea, coffee and horticulture, respectively (Kenya, 1997: 6-7). The tourism industry is the second highest single foreign exchange earner for the country after tea.

Overall, Kenya's economic performance has been declining since independence. The country's per capita income has declined as well from US$ 420 in 1980 to US$ 260 in 1998. The proportion of people living below the poverty line rose from an estimated 44 percent in 1989 to 50 percent in 1998. Gross domestic product grew at an average rate of 6.6 percent per year in the first post-independence decade. This rate declined to 5.2 percent between 1974 and 1979, 4.1 percent between 1980 and 1989, and 2.5 percent per year between 1990 and 1995 (Kenya, 1997:2). The economic growth decline was triggered by the international oil crisis of 1973 which had a structural ripple effect on the economy especially in agriculture.

Table 3.5
Kenya: Sources of employment and employment growth (in millions)

Sector	1991	1994	2001	Increase
Small scale agriculture	5.31	5.92	7.00	1.08
Large scale agriculture	0.42	0.47	0.55	0.08
Rural informal	0.35	0.62	0.98	0.36
Rural formal	0.23	0.41	0.55	0.13
Urban formal	0.74	0.81	1.08	0.27
Urban informal	0.70	1.16	1.83	0.66
Total employed	7.77	9.40	12	2.61
Total labour force	10.1	11.5	13.7	2.23
Unemployed (Percent)	23.4	18.5	12.8	--

Source: Kenya: 1997: 16

The sectoral share contributions to the GDP (Table 3.4) shows that the service sector contributes more than half the country's GDP. Also, it provides two-thirds of Kenya's modern wage employment. A prominent contributor to the service sector is the tourism industry. In 1996, tourism contributed 11.2 percent of the GDP and 18 percent foreign exchange earnings (Kenya, 1998b). Although these figures declined in the following year mainly because of insecurity, there is great potential for the development of tourism in the country.

Social situation

The decline in Kenya's economic health has had a direct effect on the social situation in the country. A good indicator of the well-being of a population is the level of child nutrition. Kenya's child nutrition appears to have stagnated or deteriorated after showing some improvement in the 1980s. The level of stunting of under-five children is currently about 34 percent of the population (Kenya, 1996b: 5) suggesting that the parents cannot grow or buy sufficient food for various reasons. Overall, 50 percent of the rural population lives in poverty and have no access to minimum food and essential non-food requirements (Kenya, 1996b: 6). As an aggregate figure, 10 million people live in poverty.

Any analysis of poverty is, however, a hazardous exercise. This is because poverty is usually defined using consumption. A person, or household is considered poor if, "despite prudent management of consumption resources at its disposal, it still finds that it cannot attain some recommended food energy intake" (Kenya, 1994f: 30). Kenya's Central Bureau of Statistics (CBS) uses a nutrient intake level of 2250 calories a day per adult plus a minimum allowance for non-food consumption. But it is clear that this figure is merely an average as the actual calorific requirement depends on several factors including body size, age, sex, environmental conditions and even lifestyle (Kenya, 1994f: 30).

Poverty is compounded by high levels of unemployment (Table 3.5). In 1996, it was estimated that 2 million people were unemployed; in the urban areas the unemployment level was about 25 percent (Kenya, 1996b: 5-6). The country must create half a million jobs every year to the year 2010 in order to keep up with the population (Kenya, 1994b: 42).

Infrastructure development

The provision of infrastructural services is critical to development. Although the term infrastructure tends to refer to all resources required for the establishment and functioning of a particular organization (Philippi *et al.*, 1994: 473), the emphasis here is on a few components of the economic infrastructure. These are public works and transport, public utilities such as power, telecommunications, water, sanitation and sewage and solid waste collection and disposal (World Bank, 1994). This is necessary because the business environment for tourism development requires improved infrastructure. Such includes roads to connect tourist ports of entry and the attractions and to allow tourism in national parks, and supply of water and electricity to the centres of the tourism industry. Indeed, an effective tourism development strategy requires careful balancing between demand for tourism and supply of facilities, and between direct investment in tourist facilities such as hotels, lodges and casinos and that made in the infrastructure necessary for supporting those facilities (Kenya, 1983: 142).

Throughout the developing countries and especially Africa there has been failure to maintain infrastructure adequately. Maintenance is overdue on 60 to 70 percent of the roads and this makes them to last only about half their projected time; 15 to 30 percent of the water and electricity produced is wasted before reaching customers; power systems work at only 60 percent at their generative capacity instead of best practice level of 80 percent; and water supply is only 70 percent of its installed capacity instead of 85 percent best practice level (Phillipi, *et al.*, 1994: 480; World Bank, 1994: 4). The reasons for the poor performance of the Third World include lack of competition because infrastructure services tend to be provided by state monopolies, services are delivered below cost, and users are unable to articulate their demands (World Bank, 1994). Yet infrastructure services are central to welfare and to economic production. Below, I consider the development of a number of infrastructure facilities in Kenya.

Transport
Many scholars have emphasized the need to examine transport services when analysing tourism in developing countries (Turton and Mutambirwa, 1996). Both land-based and air transport are crucial to tourism. Kenya's transport infrastructure comprises of roads, railway, maritime, pipeline and air transport. Road transport is more flexible and allows the movement of agricultural produce to urban areas whereas the railway is best suited for bulky goods to distant places. Air transport is used to move perishable horticultural products and flowers from farms to the markets. In addition, it is used for passenger traffic including tourists. This section focuses on these three transport modes and excludes marine and pipeline transport.

Road transport accounts for more than 80 percent of the total passenger and freight traffic in Kenya (Kenya, 1997: 104). Kenya's road network consists of 63663 km of "classified" roads of which only 8804 km (about 14 percent) is bitumenized (Kenya, 1997). In addition, there are 80,000 km of "unclassified" roads which form about 53 percent of the total road network. The latter are managed by the Ministry of Environment and Natural Resources through its Forest Department, Ministry of Tourism and Wildlife through the Kenya Wildlife Service (KWS), County Councils and other local authorities, with the municipalities and Nairobi accounting for 7,000 km (Kenya, 1997). With only about 4.7 percent of the total road network, urban roads carry more than 70 percent of all vehicles in the country because of the concentration of economic activities there. Only 45 percent of the urban road network is in "good" condition (Kenya, 1997: 109).

Although the country has tried to open up more roads, the maintenance standard is very low. Consequently, the roads are falling apart. This leads to very high transportation costs because motor vehicle spares must be replaced frequently. Also, it makes travelling a fearsome exercise because of personal discomfort, the high probability of road accidents, and the enormous amount of time consumed in travelling.

The government will need to pay greater attention to the maintenance and rehabilitation of the existing road network and to open up new roads in order to improve the efficiency of the country's productive capacity and to enhance the movement of tourists. With regard to the latter, the roads connecting Kenya's network of national parks and reserves need to be improved. The road system within individual parks must be graded for all-weather use.

Railway transportation is the second most important mode of transport after roads. Although it is the objective of the Kenya Railways to become the main carrier of both goods and passengers over long distances (Kenya, 1983: 186), the present realities show that freight haulage accounts for more than 80 percent of its total annual revenue with passenger transport accounting for only 10 percent (Kenya, 1997: 112). The number of railway passengers declined from 2.6 million in 1991 to 1.7 million in 1995. As a passenger carrier, the railway appears to be unpopular among Kenyans many of whom prefer to use road transport. Consequently, earnings from the roads are much higher than the railway (Table 3.6). The increase in revenues for the railway reflected on Table 3.6 comes more from adjustments in tariff rates than performance (Musuva, 1992).

Built as a British colonial project from Mombasa in 1896, Kenya Railways operates a network of 2,735 km of track and employs 21,000 people (Musuva, 1992: 265). The initial railway line connected Mombasa and Kisumu on Lake Victoria from where passengers and cargo to Uganda could go by lake steamer. This situation persisted from 1902 when the line reached Kisumu until the 1920s when a branch line was constructed from Nakuru to Tororo and Kampala via Eldoret. But this line did not come into operation until 1931. From the main railroad, a number of branch lines were constructed for specialized purposes during the colonial period. These are Konza to Magadi (in 1915) for soda ash mining at Lake Magadi; Nairobi to Thika (1913) and to Nanyuki (1930); Naivasha to Nyahururu (1929), Nakuru to Solai (1929), Eldoret to Kitale (1926) and Kisumu to Butere in 1920. Except for the Kisumu to Butere line and the Konza to Magadi line all these extensions were intended to serve European farming interests in the highlands. Another branch line connects Voi with Moshi (built in 1916) in northern Tanzania.

Railway commuter services have been unable to become a truly national transport service for a number of reasons. First, there is great competition with buses and other public transport services which offer faster and more accessible service. Second, the trains move too slowly. The Mombasa-Kisumu journey, a distance of 928 km, for example, takes 38 hours including a 12-hour break in Nairobi whereas the Mombasa to Nairobi trip takes an average of 22 hours or at least 15 hours with transit priority (Ongaro, 1995: 88, 151). This is partly because Kenya's railway is a simple tree-shaped single track network which tends to be very rigid. This means that should a section be impassable for whatever reason, it causes delays through the entire network or branch lines (Ongaro, 1995). Second, the railway system is not connected to several economically-deserving areas such as Kerio Valley, Nanyuki-Meru-Embu-Sagana, and Kisii-Sotik (Kenya, 1983: 186). This makes it difficult for the railway system to operate in an optimal way. Third, the Kenya Railways Corporation appears to suffer from many problems among which are insufficient locomotives, wagons and spares, inadequate maintenance, and huge operational costs (Kenya, 1983: 186;1997: 113). This problem may be largely a management one. The railways have long operated as a public corporation funded by the Kenyan taxpayer. As such, it has not been run on purely commercial principles. Besides, there appears to be no clear definition of the market targets and this makes it difficult to monitor the performance of the organization (Musuva, 1992: 275).

Yet, there is some demand for an efficient national train service for passengers. This stems from the fact that road transport is uncomfortable and much accident-prone and that it is comparatively more expensive. Another market niche for the railways is the tourism industry. Kenya's trains are slow moving and this may attract certain tourists. However, most long-distance trains currently travel at night thereby making it difficult for tourists to enjoy the country's varied physical geography.

Ever since Kenya established a domestic air transport service in 1929, air travel has become crucial in the development of tourism, the movement of horticulture products and flowers and for promoting regional integration (Kenya, 1997). A number of national parks and reserves in remote locations and Malindi at the coast are connected by air. Three airports in Kenya, namely Nairobi, Mombasa and the new Eldoret one are equipped for jet services. Malindi is also capable of handling medium sized aircraft, whereas Wilson airport in Nairobi handles chartered light aircraft both within and outside Kenya. Together with Kisumu, these airports are equipped with fire fighting systems, water supply, ambulance service, police service, travellers lounge, and customs and immigration officials.

Table 3.6
Earnings from road and rail traffic*, 1989-1993 (K£million)

	1989	1990	1991	1992	1993
Passenger traffic					
Road	244.9	285.9	358.8	421.5	438.8
Rail	8.1	10.3	11.7	12.4	14.4
Total	253.0	296.2	370.5	433.9	453.2
Freight traffic					
Road	176.6	193.0	239.1	262.5	280.8
Rail**	65.6	86.0	102.5	104.1	145.0
Total	242.2	279.0	341.6	366.6	425.8
Total road traffic	421.5	478.9	597.9	684.0	719.6
Total rail traffic	73.7	96.3	114.2	116.5	159.4
Total	495.2	575.2	712.1	800.5	879.0

*   Railway figures have been adjusted to read calendar year from 1986
** Includes other revenue.
Source: Kenya, 1994f: 181

The second tier of airports which includes Embu, Garissa, Keekorok, Kakamega, Kitale, Lamu, Kilaguni, Marsabit, Nyeri, Nanyuki, Voi and Ukunda, has runways with a mix of bitumen, murram, sand, bare soil or grass. The third tier is made up of numerous aerodromes distributed around the country. Together with the second tier these aerodromes are mainly used by civil servants on duty, during emergencies, anti-poaching patrols in wildlife areas, for shooting films, relief services, and agricultural work such as crop spraying (Ongaro, 1996).

The busiest domestic airports are Malindi, Lamu, Nairobi, Keekorok in Maasai Mara National Reserve, Mombasa, and Ukunda (Ongaro, 1996) partly reflecting the use of these airports by tourist traffic. However, airport facilities and the standards of service need to be improved at major airports to make air travel safer and efficient.

Water and sanitation

Water is essential for human survival and a necessary infrastructural service for all sectors of the economy. Current estimates indicate that 75 percent of the country's urban population has access to safe drinking water whereas only 50 percent of the rural population has access to potable water from a number of sources such as pipes, boreholes, springs, pans and dams (Kenya, 1997). However, there are wide regional variations in the availability of water. The large semi-arid and arid zone for example, has little surface water, and ground water resources are of varying quality in terms of salinity and chemical composition (see for example Krhoda, 1994b). Besides, except perhaps for certain parts of Coast Province, Kenya does not appear to have much ground water in the semi-arid area where the metamorphic rocks of the pre-Cambrian basement complex yield much lower supplies (Edwards, 1981: 89). Water is generally inadequate in Kenya in both the rural and urban areas. Domestic, industrial and commercial users do not get sufficient supplies of water.

The problem of water supply is also serious in the coastal region, especially Mombasa. Its main supply is a 270-km long pipe from Mzima Springs in Tsavo West National Park which produces about 35,000 cubic metres of water a day but also serves Voi, Maungu, Mbololo, Mackinnon Road, Samburu, Mariakani, Mazeras and Changamwe, in addition to Mombasa Island. This is supplemented with water from Marere river, Sabaki river and boreholes. The latter have been constructed by institutions, hotels and private homes. However, water supply is still inadequate. For example, in Mombasa in 1992 all sources supplied 85,000 cubic metres of water per day, compared to the demand level of 190,000 cubic metres in the low season and 220,000 cubic metres in the high season (Kenya, 1994h: 19). Both the Mzima Springs and Marere supplies which were put on line in 1953 and 1916, respectively, were established for much smaller populations than they currently serve. The pipelines are corroded and the pumps are damaged (Kenya, 1994h). The Marere pipeline from Kwale is 40 km long and has a production capacity of 9,200 cubic metres per day (Kenya, 1994h).

The majority of Kenya's urban areas including Nairobi have over-extended and grossly underdesigned water supply schemes for their populations. In many cases the quality of service is appalling either because of low pressures or broken pipes. Water is proving to be particularly troublesome to nearly all of the country's rapidly expanding urban populations.

Besides efficient water supply there should be an efficient system of sanitation and refuse management. The Kenya government summarizes the problem in the urban areas as follows:

> Currently, out of the 142 gazetted urban areas in Kenya, only 30 percent have sewerage systems. This is partly because in many urban areas, the development of water supplies has not been matched by a corresponding increase in facilities for sanitary disposal of waste-water, thereby posing serious environmental and health problems. Some of the systems do not even have the capacity to handle their full sewage load. In addition, there is an increasing need to address the issue of management of solid wastes in urban areas (Kenya, 1997: 126).

Indeed, in nearly all of Kenya's urban centres, refuse collection is a stubborn problem. In Nairobi, daily refuse collection is less than 25 percent of the refuse accumulated (Kenya, 1994f: 139). This poses a serious health hazard to the residents. The problem is probably worse in the rural areas.

Energy

Electricity is the second largest source of commercial energy in Kenya after petroleum. The latter accounts for about 67 percent of the country's total industrial and commercial energy consumption. This dependence on imported energy distorts the country's economic performance as international market prices of crude oil tend to be unstable. Of the three sources of electricity in the country, hydro power accounts for 629 Megawatts (MW) which represents nearly 75 percent of the total domestic installed capacity, while thermal oil accounts for nearly 18 percent of the total. Geothermal power from Olkaria supplies 5.4 percent of the total capacity (Kenya, 1997: 98-99). About 30 MW are imported from the Owen Falls Dam in Uganda each year.

Kenya does not generate sufficient electricity. During peak periods, demand is greater than supply. The problem is worse in dry periods when dammed water levels go low and the power plants cannot produce enough. This leads to irregular supplies of electricity leading the power company to ration supplies. This seriously affects commercial and industrial enterprises including tourism enterprises. The worst hit places are accommodation facilities where entertainment programmes are interrupted, food in storage facilities gets spoilt, and several other conveniences are affected. This causes losses. Unless the problems of water and electricity are addressed urgently, they are likely to reduce further foreign investments in Kenya.

Partly because of lack of sufficient electricity most of the non-commercial energy is provided by wood. Probably up to 80 percent of the Kenyans use wood fuel for cooking heating and other domestic purposes. This is especially so in the rural areas, where the majority of the Kenyans live. Also, woodfuel is used among the urban poor.

The heavy demand on woodfuel supplies has led to deforestation of water catchment areas. As a result, soil erosion, denuded hillsides, siltation and desertification processes have become serious. In the semi-arid areas the climax vegetation is bushland and woodland. Closed canopy forest occurs only in the small highland areas and the coast where there is ample rainfall and where the majority of the people live. Much of this forest has been cleared for various reasons including woodfuel supplies; only 1.2 million hectares of forest remain (Kenya, 1994g: 13). Should current trends persist, some 20 percent of this forest will be cleared within the next 25 years.

Communications
Communications are at the core of modern development by allowing interaction at various scales, information exchange and trade. The total number of telephone exchange connections rose from 200,000 in 1991 to 250,000 in 1995 reflecting a growth rate of 6.3 percent per year (Kenya, 1997: 119). These figures also reflect a telephone density of 9.4 lines per 1000 people. It is projected that the total telephone exchange capacity will increase from 377,000 lines in 1995 to about 675.000 lines in 2001; and that total exchange connections will increase from 250,000 lines to over 500,000 lines by 2001 thereby raising the telephone density to 15.2 lines per 1000 people (Kenya, 1997: 119).

Although these projected figures are still inadequate, the modernization and expansion of telecommunications will assist general development. This is because electronic mail systems, facsimile technology and telex have become indispensable tools of development by speeding up the flow of information for decision-making. These services require adequate telecommunication lines.

Summary and conclusion

This chapter has explained that Kenya was a British colony until 1963 when political power was passed to the African majority. The country's settler colonialism was responsible for creating national parks and reserves and provided a class of people with a demand for tourism services. Relative political and economic stability in the post-independence period led to the rapid development of the tourism industry. At the beginning of the 1990s the single party state was greatly discredited leading to the re-introduction of a multiparty political system. Multiparty politics re-ignited ethnic rivalries and tribal groups aligned themselves into opposing political forces ending up into violent conflicts in different parts of the country. By 1998, Kenya's security problem was such that it had pushed tourism to "its lowest ebb in history" (*Kenya Times,* June 16, 1998: 6).

The chapter also outlined Kenya's varied physical geography, ecological diversity and water resources. The land rises from sea level to well over 5000 m. The country's landscapes including the Rift Valley, volcanic mountains, savanna grasslands, wetlands, woodlands and bushland, tropical rainforests, and barren desert provide many options for tourism activity.

An important climatic characteristic of Kenya is the aridity of 80 percent of the country. Kenya's wildlife reserves are mainly located in this semi-arid and arid zone. The diversity of the biophysical habitats shown in this chapter provide great potential for tourism development – from beach tourism and water sports along the Indian Ocean coast, to angling, riding, canoeing, bird watching, mountain climbing, and wildlife photography in interior locations.

Kenya's social picture shows considerable poverty in the backdrop of a youthful and rapidly increasing population. Unemployment is a serious problem. Agriculture which has been the main employer steadily declined in the past few decades; its contribution to GDP is now much lower. This background is important to understanding government desire to diversify economic activities. Tourism development should be viewed in this context.

This chapter has also discussed the status of selected infrastructural facilities which are essential to Kenya's economic development. The specific indicators considered were road, railway and air transport, water and sanitation, electricity and telecommunications. The physical measures of infrastructure provision provide a picture of inadequate development and maintenance of the facilities, especially roads. There are also variations in the provision of infrastructure between the urban and rural areas, to the disadvantage of the latter. Unless urgent measures are taken, lack of adequate infrastructure could foreclose further investments in the country.

Under the structural adjustment programme being implemented in Kenya (Chapter 2), the government has started to divest from many infrastructure facilities such as telecommunications, air transport business and liberalize aspects such as electricity generation (Kenya, 1996b). Other measures will include charging urban consumers a water tariff to cover capital amortization and operation and maintenance of the systems. These steps of liberalizing certain aspects of infrastructure to allow the private sector greater participation in business, and charging user fees at cost are likely to improve the efficiency of service delivery. However, the physical works infrastructure especially road maintenance remain an unsolved problem. This is because in developing countries, public works and services tend to be in the hands of the state. Usually the state is reluctant to let go public works and equipment purchase which are capital-intensive and generate political rewards (Philippi *et al.*, 1994). Although the Kenya government promises to address road maintenance, upgrading and rehabilitation of roads with the use of the road fund in a transparent manner (Kenya, 1996b: 61), it is clear from past experience that such undertakings turn out to be hollow.

4

Tourism in Kenya

This chapter examines the basic characteristics of Kenya's tourism, provides a brief historical account of its development including the management of tourism-led conservation, and discusses its role in the economy. By inquiring into tourism's role in the Kenyan economy it is expected to focus on tourism's contribution to foreign exchange earnings and other government revenues, and employment generation. Finally, the chapter discusses ways by which Kenya's tourism industry can generate increased foreign exchange earnings and their retention within the country and expanded job opportunities. This way, tourism could contribute meaningfully to the country's development.

Kenya is one of the most developed tourism destinations in sub-Saharan Africa (Williams, 1976; Economist Intelligence Unit, 1991). As noted above, tourism is the second highest single source of foreign exchange after tea. This position reflects some decline in tourism which was the leading foreign exchange earner for the country for about a decade since 1987. In 1996, Kenya attracted 4.5 percent of the 20 million tourist arrivals to Africa (WTO, Personal communication, 2 April 1997). This formed about 0.15 percent of international arrivals of tourists in the world in that year. Although Kenya's tourist arrivals declined to 3 percent of Africa's share of arrivals from abroad in 1997, reflecting the deterioration of the country's tourism product (Chapter 6), Kenya is still one of the top African tourist destinations after South Africa, Tunisia, Morocco, Zimbabwe, and Botswana.

Basic characteristics

Kenya's tourist numbers rose steadily from 65,400 in 1964 to a peak of 814,000 in 1990. The arrivals declined to 805,000 in 1991 and 699,000 in 1992. There was a marginal rise of 4.5 percent of visitor arrivals in 1994, however, subsequent years show continuing decline. Although the arrivals in 1996 and 1997 appear to have topped 1,003 thousand and 1,000.6 thousand, respectively (Kenya, 1998a: 9), these figures are of doubtful validity as the revised government projections show only a modest increase in numbers to the year 2001 (Table 4.1). Besides, the WTO record at 717 thousand and 700 thousand for the same years are significantly different from the government data cited above (WTO, Personal communication, 1998). The WTO figures may be more accurate because of the problems of Kenya tourism in the 1990s (Chapter 6).

Statistics on various tourism indicators in Kenya are notoriously inaccurate. Government publications tend to carry different figures for a given year. Sometimes, provisional results are used which may be significantly different from final tallies for the year. The statistics presented, however, provide relative indicators of the extent and magnitude of tourism.

Table 4.2 which should be read with the above caveat in mind, provides the basic statistics about Kenya's tourism for selected years between 1972 and 1997. The country's wildlife attracts many visitors who go to the National Parks and reserves. Other concentrations of tourism are the beaches along the Indian Ocean coastline; urban tours of Nairobi and Mombasa; and museums and historical sites.

Tourist attractions, present and future

Although a variety of attractions has been developed, there is very wide scope for further expansion (Table 4.3). The country's varied tourism resources could be exploited to the full. They offer opportunities for walking and hiking at various places, and nature trails in the forests. Facilities for polo and golf could also be developed; and so can angling for trout in the country's many highland rivers and fishing both at the coast and inland water bodies. The history of the sport fishery in Kenya has been summarized by Muchiri (1995) and Ouma (1970). Briefly, sport fishing started early in the 20th century with the introduction of brown trout and rainbow trout in the highland streams of the Mount Kenya region. Subsequently, new introductions were made in the streams of the Mau escarpment, Nyandarua and Kinangop ranges, Kericho, Mt. Elgon and Cherangani hills. In 1928, largemouth bass (*Micropterus salmoides*) was introduced in Lake Naivasha. These fisheries combined with native fish species to provide a basis for recreational fishing both in the rivers and other inland waters (Ouma, 1970). Whereas the country's inland fisheries have declined mainly because of the degradation of breeding grounds and loss of feeding grounds, recreational fishing in the marine waters of the Indian Ocean is an important activity which is undertaken all year round (Ouma, 1970: 55; Muchiri, 1995). In some inland waters especially Lakes Victoria and Turkana, fishing for Nile perch (*Lates niloticus*) is not fully utilized. Better management of the fisheries including periodic introduction of fingerlings could restore the fisheries and increase the potential for Kenya's recreational fisheries.

Cruise-ship tourism at the coast remains a virgin area. Luxury ship or boat trips in the Kilindini harbour and the surrounding areas, for example, could generate a lot of income. This can also be done at other places along the coast. Another arena for development is traditional cultural shows and dances. So far, there has been a heavy reliance on Maasai cultural life to the extent that it has become an African stereotype. Kenya's cultural pluralism has much greater variety that has yet to be fully exploited.

Table 4.1
Targets for Kenya's tourism development, 1997-2001

Tourism indicator	1997	1998	1999	2000	2001
Tourist arrivals (thousands)	767	848	941	1045	1160
Foreign exchange (K£ mil.)	1790	1940	2100	2280	2470
Bednights occupancy (000s)	7190	7480	8080	8870	9070
Number of days stay (000s)	11900	12900	13200	13900	14700

Source: Kenya, 1997: 19.

In terms of spatial considerations, Kenya has great potential for tourism development in various parts of the country. These include Lake Turkana area, Mount Elgon region, Lake Victoria basin, Kerio Valley and Lamu region. Lake Turkana has a beautiful volcanic landscape, is remote, has archaeological sites of world renown, a lake with fish, and the "greatest crocodile concentration in the world" (Nyeki, 1992: 91; Rajotte, 1983). Although Siliboi National Park to the eastern shore of the lake was long proclaimed, it remains underdeveloped in terms of access routes and accommodation. Koobi Fora archaeological site with fossil remains of Homo erectus going back three million years, and the Chalbi desert could be great attractions to certain types of tourists. Similarly, the potential of the Mt. Elgon region has not been exploited. Mount Elgon has a caldera on the top with hot springs and is known for its dense mountain forest and caves. These caves harbour leopards and hyenas, whereas the cave walls attract elephant, buffalo, duiker and bushbuck which lick them for salt (Nyeki, 1992: 80). It is possible to go by car to 4000 metres altitude from where hikers can scale one of the peaks or climb the caldera walls to the floor. The mountain has different vegetation zones along different altitudes and has a rich diversity of flora, fauna and birdlife. The problem with Mount Elgon is accessibility. The roads need to be upgraded to all-weather status to allow continuous tourist visitation.

The Kerio Valley is at the bottom of the western escarpment of the Rift Valley and is drained by the Kerio river which flows into Lake Turkana. Climbing the escarpment by car as the road coils around from the Kerio River to the top at Iten provides a spectacular view. The Kerio river in places has a magnificent gorge which could be developed for tourism. Another attraction in this area is the age-old traditional irrigation system practised by the Pokot and the Marakwet (Kipkorir, Soper and Ssenyonga, 1981; Adams, 1996). Also, the Rimoi Game Reserve at the valley floor has the small Baringo elephant and a variety of wildlife.

Another relatively underdeveloped area is Lamu. The infrastructure for tourism needs to be upgraded so that Lamu's full tourist potential could be realised. However, any further tourism development would need to be socially and culturally sensitive to Lamu's Islamic culture (Sindiga, 1996b). Lamu has long remained the centre of Islamic scholarship and religion in East Africa.

Table 4.2
Kenya tourism trends, selected years 1972-1997

	1972	1976	1980	1984	1988	1989	1990	1991	1992	1993	1994	1995	1996	1997
Visitor arrivals (000)	444	446	393	512	695	735	814	805	699	826	863	691	1,003	1,007
Visitor departures (000)	428	424	363	453	677	667	728	682	670	697	865	656	981	925
Hotel beds available (000 nights)	4,980	6,983	8,325	9,204	9,704	9,631	10,495	11,037	11,465	11,909	11,909	11,562	11,355	9,517
Occupancy rate (percent)	50	51	57	51	53	55	58	59	48	43	43	44	45	52*
Visitors to national parks & game reserves (000)	522	591	609	1,011	1,096	1,255	1,532	1,519	1,367	1,428	1,429	1,493	1,489	1,365
Visitors to museums, snake parks and sites (000)	342	433	508	746	808	831	907	790	813	850	818	843	759	588
Foreign exchange earnings (K£ m)	27	41	83	152	349	432	533	597	713	1,222	1,405	1,250	1,280	1,132

* This relatively high hotel occupancy rate in a poor tourism year for Kenya is explained by the reduction in hotel bed capacity brought about by the closure of several hotels especially at the coast (Chapters 3 and 6).

Sources: Kenya, 1994c; 1995; 1997b; 1998a

Table 4.3
Tourist attractions in Kenya

Developed	Underdeveloped
Wildlife safaris	Camping
Beaches	Hiking and mountain climbing
Marine life	
Urban tours	Forests e.g. mangroves, rainforest remnants
Balloon trips e.g. Maasai Mara	
Animal orphanage	Horseriding safaris
Plantation agriculture e.g. tea, coffee	Polo
	Cruise ship and water sports
Nature trails e.g. Bamburi	
Bird watching	Golf
Angling	Camel safaris
Dhow tours	Cultural shows
Race course	Cultural pluralism
Archaeological sites, historical ruins and museums	Sculpture and handicrafts
	Fish farms
Traditional dancing	Hunting
Traditional arts and crafts	Trout fishing — Aberdares and Mt. Kenya, lakes and rivers
	Wilderness holidays e.g. Lake Turkana

Geography of tourism

The largest share of tourist bednights is in the coastal region followed by Nairobi (Table 4.4). Nairobi is a principal business centre and the air transportation hub in eastern Africa and has been able to attract some conference tourism. In addition, visitors to Nairobi can view wildlife within a short distance of the city centre at the Nairobi National Park, and go to the Kenya national museum including the snake park and the Karen Blixen museum.

Lodges are dispersed around the country within or adjacent to wildlife protected areas. However, only about seven parks receive the preponderant number of visitors to Kenya. The following receive over 100,000 visitors each per year: Nairobi, Amboseli, Tsavo West, Tsavo East, and Lake Nakuru National Parks; Maasai Mara National Reserve, and the Nairobi Animal Orphanage (Table 4.5).

The data on bed-nights occupied by country of residence of the visitors and the Kenya tourism region visited show differences in tastes and preferences of the visitors (Table 4.5). Visitors from continental Europe appear to prefer a beach holiday whereas those from other countries go to the Nairobi area and the National Parks. In 1994, for example, Europeans spent 2,220.7 thousand bednights at the coast representing three-quarters of all European bednights in the country (Kenya, 1995: 165). Of the 5 million hotel bednights occupied by country of residence in 1995, 24 percent came from Germany, 19 percent from the UK, 6 percent each from France, Italy and Switzerland, and 5 percent from the USA (Kenya, 1996a: 178). In 1983, Germans became the leading single group visiting Kenya as shown by the number of bednights. Ever since, they have occupied over one million bednights each year. This peaked at 1.8 million bednights in

Table 4.4
Hotel bed-nights occupied by country of residence, 1997 ('000)

Country of residence	Nairobi	Coast	Lodges	Others	Total
Permanent occupants*	14.6	11.2	1.3	1.2	28.3
Germany	46.1	1,036.7	43.5	8.8	1,135.1
Switzerland	12.3	244.2	13.6	2.5	272.6
United Kingdom	148.6	714.2	64.4	28.8	956.0
Italy	22.4	214.0	10.9	2.0	249.3
France	37.3	184.1	38.7	7.5	267.6
Scandinavia	34.2	98.1	15.5	4.3	152.1
Other Europe	77.0	209.2	26.4	9.3	321.9
Kenya	262.3	291.8	29.8	192.9	776.8
Uganda	22.3	9.9	0.3	4.1	36.6
Tanzania	24.3	11.7	1.1	3.5	40.6
East and Central Africa	41.1	7.6	0.2	1.3	50.2
West Africa	18.6	2.1	0.7	0.3	21.7
North Africa	12.4	1.6	0.4	0.6	15.0
South Africa	29.2	13.1	0.8	0.5	43.6
Other Africa	45.5	16.7	0.7	1.5	64.4
U.S.A.	118.8	26.8	66.2	13.9	225.7
Canada	18.1	6.3	3.9	1.6	29.9
Other America	11.4	4.6	4.3	2.9	23.2
Japan	29.8	4.9	10.7	4.2	49.6
India	18.4	8.0	3.3	1.4	31.1
Middle East	23.0	3.9	5.3	2.4	34.6
Other Asia	13.8	8.0	2.8	1.6	26.2
Australia and New Zealand	19.5	2.9	5.7	2.1	30.2
All other countries	12.1	14.5	0.7	0.7	28.0
Total	1,113.1	3,146.1	351.2	299.9	4,910.3

* Persons staying one month or more in one hotel — includes some block bookings for aircrew.
Source: Kenya, 1998a: 181

1991 although there was a downturn in subsequent years (Kenya, 1995). Residents of the UK are second ranking to the Germans since 1986. Kenya needs to market its tourism in other parts of the world to improve the geographical coverage as an insurance against the risks associated with a narrow market.

Although many visitors from the UK go to the coast as well, a significant number still opts to stay in Nairobi. Most visitors from North America and Asia choose Nairobi and the game lodges. As will become clear later, the European domination is related to foreign capital and expertise in the country's tourism industry (Dieke, 1991; Chapter 5).

Among African countries, most tourists come from Tanzania followed by Uganda (Table 4.5). This shows clearly that there is a basis for regional tourism development within East Africa (Chapter 8). Besides, this can also encourage visitors from outside the region to make an East African tour.

Table 4.5
Number of visitors to national parks and game reserves, 1990-1997

	1990	1991	1992	1993	1994	1995	1996	1997
Nairobi	152.8	168.8	156.4	164.6	163.2	113.5	158.3	149.6
Animal Orphanage	213.8	217.8	173.2	155.3	182.0	212.1	210.6	193.7
Amboseli	237.2	189.2	168.3	121.1	159.5	114.8	109.1	117.2
Tsavo (West)	78.6	119.3	103.1	102.9	105.4	93.1	93.6	88.6
Tsavo (East)	127.7	135.9	125.5	135.8	132.4	228.8	137.5	123.2
Aberdares	66.6	56.3	63.6	60.8	60.2	70.1	60.2	59.0
Lake Nakuru	174.2	174.4	139.8	178.6	164.3	166.8	156.9	132.1
Maasai Mara	180.5	143.3	138.1	133.3	138.2	133.2	130.3	118.3
Bamburi Nature Park	...	...	...	93.2	98.9	109.2	107.0	86.8
Malindi Marine	35.6	33.0	44.2	41.1	39.4	38.8	39.3	27.0
Lake Bogoria	53.8	53.0	39.4	37.2	43.2	14.2	14.2	24.5
Meru	11.1	9.1	7.1	7.4	7.9	7.3	7.8	4.1
Shimba Hills	60.0	38.2	31.9	24.8	31.6	20.0	23.4	22.5
Mount Kenya	18.7	14.6	15.5	18.0	17.2	17.2	17.1	14.8
Samburu/Buffalo Springs	...	...	...	21.5	9.2	9.1	9.1	8.3
Kisite/Mpunguti	27.1	33.1	28.0	27.5	34.8	32.4	39.9	35.1
Mombasa Marine	29.1	54.6	57.8	43.3	48.0	23.9	21.7	15.2
Watamu Marine	20.5	22.0	27.0	31.7	32.7	16.1	20.2	19.4
Hell's Gate	31.1	41.3	34.2	47.4	44.9	50.1	52.1	47.2
Impala Sactuary (Kisumu)	...	...	...	59.1	5.5	3.5	65.6	62.4
Other*	13.8	14.8	14.0	16.6	9.6	18.9	14.8	15.5
Total	1,532.2	1,518.5	1,367.1	1,427.8	1,428.6	1,493.1	1,488.7	1,364.5

* Other includes Mount Elgon, Ol-Donyo Sabuk, Marsabit, Saiwa Swamp, Sibiloi, Ruma National Park, Mwea National Reserve, Central Island National Park, Nasolot National Reserve and Kakamega National Reserve.
Sources: Kenya, 1995: 167; 1998a: 182

Motivation for visiting Kenya

Table 4.6 shows the number of departing visitors by country of residence and purpose of visit for 1996 and 1997. The number for 1997 is depressed by about 6 percent reflecting negative publicity of the country in the Western media, poor promotion and reliance on a limited source market for tourists and political violence in the country (Kenya, 1996a: 172).[1] With the decline of the total number of departing visitors was the average length of stay by the tourists. In general, the total number of days stayed by visitors declined by 21.5 percent from 13,598.2 in 1996 to 10,673.1 in 1997 (Kenya, 1998a: 177). Most departing visitors to the country go for holiday (Table 4.6). This category of visitors also records the highest number of visitor days in the country. In 1994, for example, holidaymakers spent an average of 15.5 days whereas those on business stayed for only 8 days (Kenya, 1995). Although this trend has persisted over the years suggesting that Kenya is perceived as an excellent African destination for a holiday, the number of days stayed by holidaymakers and business people in 1997 declined by 20.6 percent and 37.0 percent respectively over the previous year (Kenya, 1998a: 177). However, government categorization of the purpose of visit for guests to Kenya is somewhat rigid and does not provide for the wide range of reasons for selecting and visiting the country.

---

[1] But see Chapter 6 for an analysis of the general decline of Kenya tourism since the early 1990s.

Research conducted by the Kenya Wildlife Service among tourists visiting Kenya provides deeper insights into personal choices (KWS, 1996). When asked on why they selected Africa (Kenya) for their visit, the following range of answers was given:
- A life time's dream — Africa; animals in the wild; adventure. *"It has been a dream since I was a small boy and now it's come true."*
- To see the big animals with one's own eyes; to experience them personally.
- To appreciate the whole natural scene and to see the animals within this natural environment (wildlife experience).
- To experience a different, more exotic holiday than obtainable in other continents. *"It's for the adventure and the unknown."*
- To experience African culture; *"I want to see the people, someone told me about the culture and life of the people here."*

Table 4.6
Departing visitors by country of residence and purpose of visit, 1996-1997

Country of residence	Holiday 1996	Holiday 1997	Business 1996	Business 1997	Transit 1996	Transit 1997	Total* 1996	Total* 1997
Germany	195.2	182.7	4.6	4.3	6.7	7.7	206.5	194.7
United Kingdom	123.2	115.1	18.9	17.6	5.8	6.7	147.9	139.4
Switzerland	20.5	19.0	2.6	2.4	2.0	2.3	25.1	23.7
Italy	25.4	23.7	3.0	2.8	1.7	1.9	30.1	28.4
France	19.6	18.1	2.7	2.5	1.8	2.1	24.1	22.7
Scandinavia	16.7	15.5	2.3	2.1	1.6	1.8	20.6	19.4
Other Europe	152.2	141.7	3.4	3.2	8.9	10.2	164.5	155.1
Total Europe	552.8	515.8	37.5	34.9	28.5	32.7	618.8	583.4
U.S.A.	45.9	42.9	5.3	4.9	2.4	2.8	53.6	50.6
Canada	14.7	13.6	1.9	1.8	1.3	1.5	17.9	16.9
Total North America	60.6	56.5	7.2	6.7	3.7	4.3	71.5	67.5
Uganda	14.8	13.7	21.9	20.4	2.5	2.9	39.2	37.0
Tanzania	27.0	24.2	5.8	5.4	6.8	7.8	39.6	37.4
Other Africa	32.7	29.5	18.1	16.8	8.3	9.5	59.1	55.8
Total Africa	74.5	67.4	45.8	42.6	17.6	20.2	137.9	130.2
India	12.4	11.5	2.5	2.3	1.3	1.5	16.2	15.3
Japan	10.7	10.0	1.3	1.2	0.6	0.7	12.6	11.9
Israel	5.9	5.6	0.9	0.8	0.3	0.3	7.1	6.7
Other Asia	13.4	12.2	3.4	3.2	1.7	2.0	18.5	17.4
Total Asia	42.4	39.3	8.1	7.5	3.9	4.5	54.4	51.3
Australia and N.Zealand	14.4	13.3	1.6	1.5	1.0	1.2	17.0	16.0
All other countries	55.8	52.0	0.9	0.8	2.8	3.3	59.5	56.1
Grand total	800.5	744.3	101.1	94.0	57.5	66.2	959.1	904.5

* The total does not include "other visitors" category.
Source: Kenya, 1998a: 177.

On the reason for choosing Kenya, the following responses were obtained (KWS, 1996):
- Wildlife, the main attraction
- Most familiar African country
- Obvious choice for wildlife; more animals and more choice of different safari packages. Kenya was the *"original"* safari destination.
- Beach/safari combination
- Better developed product. *"Safaris are more professional in Kenya — they were recommended by our friends."*
- Documentaries/films for example: "Born free", "Out of Africa"
- More politically stable
- British connections — "more civilized"
- Personal recommendation
- Cheaper
- Air connections
- More brochure space
- Famous names, for example, Maasai Mara, Tsavo, Amboseli, Tree Tops.

These responses reveal that Kenya is a choice tourist destination because of its rich wildlife and/or beaches. There is a sense of the exotic and adventure expected of an African visit in general and a Kenya one in particular. It is significant that Kenya is promoted by word of mouth by people who have visited the country previously, or through a television documentary rather than by systematic marketing and promotion. These channels of information combined with the data provided by tour operators to prepare the potential tourist on what to expect to gaze at when he or she arrives in Kenya. The tourist expectation may then be reinforced by actual experience at the destination or it may be constructed and reconstructed with the gaze on the landscape (Urry, 1991). The tourist views are subjective and impressionistic. Yet the whole enterprise of tourism and the dollars it generates is about personal likes and dislikes, impressions and mis-impressions. Hence the significance of tourists' feedback about their experiences in destination areas. Their views and perceptions can become grist on the mill of the tourist planner intent on providing a pleasurable tourism product.

Also, the KWS customer survey shows that tourists make several pleasant discoveries while they are visiting Kenya. Their gaze on the physical and social landscapes is reconstructed as they experience the places in the itinerary. The following are some of the responses given (KWS, 1996):
- The friendliness and charm of most of the Kenyans met.
- *"The people have been an unexpected and significant joy — you have no idea before you come."*
- The beauty of the scenery. *"I did not expect such beautiful country side. You see so much of the poor side of the country in pictures. We've been very impressed."*
- The richness of local culture.
- The climate inland — fresher and less hot than feared.

- The high standards of food and accommodation — particularly in parks. *"I expected the hotels would be much rougher — I've been surprised by their quality — they're first class."*
- *"Tasteful lodges blending in with their surroundings."*

However, Kenya's international tourists come face to face with some of Africa's difficult roads and the poverty of its peoples. Whereas some of the tourists "didn't realise the roads would be quite as bad" thereby making "travelling time so long", others felt that they were partaking of the real life of the country, a genuine old time safari. To the latter group the following remark is typical: "I wouldn't change the roads, it gives you a sense of roughness — it's all part of the experience and what the country is all about." The disappointment of many tourists about roads can be viewed from the perspective of ambitious itineraries prepared by tour operators without considering the realities of the local infrastructure, in this case the roads. Also, the visitors were shocked at the level of poverty they saw among local people. A typical remark was: "It's a culture shock to see how these people live in huts on the roadside." They expected Kenya to be wealthier than they saw it.

The foregoing has sketched the basic characteristics and trends of Kenya tourism. Also, it has outlined the major source areas of Kenya's international visitors and their preferences with regard to the country's tourism product. This includes the factors which influence tourists to go to Kenya. In the next section, I discuss in some detail the historical and geographical development of Kenya tourism. This is the basis of the later analysis on the role of tourism in the Kenyan economy.

Development of tourism

Kenya's rich wildlife resources was the base on which the country's tourism was founded. Since 1946 when Nairobi National Park was gazetted followed by Tsavo in 1948, the Aberdares in 1950, Meru in 1966 and Lake Nakuru National Park in 1967, the government adopted a policy of game protection and opening up these areas for tourism (Appendix 3). The National Park concept goes back to the nineteenth century with the creation of the Yellowstone National Park in the USA. In Kenya it became necessary to establish parks for the preservation of wildlife which had suffered destruction from hunting especially with the use of firearms following the establishment of British rule (Ouma, 1970; IBRD, 1963: 173). Initially, a number of ordinances was made to restrict game killing but this did not always stop the poachers (Ouma, 1970: 50). Such included the game ordinance of 1903, the East African wild bird protection ordinance, 1903, the game ordinance of 1909 which created the southern reserve (Maasailand) and the northern reserve; others were the game ordinance, 1921, and the Kenya colony and protectorate ordinances and regulations, 1937 (Ouma, 1970: 41-42). Before 1930, most of the overseas visitors to Kenya were wealthy Europeans and Americans who could afford the time and resources to undertake the long sea voyage.

In subsequent decades Kenya established additional protected areas to enhance wildlife conservation. A recent count reveals 25 terrestrial National Parks, 4 marine parks, 22 national reserves, 5 marine reserves, one animal orphanage, and one national sanctuary (Figure 4.1; Appendix 3). These parks cover about 8 percent of Kenya's area and host a wide variety of wildlife including the rare roan antelope, the Hirola antelope, and bongo, the forest antelope.

Classification of wildlife conservation areas
Perhaps the categorization of protected areas in Kenya requires some clarification. The classification of wildlife conservation areas as national/marine parks, national reserves/marine reserves, and game reserves implies a concept of the ownership and management of wildlife conservation areas which is important for the relationship of local people and protected areas and the benefits accruing therefrom (Sindiga, 1995; Chapters 6 and 7).

National Parks are state lands which are managed exclusively for the conservation of fauna and flora (Kenya, 1975; 1985a; 1989). Government policy explicitly states that parks are to be used for many purposes including educational, recreational, and tourism (Kenya, 1975). As such, activities such as cultivation, livestock herding, timber harvesting and consumptive wildlife utilization, for example sport hunting, live animal capture, cropping for meat and trophies and game ranching, are excluded from parks. Kenya banned sport hunting in 1977, followed by an embargo on curio and animal parts in 1978. Several attempts to revive limited hunting since then have not yet been allowed. In contrast, national reserves are declared by the government with the consent of a local authority on any type of land. The difference with parks is that certain land uses such as herding and woodfuel collection may be allowed in reserves; however, the entire wildlife management in Kenya is vested in the Kenya Wildlife Service (Kenya, 1985b) which also collects licensing fees for tourism facilities located in protected areas.

Marine parks are similar to National Parks in administration and management. Kenya established its first marine parks in 1968, the first country in the world to do so following an IUCN resolution in 1962 (Jackson, 1973). This was done to conserve fragile marine ecosystems, a recognition of the degradation of coral gardens in the reef by tourists collecting corals, and shells and other ornamental marine life (Musyoki, 1992). Marine parks are of varied size and start at the highest spring water mark and extend to some distance. The reserves extend beyond the parks. Both marine parks and reserves are managed by the KWS. Certain types of fishing by local people are allowed in the marine reserves.

Finally, wildlife is also conserved in forest reserves owned by the state and individuals, trustlands or land held in trust for local people usually by a local authority such as a county council, and in private farms and group and private ranches (Chapter 6). Wildlife have protection under the laws of Kenya and may not be killed even when they are present on private land. So far, forest tourism remains underdeveloped (KWS, 1990; Kenya, 1994g). This is partly because wildlife and forest management are housed in different government ministries and their aims and objectives are not always shared. The forest department concedes that deforestation including the indigenous species is a continuing problem (Kenya, 1994g: 14). Yet the value of forests for biological diversity and nature tourism cannot be overemphasized (KWS, 1990: 45).

Although initial wildlife conservation was to be closely intertwined with the development of Kenya's tourism, the goals of conservation have always been much broader. The 1945 Kenya National Parks ordinance, for example, outlined the goals of the parks to be "the preservation of wild animal life, wild vegetation and objects of aesthetic, geological, prehistoric, archaeological, historical, or other scientific interest therein, and for incidental matters relating thereto" (quoted in Ouma, 1970: 40). Unlike the wildlife Act of independent Kenya noted above, tourism activity was not purposely included; it can be inferred, however, that tourism was one of the incidental aspects of wildlife conservation. As such, the intensive tourist visitation which occurred in the parks in later decades had not been planned for. Lack of roads, airstrips, and lodging facilities presented the greatest difficulty for National Parks as tourist destinations (Ouma, 1970: 50). When, later, on tourist demand, such facilities were installed, they were superimposed on an existing park without prior planning. This had potential for problems.

The first visitors to the parks in the 1950s and 1960s were interested in sport hunting, sport fishing, collection of trophies, and generally experiencing the wild. The activities included slaughtering game for food, skins, ivory; capturing live animals for sale abroad; and photography. Kenya became world famous for sport hunting and tourism in general following the visit of American President Theodore Roosevelt earlier in the century and that of Queen Elizabeth II of the United Kingdom. As noted above, the creation of National Parks was a step in biodiversity conservation. It was not intended expressly to serve the needs of the incipient wildlife-based tourism. In the initial period of tourism development, the government role was somewhat limited. This might explain the later ambivalent attitude towards tourism planning.

Before 1940 Kenya had no tourism policy and there was no organization dealing with tourism. The East African Publicity Association (EAPA) was formed in 1938 to coordinate tourism activities, not only in Kenya but East Africa as a whole (Chapter 8). The outbreak of World War II did not allow the body to function. EAPA was succeeded by the East African Tourist Travel Association (EATTA) in 1948 to coordinate tourism business (Ouma, 1970). Over the next one and a half decades, EATTA was involved mainly in matters of tourism promotion and transport. There was relatively little done to plan and develop tourism as part of the colony's sectoral planning. This was the state of Kenya tourism at independence. The major preoccupation appeared to be opening up access roads in the parks to allow tourists to visit both in the wet and dry seasons (Popovic, 1972). One thing is clear, however, virtually all tourism income to the country was associated with wildlife (IBRD, 1963: 173). The money was drawn from transport, tour guides, professional hunters, and equipment and materials for hunting and photography procured from Kenyan firms. Income was also obtained from the sale of safari clothes, shoes, arts and crafts.

Figure 4.1

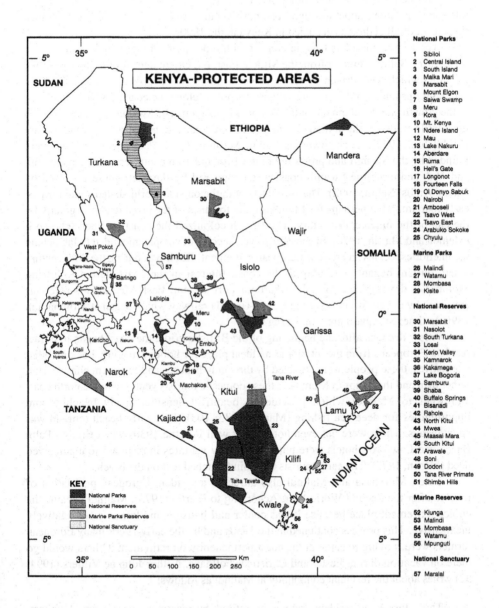

Origins of beach tourism
Parallel to the development of wildlife tourism was beach tourism at the Indian Ocean coast. Although it expanded to become a crucial part of the country's tourist industry, beach tourism started without much planning either (Popovic, 1972: 99). This raises interesting questions about its origins and how it could expand quickly to claim more than 60 percent of all bednights occupied in Kenya in the 1990s.

The Kenya coast has been in contact with other parts of the world for more than 2000 years. Sailors came in from the Middle East, the Orient and from southern Europe in *dhows* which were driven by the monsoon winds. These people mixed with the local Bantu groups and founded trading settlements dotted along the coast. These contacts led to the growth and development of the Swahili civilization. The Swahili participated in the mercantile trade on the Indian Ocean and founded an urban, literate, Islamic culture (Middleton, 1992). Such towns as Lamu, Malindi, Gedi, Pate and Mombasa were founded by the Swahili and prospered in the 14th and 15th centuries. Between the 16th and 18th centuries the Swahili coast was conquered by the Portuguese followed by Omani Arabs (Salim, 1992). These contacts with the outside world abated some form of early tourism. Save perhaps for Mombasa, the fortunes of the coast declined greatly by the end of the nineteenth century. The British colonized the coast but then ignored it (Memon and Martin, 1976). In subsequent years, coast development tended to lag behind the interior especially in areas of European settlement. But it was during the 20th century when tourism began to develop at the coast. Interest in the coast started following Mombasa's development as a deep-harbour port serving East Africa. This role was enhanced by the construction of the Kenya-Uganda railway which began at Mombasa in 1896. In time, Mombasa grew into a big town.

A few decades after the beginning of the British period, the coast began to attract resident Europeans from the interior as an ideal place for holiday making. Lacking other alternatives, these people were attracted by the sandy beaches and the warm climate. But, rather than end their trips in Mombasa, these domestic tourists ventured to the north coast and went to Malindi which provided a beautiful seaside, sandy beaches, and opportunities for deep-sea fishing (Martin, 1973: 103). This early beach tourism was spontaneous. There were not even hotels until well into the 1930s when Brady's Palm Beach and Lawford's hotels were put up as family ventures in response to a perceived need (Martin, 1973). The early tourists to Malindi pitched tent on the beach.

Later, Mombasa and Malindi also attracted a resident European population of retirees after the Second World War. According to Martin (1973), Malindi became the choice retirement place because it was cooler and housing and labour were relatively inexpensive. This process continued in the 1950s and by the early 1960s many European farmers were moving to settle at the coast permanently on retirement. Others would go there on vacation during Easter and Christmas holidays. Author John de Villiers (1994: 32) writes about the resultant community at Malindi as follows:

> This close-knit, resident faction of retired businessmen, pensioners, hoteliers, shopkeepers, small-scale coastal farmers, charter operators and a few old folk waiting to die, was probably not much different from a coastal residentia in any other place or country, though it did boast a nobility, black, white and brown ... it included the mandatory sprinkling of millionaires, retired, active and in transit, some politicians

and senior civil servants, the infamous and moderately famous, leading fishermen rich or poor .....

As Kenya became independent, coast tourism could be summarized as a place for resident Europeans to spend their holidays and a slowly emerging international tourist activity.

Post-independence tourism developments
Foreign visitors went to the coast only after 1962 on the first all-inclusive package holidays (Jackson, 1973). These tourists took advantage of the relatively cheap charter flights to Mombasa and were mainly Germans and Italians. This marked the beginning of mass tourism in Kenya. The numbers of the visitors increased tremendously after 1965.

As this influx of visitors had not been planned for, private investors made ad hoc responses to meet the demand. For example, up to 1970, most of the bed space expansion took the form of alterations and extensions to existing hotels (Kenya, 1971a). Coast tourism at this stage attracted little new investment because of the relatively underdeveloped physical infrastructure. Water supply was inadequate, the access roads were poor and communication facilities were meagre. Mombasa airport had poor facilities for handling aircraft. Further, there were delays and uncertainties in ferry operations especially across the Likoni channel connecting Mombasa Island to the south coast and across the Kilifi creek connecting Mombasa and Malindi. The government moved in, for the fist time, to attempt to salvage the situation with some kind of planning for existing tourism and future development (Kenya, 1971a). A plan for 3100 new beds at the coast by 1974 was inaugurated (Kenya, 1970). In addition, an interministerial working party was established to map out strategies for future development of coast tourism (Kenya, 1971a). Consequently, the physical infrastructure such as roads, electricity and water were expanded in the 1970s. Also, the government encouraged private developers and investors to participate in coast tourism. The KTDC provided the required investment finance (Chapter 5). In the meantime, private investors moved in and constructed hotels along the beaches wherever they could obtain land. There was neither government control nor regulation. The result was a ribbon-type spatial structure of hotels along the coastline. The government merely responded by providing infrastructure after investment decisions and actions had been made without prior planning.

For Kenya as a whole, tourism grew rapidly in the immediate post-independence period. The number of visitors increased by 24 percent in 1965 over the previous year. This was the highest rate of increase achieved over a period of ten years (Kenya, 1966b: 51). The number of visitors multiplied many times in the coming few years rising from 80,000 in 1965 to 339,000 in 1970 (Kenya, 1966b: 51; 1971b: 123). The government tended to appreciate this phenomenal increase in tourist numbers because it was associated with employment creation. Tourism led to 20,000 additional jobs in direct employment between 1968 and 1974 and a further 7,000 in agriculture and distribution (ILO, 1972: 211). However, tourism also induced a demand for other services in accommodation, entertainment, and distribution. The stage had been set for tourism to play an important role in the Kenyan economy in the future.

Management of tourism-led conservation

As already noted, Kenya's tourism primarily relies on biodiversity conservation. The management of biodiversity is in turn vested in the Kenya Wildlife Service (KWS) which was created as a quasi-government organisation by an Act of Parliament in 1989 to succeed the Wildlife Conservation and Management Department (WCMD) (Kenya: 1985a; 1985b). The latter was itself formed in 1976 and combined the functions of the former National Parks and the Game Department. The KWS is charged with the responsibility of wildlife management throughout Kenya both inside and outside formal protected areas.

The establishment of KWS followed a period of decline in wildlife resources, long the lifeline of Kenya's tourism industry. The numbers of visitors to the parks and reserves increased from 566,000 in 1979 to 987,000 in 1985, and to 1,532,000 in 1990 (Kenya, 1994f; 1984b; 1989), showing the significance of wildlife to tourism. As such, the policies for wildlife conservation and management had to meet with the objectives of tourism development (Kenya, 1979). But the increase in the numbers of tourists in Kenya's protected areas in the 1970s and 1980s coincided with falling standards in park management, a crumbling infrastructure and low staff morale. Overcrowding by tourist traffic in the parks and reserves led to animal harassment and overutilization of resources. In 15 years, 85 percent of the country's elephants and 97 percent of its rhinos disappeared. This was a result of poaching, that is, illegal game hunting for commercial purposes. The elephant was killed for its ivory which is used for carvings and trinkets; the rhinoceros was hunted for its horns which are used to prepare traditional medicines in the Orient, and carvings; and the lion for its skin which is used for decoration and its claws which form an important element in traditional medicine especially among the Waswahili of the East African coast. The leopards and cheetahs were sought for their ornamental skins which are used for clothing materials, hats and other decorations. Poaching reduced certain species of animals drastically. In many areas including National Parks and national reserves, poaching had either eliminated entire elephant populations or reduced their densities to unviable levels (Poole, 1992).

Poaching depends on a complex international market (Burnett and Conover, 1989). The price of ivory, for example, encouraged elephant destruction. A kilogramme of ivory which was going for US$ 10 in 1970 sold for US$ 300 by 1989 (Poole, 1992: 29). Between 1973 and 1989, poaching was so severe that Kenya lost an average of 5,000 elephants every year. Elephant populations were reduced from an estimated 130,000 in 1973 to about 20,000 in 1993 (Kenya, 1994f: 139; Poole, 1992: 29, 31). White rhinos were dramatically reduced as well. For example, in the Meru National Park to the east of Mount Kenya, the last native black rhino was killed in 1991 whereas the previously abundant white rhinos had been exterminated by 1989 (Dougherty, 1994: 18).

The 1970s had been particularly good years for the Kenyan economy. There was a boom in coffee trade as frost devastated Brazilian coffee in 1974. The smuggling of Uganda coffee across the border into Kenya brought in a lot of money into the economy. In the domestic market, demand for luxury commodities went up and with it demand for ivory and rhino horns (Sindiyo and Pertet, 1984: 13). This fuelled poaching. Yet, poaching can only succeed when there is corruption by government officials charged with wildlife protection (Burnett and Conover, 1989; Western, 1992a). In the Kenya case "indifference, laxity and corruption contributed to poaching" (Western, 1992a: 22). Poaching and widespread insecurity and lawlessness were caused by the easy availability of guns in Kenya from the political instability in Somalia and Ethiopia. Under the circumstances, tourists could not enjoy their trips into protected areas. Violence was unleashed on some of them.

In addition, the many negative environmental impacts of tourism on national parks and reserves led to serious questions about the relative contribution of parks as compared to beaches to the country's tourism industry. Further, Kenya's international tourism was affected by the closure of the Kenya-Tanzania border in 1977 following wrangling within the East African Community (EAC), an economic organization hitherto grouping the three East African countries (Chapter 8). Prior to this, most tourists to Kenya had always crossed the border into Tanzania. Finally, the Kenya government banned hunting and trade in game trophies in 1977 and 1978 respectively in the expectation of curbing poaching. Ironically, the banning of sport hunting had the short term effect of reducing the number of tourists to the wildlife areas (Sindiyo and Pertet, 1984). It did not stop the poachers who roamed freely in Kenya's National Parks and reserves eliminating their choice animals.

Because of a long period of decline in the standards of wildlife conservation and management, the future of wildlife tourism became quite shaky. From the mid-1980s Kenya's parks were in a terrible state (Olindo, 1991; Western, 1992a; 1992b). This was highly publicized in the Western media. The problems of wildlife tourism prior to the establishment of the KWS may be summarized as follows: insecurity in the parks associated with poaching and elimination of popular wildlife species, especially elephants; the deterioration of the parks' infrastructure, especially roads, and overcrowding. Under the circumstances, the government created a quasi-government organization which could have some autonomy by conducting its business outside the strictures of the civil service.

The principal goals of the KWS include conserving the natural environment of Kenya and its fauna and flora for the benefit of present and future generations; using wildlife resources in a sustainable manner for the economic development of local communities and the country as a whole; and protecting people and property from injury or damage (KWS, 1990). Among the strategies to achieve these goals are several elements intended to enhance tourism. This is a recognition that conservation qua conservation is itself not sustainable. Hence the emphasis on tourism-led conservation. Conservation attracts tourism revenues and the money is used partly to foster conservation.

The KWS therefore seeks to encourage the development of environmentally-sensitive tourism, maintain adequate security in conservation areas, restore and maintain park and reserve infrastructure, enable rural people to benefit from wildlife conservation, minimize conflicts between wildlife conservation and human settlement, educate people about wildlife, manage the protected areas according to plans and to increase cooperation with other sectors, among other strategies (KWS, 1990). As a quasi-government organization, the KWS is allowed to spend the resources that it generates from the parks through gate fees and licensing of various activities. A few years ago, the KWS opened a tourism division within the organization. This should complement the activities of the KTB in packaging and selling Kenya's tourism product in a systematic way (Chapter 5). Already, the KWS has issued a glossy 36-page colour National Parks and reserves tour planner which provides invaluable information, maps and addresses of important places (KWS, no date). Such effort will yield great promotional and marketing dividends for Kenya's tourism industry.

Tourism and the economy

Recognition of the economic benefits of tourism led the newly independent government to create a Ministry of Tourism, Forests and Wildlife. This emphasized the environmental and especially the wildlife basis of the country's tourism industry. A World Bank economic development mission at the dawn of independence in 1962 set the tone of Kenya's future tourism policy. Tourism would be nurtured because it was an important foreign exchange earner, would stimulate domestic income, and generate employment in other areas related to tourism (IBRD, 1963: 170). These objectives which were further elaborated and articulated by the subsequent national development plans (Kenya, 1966a; 1970; 1974;1979; 1984a; 1989; 1994a; 1997) may be summarized as follows:
1) to increase the contribution of tourism to the growth of the country's gross domestic product (GDP);
2) to increase foreign exchange earnings from the sector and maximize the retention of foreign exchange in the economy;
3) to create and expand employment opportunities;
4) to improve the quality of service offered by tourism enterprises; and
5) to conserve wildlife and protect the environment.

These objectives show the Kenya government's continued enthusiasm in tapping tourism's economic outcomes and preserving biodiversity.

The Kenya national economic statistics published in various government policy documents do not show tourism as a separate category in the national accounts (for example, Kenya, 1997; 1994d). Tourism statistics tend to be subsumed under services. Over the period 1982 to 1993, the absolute size of the tourism sector using 1982 constant prices grew from K£ 306.7 million to K£ 479.6 million representing an annual growth rate of 4.18 percent (JICA and Kenya, 1995d). The share of tourism in the GDP increased from 9.97 percent to 11.06 percent or an average of 10.9 percent, over the same period. In relative terms, the share of the tourism sector in real GDP was fourth ranking after agriculture (28.5 percent), government services (15.3 percent) and manufacturing (13.1 percent) (JICA and Kenya, 1995d). At present, the tourism sector contributes about 11 percent of the GDP (Kenya, 1998b: 18). This shows the important contribution which tourism makes to the Kenyan economy. Below, this contribution is examined more closely by focusing on tourism's performance indicators, namely, foreign exchange earnings, employment generation and its share in government revenues.

Foreign exchange earnings

Since independence, tourism has played a leading role in the country's foreign exchange income. It has maintained its position among the three leading export earners; the others are coffee and tea (Table 4.7). As such, tourism is an important contributor to the GDP and the foreign exchange reserves necessary to allow the importation of capital goods required for development and to service foreign debts.

Over the years, however, real dollar tourism earnings have been declining essentially because of the depreciation of the Kenya shilling (Sinclair, 1990). Also, per capita real earnings in tourism has been declining (JICA and Kenya, 1995d; Sinclair, 1990). The foreign exchange earnings per foreign tourist per day in 1993 was Ksh. 500 calculated on the basis of constant prices for 1982 (JICA and Kenya, 1995a). This figure which has been stable over the years represents US$ 9 at 1997 foreign exchange rate and demonstrates the low earnings per tourist for Kenya from international tourism. Also, although the absolute size of foreign exchange receipts from tourism grew by a compound annual growth rate of 3.97 percent between 1982 and 1993, average per capita tourist receipts declined by an annual compound growth rate of -2.09 percent (JICA and Kenya, 1995d).

Table 4.8 shows the gross tourist per capita expenditure per day over a period of some years. Although these are crude figures, they do emphasize the fact that the phenomenal increase in the numbers of tourists over the past three decades has not translated into high foreign exchange earnings for the country. This is related to the dominance of all-inclusive package tourists. For example, although tourist expenditure rose from K£ 16.7 million to K£ 18.5 million between 1969 and 1970, the average expenditure per visitor day declined from Ksh. 135 in 1969 to Ksh. 120 in 1970 (Kenya,

Table 4.7
Tourism's contribution to Kenya's total export earnings (percent)

Year	Tourism	Coffee	Tea	Year	Tourism	Coffee	Tea
1964	12	19	8	1979	16	27	15
1965	13	17	8	1980	17	21	11
1966	16	21	10	1981	18	21	12
1967	17	18	9	1982	22	25	14
1968	19	14	12	1983	20	24	19
1969	17	17	12	1984	20	26	24
1970	17	20	12	1985	25	29	24
1971	21	17	11	1986	25	40	18
1972	21	19	12	1987	37	25	21
1973	13	20	9	1988	37	26	20
1974	11	16	8	1989	42	20	27
1975	14	15	10	1990	43	18	26
1976	12	27	9	1991	37	14	24
1977	11	41	15	1992	40	12	28
1978	16	32	16	1993	34	15	26

Sources: Sinclair, 1990; Kenya, 1994d; tourism's contribution between 1989 and 1993 was calculated using data from Table 4.2 and Kenya, 1994d.

Table 4.8
Average expenditure of international tourists to Kenya (excluding international travel)

Year	Average length of stay (days)	Total expenditure per person (US$)	Expenditure per person per day (US$)
1982	16.2		
1983	15.9		
1984	15.9		
1985	15.9		
1986	15.9		
1987	16.0	536	33.5
1988	16.0	567	35.4
1989	14.4	571	39.6
1990	14.4	572	39.8
1991	13.7	537	39.0
1992	13.4	565	42.2
1993	13.9	500	36.0
1994	13.6	488	35.9
1995	12.2	657	-
1996	13.3	554	-
1997	11.8	-	-

Sources: WTO, Personal communication, 2 April 1997; various Economic Survey documents issued yearly by the Kenya Government.

1971b: 123). Ten years later, the problem of lack of real growth in receipts persisted. This was attributed to many tourists resorting to package and charter arrangements. In 1979, the ratio of private to package tours was 5:3; about 40 percent of the tourists came on package arrangements (Kenya, 1980: 160). The recognition of the problem did not lead the government to reverse mass tourism. Instead, it opted for lower spending package tourists in earnest. The government proceeded as follows:

> In order to maintain growth in tourist earnings and achieve the Development Plan targets, it will be necessary to attract such tourists in larger numbers in the face of powerful competition from other tourist areas in the world, and it will be increasingly important to offer them good value for money on their visits here. This means that publicity overseas will have to be stepped up, more tourist attractions developed, greater attention paid to ensuring that all tourists feel they are welcome as visitors in Kenya, and prices kept as low as possible, consistent with providing the facilities tourists expect, and the returns to investment which the economy needs (Kenya, 1971b: 123).

The government challenge to allow more tourists may be understood from the perspective of increasing economic benefits from tourism. However, those benefits were not commensurate to the price that the country was paying to sustain mass tourism in terms of infrastructure development and maintenance (roads, airports, public utilities, National Park development, hotels, air travel, tour operations, and personnel training) and the serious social and environmental impacts created (Hazlewood, 1979; Mitchell, 1970; Sindiga and Kanunah, 1998). Indeed, during the 1970s, the Kenya government made very large investments in airports. This included reconstructing Mombasa airport between 1976 and 1978 at a cost of K£ 11 million so that it could handle direct flights from Europe; and building a new terminal at the Nairobi airport at a cost of K£ 28 million in order to deal with large tourist flows (Hazlewood, 1979: 105). Also, Kenya has tended to emphasize large hotel structures which require imported materials and drain on foreign exchange reserves (Elkan, 1975).

Nonetheless, the government appears to have come to terms with the problem when it complained that

> The fees and taxes levied on foreign tourists are heavily subsidised and do not reflect the true cost to the Kenyan tax payer of developing and preserving tourist attractions (Kenya, 1989: 187).

In addition, it appears that the average spending per tourist day of Ksh. 630 recorded in 1987 was not sufficient to pay for even a domestic tourist (Kenya, 1989). The problem of "package" tourism was discussed in Chapters 1 and 2 and will be broached again in Chapter 5 while examining the structure of international tourism in Kenya.

Kenya is, however, fortunate in the sense that its economy is reasonably big and can save some foreign exchange earnings by reducing imports for the tourist industry. Unlike many of its neighbours, most of the food and beer used in tourism enterprises are produced in the country. Summary (1987) found high backward linkages in food manufactures, banking, hotels and restaurants; and high forward linkages in agriculture, paper products, metal products, petroleum, trade, transportation and other miscellaneous services. While noting that petroleum is imported and the country spends a large amount of foreign exchange to do so, she was able to conclude that the "tourist industry has increased its linkages with other important sectors of the Kenyan economy since 1968. Imports of intermediate goods by the tourist industry are not excessive, at least when compared to the economy as a whole" (Summary, 1987: 538-9). About a decade ago, when tourism's foreign exchange receipts represented 22 percent of all foreign earnings for the country, it was estimated that 80 percent of the money was derived from local sources and therefore retained in Kenya (Kenya, 1991a: 147). This shows that tourism's export earnings have a relatively low import content of only 20 percent.

Although tourism's backward linkages with agriculture are strong, it appears that these links are forged between large hotels and large agricultural producers thereby excluding small-scale farmers (Rajotte, 1983). This may minimize tourism's trickle-down effects to the many peasant producers.

From the perspective of tourist expenditure, including airfare and payments to overseas tour operators, the proportion of tourist income accruing to Kenya is relatively low. As noted above, this is because of the predominance of institutionalised tourists whereby the trips are paid for overseas. The overseas tour operators are in a stronger position in bargaining for a bigger share because they determine the demand for Kenya's tourism in their countries (Sinclair, 1990: 41). Besides, the greatest foreign exchange leakage from tourist expenditure occurs through foreign airlines (Sinclair, 1992). For Kenya, the total leakage has been calculated to be between 62-78 percent for beach-only holidays including the cost of international travel for tourists using foreign airlines, compared to 12-23 percent for those using Kenya Airways (Kenya, 1991a: 152). It has been shown as well that the foreign exchange leakage drops to 35-45 percent for beach plus safari holidays even with the use of foreign airlines to travel to Kenya (Kenya,

1991a: 153). This means that domestic travel within Kenya greatly reduces the size of foreign exchange leakage. However, the situation is much more complicated than this.

Kenya's tourism enterprises including hotels, tour firms and travel agencies are owned and managed by foreign nationals from developed countries. These firms arrange all inclusive tours which tend to be cheap. Most of these tourists make prepayments abroad and such foreign exchange is never really remitted to Kenya. As such the money is not available to be used in the country's development efforts. As a singular avenue, Kenya loses a lot of foreign exchange through beach-only holiday makers. The popularity of beach holidays is related not only to the relatively low tariff but also the absence of the element of local travel. Besides, beach holidays attract low-paying tourists compared to the visitors to Nairobi and lodges up-country.

Employment

Knowledge of the employment record of a sector of the economy is important for socio economic development and the well-being of the people. The more the jobs created, the greater the multiplier effects of the sector to the rest of the economy. Employment allows people to participate in ordered economic activity with dignity and in a productive way. For tourism, it is necessary to know its capacity for employment generation because of the immense investments in infrastructure and the opportunity cost that local people forego for tourism-related conservation and for hosting tourists. Such resources could be invested in alternative sectors which promise higher returns. Finally, it is relevant to inquire into tourism's employment record because of the relatively high unemployment level in Kenya. Such unemployment and underemployment could stifle economic development because of high dependency on a relatively small productive sector.

Table 4.9 shows employment figures in tourism in Kenya for a number of years. Direct employment in tourism appears to have increased from 20,000 in 1970 to 170,000 in 1994. Tourism employment formed about 7.6 percent of the modern sector wage employment in the country in 1988. This figure shows a slight improvement of 9.1 percent in 1996. This is because, since 1990, the growth in the tourism sector declined (Chapter 6). In general, 93 percent of the employment generated in tourism is in the private sector with a small proportion in the public sector (Table 4.9).

Employment figures in tourism are not disaggregated in any sense. This makes it difficult to obtain a detailed picture of the industry. For example, hotel and restaurant figures are usually lumped together and so are laundry and house-keeping. However, the accommodation sector tends to generate the most employment. Of the 170,000 workers in tourism in 1994, 61 percent were in accommodation establishments, 16 percent in tour operations, 6 percent in travel agencies, 11 percent in curio shops and entertainment and 6 percent in the central government (Sindiga, 1996a: 19). In addition, there is little information on nationals and expatriates; and supervisory management ranks and those in subordinate positions. If such data were available, they would provide invaluable insights into the employment structure of the tourism industry. The aggregated data at hand are nevertheless useful for indicating the general magnitude of employment in tourism.

Tourism is thought to create employment in other sectors of the economy; however, there are no precise figures to show the extent and magnitude of such job creation

Table 4.9
Direct employment in tourism in Kenya

	1977	1979	1982	1984	1985	1986	1987	1988	1989	1990	1991	1992	1993	1994
Modern sector employment (000s)				1,119	1,174	1,277	1,274	1,345	1,388	1,409	1,442	1,463	1,475	-
Tourism public sector				5,600	5,900	5,300	8,200	8,400	8,900	9,300	7,900	7,800	7,000	-
Tourism private sector				79,200	83,800	88,100	92,700	98,000	101,400	104,600	108,800	110,900	114,100	-
Total	28,000	32,000	49,000	84,800	89,700	94,400	100,900	106,400	110,300	113,900	116,700	118,400	121,000	170,000
Average tourism sector employment (percent)				7.6	7.6	7.7	7.9	7.9	8.1	8.1	8.1	8.1	8.2	-
Public sector share (percent)				6.6	6.6	6.7	6.1	7.9	9.1	9.2	6.8	6.3	5.8	-
Private sector share (percent)				93.4	93.4	93.3	91.9	92.1	91.9	91.8	93.2	93.7	94.2	-
Growth in tourism sector employment (percent)					5.78	5.24	8.89	5.45	3.67	3.26	2.46	1.46	2.28	-

Sources: Jica and Kenya, 1995d: Annex 4 - A81; Kenya, 1994b: 73; Popovic, 1972: 108

(Sindiga, 1994). In Chapter 2, it was shown that even direct employment in tourism is highly variable with one hotel bed estimated to create from 0.80 jobs to three. Elkan (1975) estimated one hotel bed for 0.84 jobs for Kenya, whereas another estimate gives 1.4 employees per bed (EIU, 1991). Bachmann (1988) estimated 0.6 additional jobs in the tourism sector for each hotel bed. His estimate includes informal types of work such as tour guiding especially along the beach, professional friendships and following tourists, and prostitution. In addition, one job was indirectly created in agriculture, trade and handicrafts. Bachmann concluded that 20 to 25 percent of the Malindi population derived a livelihood from tourism. However, the figure went down to 9 to 10 percent for Malindi Division (now District) as a whole and merely 5 percent of the population in Kilifi District (Bachmann, 1988: 281). A presidential committee on employment estimated that for every person directly employed in tourism there is at least another person employed through backward and forward linkages and through the expenditure of incomes earned in tourism (Kenya, 1991a: 147). Tourism provides a market for processed and unprocessed farm products, curios and souvenirs, construction, transport and financial services. Despite the conclusion that directly and indirectly tourism generates labour intensive activities, the employment contribution of the tourism sector may not be very high. In fact, Summary (1987) also found that the wages paid by Kenya's tourism industry are rather low. She argues that

> Employment generated by tourist expenditures is what would be predicted by tourism's share of Gross Domestic Product (GDP). Wages and salaries paid directly and indirectly are slightly below what would be predicted by tourism's share of total employment (Summary, 1987: 538).

She concludes that the Kenyan tourist industry is "less labour absorbing than the overall economy, and that wages paid in the tourist industry are below the average for the modern economy as a whole" (p. 538).

Kenya's tourism industry is unable to generate many jobs, partly because of the structure of the industry which allows some of the employment to be generated abroad. Tour operators located in developed countries usually supply inclusive holiday packages to travel agents also located there. They obtain block airline seats on scheduled flights or charter aircraft. Travel agents in turn retail the tour packages to individual holiday makers at a commission; usually 9 percent for the economy class and 24 percent for a first class ticket in a non-package trip (Sinclair *et al.*, 1992). These negotiations and transactions are done abroad without reference to local tour operators in Kenya. The international tour operators then make block bookings of hotel rooms in advance and obtain large discounts due to their bargaining power and ability to source the tourists (Sinclair, 1990). The accommodation prices are usually negotiated in Kenya shillings thereby allowing the overseas operator to pay less because of frequent local currency depreciation. Typically, discounts of up to 30 percent less the price in Kenya shillings are obtained in mid-season and up to 50 percent during the low season (Sinclair *et al.*, 1992: 58).

Kenya's tourism industry loses much revenue through pre-paid all-inclusive tours arranged overseas. Although contractual relations allow the overseas tour operators to pay more than one month after the tourists have left Kenya (Sinclair *et al.*, 1992: 58), a large proportion of the money paid abroad never reaches the country (Sinclair, 1992: 557;

Kenya, 1991a). This means that many local tour operators merely act as agents to the overseas tour operators. Their role is relegated to meeting and transporting tourists from the airport to hotels and sometimes acting as tour guides (Sinclair et al., 1992). Also many of the Western tour firms have their own locally registered tour companies which take care of the ground logistics of the tourists while in Kenya. Such include Jetset, Universal Safari Tours, Franco Rosso, Kuoni, I Grandi Viaggi, Touristic Union International (TUI) of Germany, Pollman's (owned by TUI), Hayes and Jarvis, United Touring Company, British Airways Speedbird, and so on (Jommo, 1987; Sinclair, 1990; Sinclair et al., 1992). There are other instances in which Western tour firms or airlines also own accommodation facilities in Kenya. Such arrangements are described below in Chapter 5. Here, suffice to say that the transnational nature of the tour operations business heavily reduces foreign exchange retention within Kenya and this makes it difficult to generate much local employment. This raises serious doubts that tourism could become the basis of African economic development.

In terms of quality of employment in tourism, it has been noted that supervisory and management positions both in accommodation facilities and tour operations are held by expatriates. Like in other African countries, this leaves subordinate roles as drivers, porters, waiters, labourers, and housekeepers for local people. These low level jobs are poorly remunerated and produce limited multiplier effects (Farver 1984; Ankomah, 1991). Farver (1984) argues that subordinate tourism jobs are not productive and make little contribution to the economy.

One of the reasons which is frequently advanced to explain expatriate domination in the managerial and supervisory positions is that there are no local skills (Ankomah, 1991). Although this might be true for sub-Saharan African in general, it is not so for Kenya (Appendix 4). Despite, the government's stated policy of Kenyanisation, expatriate personnel come with the substantial foreign investment in tourism in the country. Most of the large tourism enterprises are joint ventures with local capital and are managed through management contracts which cover "financial arrangements, government concessions, level of protection and fees to be paid to the parent company for technical and management services. It is obvious that foreign firms will push for the highest fees possible and for quite a high level of management control (particularly at senior levels)" (Swainson, 1980: 230-1). The management contract will therefore specify the number of expatriate technical and managerial staff for a given venture and this tends to perpetuate expatriate presence even in the face of a supply of local skilled personnel. The solution to the problem therefore lies in the progressive indigenisation of the ownership of tourism enterprises.

Also, tourism employment in Kenya tends to be seasonal, reflecting the annual pattern of tourist visits. The peak tourism season is September to March. The volume of traffic flow is very small between April and July. This affects tourism enterprises especially accommodation facilities because very few beds are occupied. This leads to many employees being declared redundant. Such workers in casual employment are not well paid and their termination seriously affects family welfare (see also Chapter 2).

Government revenue

Quantitative data on governments' direct earnings from tourism are lacking. Only qualitative generalizations can be offered. Apart from injecting foreign exchange earnings into the economy, tourism generates government revenue through various taxes. Such include customs and excise duties for imports; sales tax and value added tax for goods bought in the local market; accommodation tax and training levy on hotel guests; concessional or rental fees paid by game lodges and camp sites; and trade licenses and company taxes paid by various enterprises. The government also charges income tax on the personal emoluments of the employees in the tourism sector. However, government tourism revenue is much smaller. Most of the earnings accrue to the private sector which controls the industry.

Summary and conclusion

This chapter has indicated that Kenya has a large variety of tourist attractions. Most of them, however, remain undeveloped or underdeveloped. The popular wildlife safari-beach tourism dichotomy tends to conceal the true picture of Kenya's tourism potential. Although Kenya is a valued destination for wildlife safari enthusiasts, only a small part of the country is developed to receive visitors. Wildlife tourism could be geographically diversified in order to disperse tourists thereby preserving the environment. Besides, tourism appears to be the only viable economic activity in certain remote areas of the country. As the government points out, "tourism is essential to uplifting the levels of income together with opening up these areas" (Kenya, 1998b: 18).

The preceding discussion has also shown that Kenya's tourism started as domestic tourism by the resident European community in the colonial period. This was so both for wildlife tourism and beach tourism at the Indian Ocean coast. The development of domestic tourism became the basis on which international tourism flourished especially in the post-independence period.

Kenya's post-independence tourism history shows a great increase in the number of tourists. However, per capita real earnings in tourism have been declining over time. This suggests that the Kenyan taxpayers who have put up and maintained expensive infrastructure such as airports, large hotels, National Parks and reserves and roads for the tourism industry actually subsidize the all-inclusive package tourists. Also, tourism generates little employment and on average pays wages which are below those of the modern sector economy as a whole. These conclusions raise serious questions as to the contribution of tourism to the African economy and whether tourism could become the basis of African development.

It appears that the structure of Kenya's tourism industry provides room for heavy financial leakages in favour of the international operators. This imbalance translates to diminished foreign exchange earnings and only a small employment capacity. It is clear that only when Kenya will increase its rate of retention of tourist expenditures can the tourist sector be truly developmental. This must also be accompanied by increasing local expenditure per tourist. In particular, ways and means of increasing per capita tourist expenditures for the highly competitive beach holidays must be sought. Kenya must continue to offer a very high quality tourism product by segmenting the beach holiday market according to income levels of tourists. In other words, the cheap holiday should continue to be offered; in addition, the potential for up-market cruise-ship tourism and water sports which remain underdeveloped could be exploited (Table 4.3). This is because Mombasa and other coastal ports have good docking facilities and could be used for luxury cruises and other shipping with stops in various towns for local shopping.

The point being pressed is that Kenya must diversify its tourism product by developing up-market activities. The country could also geographically decongest existing tourism attractions by opening up new ones. These opportunities exist at the coastal mangrove forests, Lake Victoria and its environs, mountain and hill areas and large parts of northern Kenya. Should these areas be developed, it would lead to the diversification of demand (Sindiga, 1996a: 28). A larger proportion of tourist expenditure is likely to be retained by increasing wildlife safari holidays for which Kenya is well known. This could be done either singly or in combination with beach tourism. This is likely to exploit Kenya's comparative advantage in wildlife tourism resulting in less price pressure than is experienced with beach holidays thereby generating greater incomes and employment (Kenya, 1991a: 155). Further, a geographical dispersion of tourism activities would spread the benefits and provide the linkages to the local economy; in the process; it will uplift the levels of income, open up remote areas and offer fresh hopes for a decent livelihood for the resident population (Kenya, 1998b). Instead of the present practice where the tourism industry links more with curio and souvenir shops in Nairobi and at the coast, tourism will become more directly linked with small-scale local producers. Ultimately, the country will enjoy greater incomes and employment.

Another way of diversifying tourism and increasing local tourist expenditure is through the encouragement of conference and business tourism. Typically, these categories of visitors stay for shorter periods in comparison with holiday makers. However, they tend to be up-market, high spending people and are more likely to bring greater income to the country (Kenya, 1991a: 155).

Yet, further development of domestic tourism could generate more employment (Chapter 6).[2] Although domestic tourism itself will not raise foreign exchange earnings, it can make savings on overseas travel expenditure and increase the number of jobs in tourism (EIU, 1991: 64).

---

[2] Domestic tourism is promoted for many reasons among which are increasing investment in the tourism industry, redistributing incomes across the country, and conserving foreign currency by having Kenyans visiting their own country rather than travelling abroad (Chapter 6).

5

The structure of Kenya's tourism industry

The Ministry of Tourism and Wildlife (MTW) coordinates policy, planning and personnel training in tourism. In addition, it oversees the Kenya Wildlife Service (KWS) which is charged with the management and conservation of wildlife (Chapter 4). The MTW comprises of the tourism department which carries the marketing and licensing sections; the administrative department which has personnel, finance, supplies and planning sections; and the fisheries department. Also, the MTW has six quasi-government organisations with certain responsibilities as follows: KWS (wildlife management), Kenya Tourist Development Organisation (KTDC; local investment in tourism enterprises), African Tours and Hotels (AT&H; hotel management), Bomas of Kenya (promotion of African culture), Utalii College (tourism and hospitality training), Catering Levy Trustees (funding for tourism training), and Kenya Tourism Board (tourism product packaging, marketing and promotion). Detailed vignettes of some of these organisations appear as Appendix 5.

In the private sector, there are a number of representative organisations. These include Kenya Airways (KA), Kenya Association of Tour Operators (KATO), Kenya Association of Travel Agents (KATA), Kenya Association of Hotelkeepers and Caterers (KAHC), Kenya Budget Hotels Association (KBHA), Mombasa and Coast Hotelkeepers Association (MCHA) and Ecotourism Society of Kenya (ESK). These associations are said to be all active (UNDP and WTO, 1993). The roles of some of these private sector organisations are briefly presented in Appendix 6.

This chapter discusses the structure of the tourism industry in Kenya. In the first part I examine investment in the tourism industry followed by marketing and promotion of tourism. The second part is an analysis of the structure and ownership of the tourism enterprises in the country. Who owns the tourism industry in Kenya? What is the extent and magnitude of indigenous ownership of tourism enterprises? These are some of the questions which are tackled in this chapter. The pattern of ownership will have implications on the country's foreign exchange earnings and retention, and tourism's capacity to generate employment (Chapter 4).

Investment in the tourism industry

Although increasing the participation of Kenyans in the private sector is a long stated policy of the Kenya government (Kenya, 1989: 29), the country has maintained an open door policy to foreign investment. In the tourism sector, there has been a disproportionate presence of foreign investment and participation to the disadvantage of Kenyans (Jommo, 1987; Sinclair, 1990). Foreign involvement is particularly strong in the development of accommodation facilities, tour operations and travel business. As will be shown below, many of the tourism enterprises have been developed as joint ventures between foreign investors and Kenyans, usually to the disadvantage of the latter. Below, I discuss Kenyan investment in the tourism industry with specific reference to the Kenya Tourist Development Corporation (KTDC).

Local investment in the tourism industry
At independence, Kenya's tourism industry was dominated by European settler interests and foreign participants. Indeed, the independent Kenyan government had to define its policy on tourism as a whole. A World Bank economic mission to Kenya at the eve of independence in 1962 defined the prospective role of the government in the tourism sector as follows:

> The primary role of the Government should be to take the lead in the creation and maintenance of an atmosphere conducive to drawing visitors to the country, the provision of some assistance in the establishment of representation in principal foreign centres of population, the provision of basic facilities in Kenya required to make local travel and sight-seeing reasonably easy, safe and interesting, and in the enactment of such legislation as may be needed to ensure safety of travellers and preservation of national points or things of interest (IBRD, 1963: 171).

On the matter of tourism enterprises, the mission opined that both public funds and private investment would be needed; however, the private sector would make important contributions because it would enjoy greater benefits from the tourism industry (IBRD, 1963).

After independence, there were few African entrepreneurs and little indigenous capital for investment in the tourism industry. Consequently, the state undertook to mobilize both financial and human resources so as to assure rapid economic development. This led to a multiplication of state enterprises not only in tourism but in other spheres of economic life. The KTDC was one such state enterprise. It was established under the KTDC Act on November 9, 1965 and commenced operations in 1966. The main purpose of the KTDC was to facilitate the promotion and development of tourism investments on behalf of the government. The objectives of the KTDC as spelt out in the Act are as follows:

1) to investigate, formulate, implement and/or finance tourist projects such as hotels, lodges, restaurants, recreation facilities, tour operations, travel agencies; and to assist enterprises intended for the development, preservation or study and improvement of the country's wildlife and natural resources;
2) to undertake improvement and/or expansion of new or existing enterprises as well as their promotion; and
3) to carry out projects or activities related to the tourism industry, and intended for that industry's improvement.

During Kenya's first post-independence decade the KTDC made financial investments in hotels and lodges so as to alleviate the acute accommodation shortage in Nairobi, game parks and the coast. Such investment was initially done as joint ventures between the KTDC and a number of international organisations and multinational corporations including Commonwealth Development Corporation, German Development Company, British Airways, International Finance Corporation, Hilton International, Inter-Continental Hotels Corporation, and so on (NCCK, 1968). Later on, the KTDC decided to invest in geographically dispersed locations in the country with the hope that this would stimulate tourism in those areas. Such businesses which included Homa Bay Hotel, Mount Elgon Lodge, Meru Mulika Lodge, Marsabit Lodge, Maralal Safari Lodge and others, were financially risky and failed to provide returns to investment. Perhaps because of lack of planning capacity and market research, KTDC failed to develop tourist attractions to complement hotel development (Sindiga and Kanunah, 1998).

Up to 1996, the KTDC had participated either alone or with others in more than 200 tourist enterprises through a number of investment programmes. First, its equity investment programme is associated with some of the major hotels, lodges and tour operations, usually through direct equity participation (Table 5.1). This was the case with AT&H in which the KTDC bought equity shares to become the majority shareholder (Appendix 5). In time, AT&H expanded to provide accommodation facilities and conduct tour operations business. In this regard, AT&H became the only indigenously owned company in the tourism business with the capacity to manage hotels and conduct tour operations. However, structural adjustment programmes of the 1990s made the KTDC to divest from a number of these ventures. The KTDC has sold its stake in Panafric Hotel, Tea Hotel Kericho, Lion Hill Camp, Robinson Baobab Club, and Pollman's Tours and Safaris. KTDC will also divest from several of its businesses such as the Ark Ltd, Buffalo Springs Lodge, Maralal Safari Lodge Ltd, Marsabit Lodge, Meru Mulika Lodge, Milimani Hotels Ltd, Safari Lodge Properties Kenya Ltd, Mount Elgon Lodge Ltd, International Hotels (K) Ltd., Kabarnet Hotel, Mountain Lodge Ltd, Tourism Promotion Services Ltd., and Kenya Hotel Properties Ltd.

Second, KTDC runs a commercial loans programme by which 23 businesses from all provinces have benefited (Table 5.2). Third, there is a revolving fund loans programme which was set up primarily to assist in the Kenyanisation of the ownership of tourism enterprises. KTDC provided loans on favourable terms to assist Kenyans to purchase facilities, develop new ones, and extend and modernise existing or newly acquired facilities.

The demand for these loans was very high and KTDC was unable to cope with it. Besides, rather than enhancing the Kenyanisation programme as happened in its early years, the KTDC became biased towards commercial loans (Sinclair, 1990: 17). Further, the recovery rate for loans already disbursed was so low that the programme could not continue without further disbursements from the Treasury in an environment of tight fiscal policy. In fact, even KTDC's equity investments in tourism enterprises stopped more than ten years ago because huge sums of money got tied up in capital development projects. Also, in the late 1980s, the KTDC received a rather low rate of return of equity investment of only six percent thereby failing to meet its obligations to the Treasury (Sinclair, 1990: 17).

Although current government plans are to turn the KTDC into an investment bank for tourism (Kenya, 1994c), its previous investment policy should be reviewed. Such a review should instil commercial principles in whatever future role it plays in tourism. One of the proposals is for KTDC to support small and medium-sized hotels, lodges and restaurants for domestic tourism. However, KTDC is said to be reluctant to do this because of the fear of recovering its money from neophyte businessmen and women (JICA and Kenya, 1995d).

Finally, KTDC ran an extension service programme to instruct inexperienced Kenyans on tourism business operations and management. This programme was intended for KTDC's loanees under the revolving fund programme to ensure that the money loaned out was used for the intended purpose and to enhance loan recovery.

In future, KTDC will need a source of funds for assisting in the development of new tourism enterprises. As the country prepares to receive additional tourists at the onset of the new millennium, much more expansion and modernisation of tourism facilities will be required. KTDC could play a central role in such investment programmes because of the expertise it has accumulated by virtue of three decades of participation in tourism development. In this regard, the Kenya Government appears to have identified KTDC as a strategic institution to act as the Government investment organ in the tourism industry (Kenya, 1998a: 184). In addition, the KTDC will be a catalyst for building confidence thereby attracting investment in the industry and providing information to potential investors. Besides, government policy now allows tax incentives for local investment in the tourism industry. Specifically, the government will allow "zero rating under the Value Added Tax for locally financed tourist hotel development and refurbishment" (Kenya, 1998b: 19). This will encourage further investment in tourism.

Tourism promotion and marketing

Until the mid-1990s, the Ministry of Tourism and Wildlife was charged with the responsibility of product development, marketing and tourism promotion. As part of its international marketing and promotion, the government opened tourist offices in London, Zurich, Frankfurt, Stockholm, Paris, New York and Pretoria; and two local ones at Mombasa and Malindi. The role of the tourist offices was to provide up to date

Table 5.1
KTDC investments and loans as at 30 June 1994

Project	% shares held	Equity (Kshs)	Loan (Kshs)	1994 (Kshs)	1993 (Kshs)
Zimmerman (1973) Ltd	51.0	1,071,000		1,071,000	1,071,000
Embu Hotel Ltd	28.5	216,000		216,000	216,000
Meru Mulika Lodge	91.7	5,653,740	2,124,823	7,778,563	7,503,366
The Ark Ltd	5.6	549,340		549,340	549,340
Kenya Safari Lodges & Hotels	63.4	6,407,550		6,407,550	6,407,550
Mountain Lodges	39.7	604,940		604,940	604,940
Safari Lodge Properties (K) Ltd	33.3	6,446,500		6,446,500	6,446,500
International Hotel (K) Ltd	33.1	10,485,500		10,485,500	10,485,500
Kenya Hotel Properties	33.8	12,264,040		12,264,040	12,264,040
Tourism Promotional Services	14.9	11,567,050		11,567,050	4,027,050
Bomas of Kenya Ltd	100.0	5,080,000	10,708,239	15,788,239	15,788,239
Mt. Elgon Lodge	72.9	1,345,780	1,292,458	2,638,238	2,638,238
Homa-Bay Hotel Ltd	99.3	6,218,200	2,296,517	8,514,717	8,564,717
Sunset Hotel Ltd	95.4	11,450,000		11,450,000	11,450,000
Marsabit Lodge Ltd	88.7	2,942,700	377,315	3,320,015	3,320,015
African Tours & Hotels Ltd	52.6	4,691,900	6,148,983	10,840,883	10,840,883
Lion Hill Camp Ltd	29.8	1,342,600		1,342,600	1,342,600
Maralal Safari Lodge	15.5	802,000		802,000	802,000
Pollmans Tours & Safaris	49.0				300,000
Utali Investments Ltd	100.0	2,000,000		2,000,000	2,000,000
Kabarnet Hotel Ltd	98.2	5,432,120	16,149,370	21,581,490	21,581,490
Milimani Hotel Ltd	50.0	7,250,000	351,884	7,601,884	7,733,732
Kakamega Hotel Ltd	80.0	4,000,000	15,342,823	19,342,823	19,587,725
Buffalo Springs	41.0	1,000,000	4,301,142	5,301,142	5,301,142
Mombasa Island Hotel Ltd	...	1,544,916		1,544,916	1,544,920
Solar Hotel Ltd	...		400,082	400,082	400,082
Kitale Hotel Ltd		545,787		545,787	449,590
Gasden Co Ltd	...		3,000,000	3,000,000	3,000,000
African Tours & Hotels Preference Shares		29,100		29,100	
Total		110,940,763	62,493,636	173,434,399	166,220,659
Revolving Fund Principal Loan				42,502,837	36,818,717
Revolving Fund Interest				22,238,082	24,668,237
Commercial Fund Interest				5,935,842	5,141,160
Grand Total				244,111,160	232,848,773

Source: Ngetich, 1996

Table 5.2
KTDC commercial fund loan from inception up to 31.03.93 by province

	Total amount		Loanees for lodges and hotels development		Other business	
	No.	Ksh.	No.	Amount	No.	Amount
Nairobi	7	38,919,611	6	25,421,611	1	13,498,000
Coast	5	10,220,100	4	8,688,000	1	1,532,100
Rift Valley	3	50,624,569	1	50,624,569	-	-
Central	1	800,000	1	800,000	-	-
Western	3	16,753,661	3	16,753,661	-	-
Nyanza	2	3,917,977	2	3,917,977	-	-
Eastern	2	1,926,941	2	1,926,941	-	-
North Eastern	-	-	-	-	-	-
Total	23	123,162,859	21	108,132,759	2	15,030,100

information on tourism in the country and cooperate with tour operators, airlines and all the other stakeholders in tourism and travel. Another purpose was to work with the mass media and members of the public in building a positive image of the country. However, the government was not well equipped to undertake all these tasks. In 1996, for example, the entire tourism department had an annual budget of only K£ 3 million for its operations, and the running of the tourist offices. This made it impossible to sell Kenya's tourism product. But the problem went beyond the restrictive budget. The tourism department lacked qualified marketing personnel. This left the staffing of tourist offices in the hands of civil servants many of whom knew little about tourism and tourism marketing. Who when marketed and promoted Kenya's tourism?

Without an aggressive marketing and promotional campaign overseas, Kenya's tourism benefitted from the work of private tour operators and travel agents both at home and overseas. The private sector contributed 60 percent of the promotional costs of participating in international fairs, exhibitions, seminars, workshops, and road shows with the government meeting the balance (Mbova, 1996). Also, Kenya's reputation as an African tourism destination was passed by word of mouth by people who had already visited the country. Kenya's varied environments, its wildlife and bird populations have always been subject of many documentary films, books and magazine articles. These provided free publicity to the country's tourism. By the mid-1990s, it was clear that these were insufficient to allow the country to maintain a competitive edge as a tourism destination. The publicity given to Kenya by the international mass media focusing on insecurity, political violence and the collapsed road network had a negative effect as exemplified by diminished tourist arrivals.

It is in the backdrop of this situation that the Kenya government established the Kenya Tourism Board (KTB) in 1996. It is expected that the KTB will solve some of the persistent tourism promotion and marketing problems of the past. The KTB must also tackle the problem of tourism planning and coordination. The latter was expected to be done by the Ministry of Planning and National Development; however, planning coordination has been weak or even non-existent (JICA and Kenya, 1995d). And so has been strategic coordination with the large private sector in tourism promotion. It is expected also that the KTB will intervene on behalf of the tourism industry to cut the long and cumbersome licensing procedures.

The establishment of the KTB was the government's answer to the serious downturn of Kenya's tourism since 1990 (Chapter 6). The board has a number of goals as follows (Daily Nation, 1996):
1) to promote and market Kenya as a tourist destination, both locally and overseas;
2) to establish public relations services to address issues raised by visitors and to facilitate conflict resolution among the stakeholders in the tourism industry;
3) to monitor the quality and standards of facilities available to tourists and advise both the private sector participants and relevant government agencies;
4) to work in partnership with national, regional and international organisations and local authorities so as to improve the tourism business environment; and
5) to initiate education and awareness programmes locally and abroad and to develop and maintain the capacity for quick, professional and effective responses to issues which adversely affect Kenya's tourism.

To allow the KTB to operate effectively, it will be funded from the catering training and tourism development levy on accommodation and other tourist establishments and the Kenya Government. Besides, an endowment fund provided by the European Union will provide a stable source of funding for the board (Kenya, 1998b: 19; *Weekly Review,* May 22, 1998, p. 17). Should KTB's goals be met, its role and position in tourism industry will be central in Kenya's tourism development.

Structure and ownership of tourism enterprises

This section discusses the structure and ownership of tourism enterprises in Kenya. The discussion is constructed around accommodation facilities, tour and travel operations, and the curio/souvenir trade.

Accommodation facilities
Kenya has about 3,000 accommodation facilities dispersed across the country. Of these, less than half are registered by the government (UNDP and WTO, 1993; JICA and Kenya, 1995d). The accommodation subsector is an important portion of tourism because it accounts for the majority of the employment in the industry. Also, it has the highest proportion in terms of value added, multiplier effects and investment potential (Jommo, 1987).

The MTW classifies hotels according to very detailed information using a star system (Appendix 7). A myriad factors such as number of beds, size of rooms, restaurant facilities, suites, air conditioning, swimming pools, shops, sports, communication facilities, and general environmental ambience are used to determine the classification of each facility (Sindiga, 1994). In general, the classification of hotels reflects level of sophistication in furniture and interior decor from relatively simple in one star to high quality in the five star. Also, it reflects the tariff structure from relatively low to very expensive.

The distribution of accommodation facilities shows that the coast has the largest share comprising of about 52 percent of the national total or about 20,000 beds (Table 5.3). Nairobi and the Central region have the second largest share of beds which forms about 31 percent of the national bed capacity.

About 25 percent of the classified hotels are in Nairobi (EIU, 1991). In general, most large hotels in Kenya are owned by foreigners exclusively or foreigners with local participation usually by the state through one or other institution. Despite claims to Kenyanizing business enterprises, "the majority of middle and upper category hotels are still joint ventures with foreigners" (Sinclair, et al., 1992: 60). African participation in ownership is minimal (Hazlewood, 1979).

About 78 percent of the major hotels at the coast, 67 percent in Nairobi and 66 percent of the lodges have some foreign investment; wholly foreign-owned hotels at the coast are 16 percent of the total, Nairobi 17 percent, and lodges 11 percent (Sinclair et al., 1992: 59). Jommo's (1987) study found total foreign investment in one form or other in 51 percent of the tourist hotels in Nairobi, 78 percent in North Coast, 73 percent in South Coast, and in 39 percent of the total lodge capacity. Bachmann (1988: 230) found that 60 percent of the international hotels in Malindi, 55 percent in Watamu and 53 percent in Lamu are foreign-owned.

Foreign investment in Kenya goes back to the period starting 1945 (Swainson, 1980). After independence, many multinational companies began to enlarge by taking over smaller units. Lonrho, the British conglomerate, for example, acquired about 50 subsidiaries in Kenya between 1966 and 1973 (Swainson, 1980: 214). In the contemporary time, Lonrho has equity shares in the Norfolk Hotel, Mount Kenya Safari Club, Ol Pejeta Ranch, Mara Safari Club and Sweetwaters Tended Camp (Sinclair et al., 1992).

Kenya's hotel industry began as small family ventures in the colonial time. The owners were resident Europeans. During the 1960s nearly all the hotel business was in private hands with the Block family, the then owners of the Norfolk and New Stanley hotels, holding the biggest share in the industry. Others were Brunner Hotel owned by the Brunner family, New Avenue and Mayfair hotels owned by the Nanji family, Fairview Hotel in Nairobi and Manor Hotel in Mombasa, both owned by the Szlapak family and Hotel Ambassadeur owned by the Hindocha group of Miwani (NCCK, 1968). Two other hotel companies, AT&H and Inns of Africa Ltd, which owned Tsavo Inn, Park Inn and Dolphin Inn (Mombasa), had European and African directors. This picture of accommodation facilities at about 1967 shows both European and Asian ownership of hotel businesses. After this, foreign investment through multinational corporations began to get into the hotel industry. Also, indigenous ownership of the hotel sector did not go to individuals but the state through a number of quasi-government organisations and in particular the KTDC.

Table 5.3
Number of beds of classified hotels and lodges by tourism region

Tourism region	5 star	4 star	Classified 3 star	2 star	1 star	Non-classified	Total
Central	3,671	1,339	2,680	1,813	1,603	762	11,868
% in the region	30.9	11.3	22.6	15.5	13.5	6.4	100.0
% in the nation	36.7	14.3	32.9	43.5	70.5	19.1	31.2
Maasailand	232	1,054	774	164	0	1,251	3,475
% in the region	6.7	30.3	22.3	4.7	0.0	36.0	100.0
% in the nation	2.3	11.2	9.5	3.9	0.0	31.3	9.1
Western	100	77	570	354	244	176	1,521
% in the region	6.6	5.1	37.5	23.3	16.0	11.6	100.0
% in the nation	1.0	0.8	7.0	8.5	10.7	4.4	4.0
Turkana	0	0	0	0	0	64	64
% in the region	0.0	0.0	0.0	0.0	0.0	100.0	100.0
% in the nation	0.0	0.0	0.0	0.0	0.0	1.6	0.2
Northern	0	0	0	0	0	48	48
% in the region	0.0	0.0	0.0	0.0	0.0	100.0	100.0
% in the nation	0.0	0.0	0.0	0.0	0.0	1.2	0.1
Tana River Basin	0	0	0	0	0	12	142
% in the region	0	0	0	0	0	8.5	100.0
% in the nation	0.0	0.0	0.0	0.0	0.0	0.3	0.4
Coastal	5,817	6,402	3,930	1,715	428	1,404	19,696
% in the region	29.5	32.5	20.0	8.7	2.2	7.1	100.0
% in the nation	58.1	68.1	48.2	41.1	18.8	35.1	51.8
Eastern	185	524	74	124	0	278	1,185
% in the region	15.6	44.2	6.2	10.5	0.0	23.5	100.0
% in the nation	1.8	5.6	0.9	3.0	0.0	7.0	3.1
National total	10,005	9,396	8,158	4,170	2,275	3,995	37,999
% in the nation	26.3	24.7	21.5	11.0	6.0	10.5	100.0

Source: JICA and Kenya, 1995d

One of the earliest multinational corporations to enter the Kenya hotel industry was Inter-Continental Hotels Corporation (owned by Pan-American World Airways). Together with the International Finance Corporation, an affiliate of the World Bank, KTDC and Development Finance Company of Kenya (DFCK), they formed the Kenya Hotel Properties company which constructed the 800-bed Nairobi Intercontinental Hotel at a cost of K£ 5.2 m (Jommo, 1987; NCCK, 1968). This company later constructed the Mombasa Intercontinental Hotel on the Shanzu beach and has a management contract for Mount Kenya Safari Clubs, the exclusive all-suite facility in Mt. Kenya region and Nairobi.

Another example of the entry of multinational companies was Hilton International, owned by Trans-World Airlines of the USA. Hilton International joined up with Kenya government through KTDC, Block Hotels, International Finance Corporation, El-Al Israel Airlines and Standard Bank to form International Hotels (K) Ltd company which developed the 200-bed Nairobi Hilton at the centre of Nairobi, and Taita Hills and Salt

Lick lodges in Tsavo (NCCK, 1968; Jommo, 1987). Other examples of major hotels in which foreign investment was injected include Robinson Baobab at the coast in which Barclays Overseas Development Corporation of the U.K. and TUI of Germany invested; Diani Reef — Sonotels International of the Netherlands and Hobby Hotels of Germany; Whispering Palms Hotel — TUI; Two Fishes Hotel — TUI; Diani Sea Lodge — TUI; Mombasa Beach — British Airways; and Serena — Lufthansa (Jommo, 1987).

This list is only intended to be illustrative rather than exhaustive. The ownership of some of the properties has in some cases changed hands. However the pattern of ownership reflecting a dominance of foreign interests carries forth to the present. Like the fashion in other areas of the economy, the pattern of foreign investment in hotels in Kenya shifted in the 1970s to emphasize joint ventures or partnerships involving international finance agencies, multinational corporations and local state and private capital (Swainson, 1980: 214). A joint venture provides access to knowledge, expertise and joint distribution channels thereby increasing output and profitability (Sinclair *et al.*, 1992). There are other cases in which franchising agreements are used. This agreement is somewhat like a management contract. Here, a local company associates with a foreign one through using its trade mark, for example Holiday Inn. Production, knowledge, marketing and quality controls are assured through periodic checking and/or by maintaining a resident representative (Sinclair *et al.*, 1992). However, the responsibility and risks of the operations are vested in the local company.

Apart from multinational corporations, foreign investment in Kenya's tourism is made by individuals, families and small companies. In Malindi, most hotels are owned by Germans and Italians, some of whom are absentee landlords periodically shuttling between the Kenyan coast and Europe (Bachmann, 1988; Jommo, 1987). Foreigners also own private cottages and apartments which are made available for tourist use thereby undercutting hotels (Jommo, 1987). The Germans and Italians have also gone into tourism-related businesses such as boutiques, bars and entertainment (Jommo, 1987).

Contrary to earlier optimism that substantial indigenous ownership of tourist hotel accommodation has been attained (Kenya, 1983: 145), the data reveal a different picture. Both ownership and management of large hotels remains in the hands of foreigners. Should the government steer the privatization programme carefully, government-owned shares in accommodation facilities may go to indigenous people. But it is possible that a good proportion could be purchased by foreign investors. It appears unlikely that the structure of ownership will change much without policy interventions. But it would be pointless to reform policy unless local capital can be raised and the necessary improvement and availability in the human element.

Tour and travel operations
Although tour operations and travel agency business can be separated, the two are frequently combined in one venture. Nevertheless, the two are represented by different associations in Kenya, namely KATO and KATA (Appendix 6). Just like the growth in the numbers of tourists in the country, tour operators and vehicle hire enterprises grew from 82 in 1970 to 288 in 1980, 1240 in 1990, and 2238 in 1994 (Kenya, 1991: 149; Table 5.4).

Table 5.4
Distribution of tour operators by region, 1997

Tourism region/ district	No. of operators	Share (percent)	Tourism region/ district	No. of operators	Share (percent)
Nairobi	1,113	49.7	Maasailand	31	1.4
Central	84	3.8	Kajiado	10	0.4
Nakuru	27	1.2	Narok	21	0.9
Lakipia	25	1.1			
Samburu	3	0.1	Coast	973	43.5
Nyeri	10	0.4			
Murang'a	1	---	Turkana	2	0.1
Kiambu	9	0.4			
Machakos	2	0.1	Kenya	2238	100.0
Meru	5	0.2			
Isiolo	2	0.1			
Western	35	1.6			
Baringo	3	0.1			
Uasin Gishu	6	0.3			
Trans Nzoia	7	0.3			
Kericho	1	---			
Kisumu	16	0.7			
Kakamega	2	0.1			

Source: Interview with Kenya Association of Tour Operators (KATO), January 1998.

The Kenya tour operators organise holiday packages which include accommodation and transport. They sell these to domestic and foreign tourists either on individual or group basis through travel agents and foreign tour operators (Sinclair, 1990). The tour operators are able to organise specialized packages depending on demand. Such may include educational tours, cultural tours, bird watching, sea tours, tea plantation tours and so on.

Tour operators usually meet foreign tourists at the airport, arrange their transport to hotels, explain local immigration and customs requirements, airport tax, the itinerary and other matters of interest to the tourists. They may perform this role on their own behalf or as agents of a foreign tour operator. Table 5.4 shows the distribution of tour operators by tourism region of the country. Nearly half of the tour operators are located in Nairobi with the coast taking 43.5 percent as the second single largest concentration. The remaining are widely dispersed around the country mainly in areas of wildlife conservation. This geographic pattern of tour operators reflects the enclave nature of tourism in the country.

In terms of size, tour operator companies range from small offices of half a dozen employees in one location to big ones with several branch locations and as many staff as 500 (JICA and Kenya, 1995d). The big ones tend to be foreign-owned companies such as UTC, Abercrombie and Kent, Pollman's and others.

As noted above, tour and travel operations facilitate tourism through making arrangements for air travel, hotel bookings, organising tour packages, and providing transport and tour guides. But in these activities foreign companies play a dominant role. Whatever balance is left is taken up by Asian businessmen. There is little participation by

Africans in ownership or management of tour operations (Hazlewood, 1979: 105). Africans tend to have small companies which obtain subcontracts from the big tour operators for a small fee (Jommo, 1987). As such the developmental effect of tourist on local people is doubtful.

A few examples would suffice to illustrate the foreign domination of tour operations. Many of the businesses tend to be vertically integrated. This means that, for example, a tour operator owns an airline and a hotel chain at the same time. In Kenya, many international tour operators have local subsidiaries. They access the tourists in Western Europe or North America, put them on their aircraft to Kenya where the ground handling is done by their local subsidiary tour firm and accommodation is provided by hotels which they own (Bachmann, 1988; Sinclair *et al.*, 1992). For example, Africa Safari Club (ASC) of Switzerland is a vertically integrated tour company with its own charter planes, safari vehicles and several hotels at the Kenya Coast (Jommo, 1987; Bachmann, 1988). In addition, ASC owns a domestic air charter service in Kenya, Skytrail Ltd (Jommo, 1987). So dominant did ASC become in the Kenya coast tourism business that it advertised that it was able "to offer a two-week holiday, including return flight, and full-board accommodation for a minimum of less than a third of the cheapest Swissair excursion ticket to Nairobi" (Jommo, 1987: 49). Under such dominance of foreign business interests, it does not surprise anyone that there is a heavy leakage of foreign exchange earnings from the Kenyan economy. But the ASC company is not isolated.

The German owners of the international tour operator TUI also own equity in Pollman Tours of Kenya and several hotels including Whispering Palms, Two Fishes Hotel and Diani Sea Lodge. Their operations are vertically integrated. They monopolize travel packaging, management, investment advisory, and local tour operations through Pollman's (Jommo, 1987). Franco Rosso is an Italian tour firm. It owns Tropical Village in Malindi and Leopard Beach Hotel at Diani, among other properties; in addition, it is involved in local tour operations. The United Touring Company (UTC), a subsidiary of the British firm BET Traction, owns the expansive Block hotel chain. Sinclair *et al.* (1992) note that UTC has hotel management, touring, travel and "self-drive" divisions and combine these with serving as local agents for major overseas tour operators. Other foreign tour companies with equity in hotels in Kenya include Kuoni, Hayes and Jarvis, Universal Safari Tours and I Grandi Viaggi (Sinclair *et al.*, 1992). The vertical integration of tourist operations extending from tour firms to airlines and hotels is the most common organizational structure of tourism in developing countries (Farver, 1984). It ensures that the foreign exchange earnings from African tourism remain overseas or are repatriated to developed countries.

Role of Kenya Airways in tourism

Since 1987, Kenya Airways (KA) has provided charter flights from Europe, initially from Italy and France, although it was expected to expand to other countries (Sinclair, 1990). These flights are provided by Kenya Flamingo Airways (KFA) which is a subsidiary company of KA. In doing international air charter business, Kenya is considered to be an unusual African country as this allows KA to tap into the lucrative international air charter business. This is because of the practice of European tour operators chartering a full plane and paying for it in foreign currency before the journey is made (Sinclair, Alizadeh and Onunga, 1992: 58). However, most tourists prefer to travel in their own country's airline or one of the old and big names in Western airline business. KA must negotiate bilateral agreements to obtain profitable routes but this is not always successful (Sinclair *et al.*, 1992).

Even for air charters, Western European countries form powerful cartels that make it difficult for an African country airline to succeed. For example, as an effort to provide business to KA's regular scheduled flights on the London-Nairobi route, Kenya initially declined to give British tour operators landing permission for charter aircraft. European tour operators responded by arranging short flights to Rome for London-based tourists to catch a charter flight to Kenya thereby circumventing the country's regulations (Sinclair *et al.*, 1992).

KFA enjoys the advantages of flying to any part of the world without the restrictions usually imposed on a scheduled airline and to provide high quality services to high paying tourists (Sinclair, 1990). In addition, charter business allows KFA the flexibility of cancelling flights if the demand is low. Besides, KFA can negotiate favourable terms for its services and obtain pre-payment for planned trips (Sinclair, 1990).

Kenya Airways (KA) was established as Kenya's national carrier in 1977 on the collapse of the East African Airways which was run by the defunct East African Community. It has a small fleet of aircraft which includes airbuses, Boeing and Fokker. KA runs scheduled international services to a number of European routes and provides services to Rome, Frankfurt, Paris, Amsterdam and London. However, KA has in recent years discontinued scheduled flights to a number of European routes including Nairobi-Zurich, Nairobi-Frankfurt and Nairobi-Rome. Rival local companies have sought to be licensed to operate on some of the routes abandoned by KA. Specifically, East African Safari Air (EASA) has applied for national carrier status and to fly ten scheduled flights to European destinations which are not covered by KA or those abandoned by it (Otieno, 1998: 31). Should the rival be licensed, it will not only provide competition to KA but will open up additional routes thereby encouraging tourism, providing jobs and bringing into Kenya new investment (Otieno, 1998).

KA has an international service to India as well. In addition, KA has scheduled domestic flights to and from Nairobi, Mombasa, Malindi and Kisumu. Some of these domestic flights are conducted either singly or in conjunction with other operators such as Eagle Aviation. EASA operates domestic charter flights mainly to Mombasa. In addition, charter flights to various national parks and reserves are provided by private air operators, most of whom are based at Wilson Airport in Nairobi. Until 1996, KA was a fully government-owned airline and had a notorious history of loss-making and an inability to keep to its timetable of flights. For a few years prior to 1996, KA was restructured to become a viable and profitable airline. The government then divested its majority shares from KA. As a result of the privatization programme 51 percent of the shares are owned by members of the public with 26 percent of the equity shares held by Koninklijke Luchtvaart Maatschappij (KLM), the Royal Dutch Airlines, and only 23 percent by the Kenya government. The association with KLM is expected to strengthen the financial and administrative management of KA. Besides, the latter will benefit from transfer of technology and know-how from an experienced and successful international airline. The prospects of KA playing a significant role in international tourist transport appear promising. Ultimately, the leakage of Kenya tourism's foreign exchange on account of international air transport will be greatly minimized to the advantage of the Kenyan economy.

Curio/souvenir business
At independence, the curio business promised to provide a share of the tourism earnings directly to Africans. These Africans were assisted in the efforts to produce and market tourist arts and crafts by the KTDC. Consequently, curio shops sprang up in the 1960s in the areas of major tourist concentrations. Although the number of licensed curio shops subsequently increased from 49 in 1970 to 147 in 1980 and 532 in 1990 (Kenya, 1991a: 149), the number of African owned businesses actually declined. This reversal in the fortunes of the Africans came in the 1970s to allow Asians to dominate the business (Jommo, 1987). Whereas Africans could not raise sufficient capital to put into the business, pay for expensive building premises and associated overhead costs in central Nairobi, Asians had the advantage of utilizing family resources. Moreover, building ownership among Asians in Nairobi is high. This is an additional advantage to a budding Asian businessman. However, the greatest asset the Asians have is the network of caste identity and through this they assist one of their own with accommodation, employment and loans for starting a business (see for example Zarwan, 1975). However, there are many small scale curio businesses run by Africans in temporary kiosks or on the streets of the urban centres. Such curio traders, however, suffer from frequent harassment by local authorities with their kiosks and merchandise destroyed. An excellent example is the 1998 burning of the Kigali Road market, probably the most extensive curio market in Nairobi. The traders lost millions of shillings worth of crafts and kiosks.

Although women make all kinds of wares including baskets, necklaces, beads and so on, they never really obtain proportionate returns (Chapter 6). Middlemen purchase these at throw-away prices and then sell them expensively in the market. At the coast, curios are sold by hawkers, commonly called beach boys (Peake, 1989), along the beach. Although some of the handicrafts are produced by women's groups in Mombasa, payments are made to individuals according to personal output. Many of the women, however, do not make sufficient quantities because they are unable to raise investment resources as they are not paid quickly after delivering their merchandise (Maas, 1991: 48-49). As a result, they do not benefit much from tourism.

Summary and conclusion

This chapter dealt with indigenous Kenyan investment in tourism enterprises and in marketing and tourism promotion. Also, it analysed the structure and ownership of tourism enterprises in order to expose the problems which hinder tourism's contribution to local development.

The findings show that the tourism industry is dominated by the private sector. In addition, there is substantial foreign ownership of tourism enterprises especially in the accommodation and tour operation sectors. Although a substantial fraction of tourism enterprises is fully owned by foreign companies, the majority are joint ventures with local capital. There is little indigenous African ownership of the middle and large hotels in the country. African ownership, however, dominates the small and medium sized hotels.

Tourist hotels started in the colonial period as family businesses by resident Europeans. During the 1960s, most of these family operations sold equity shares usually to multinational corporations with some shares being held by KTDC on behalf of the Kenyan public. The development of joint venture business in the hotel industry started and quickly took root in the country. Such joint ventures assured that the participating foreign investors managed the businesses and controlled the financial transactions usually in their own interest rather than that of the country. The push towards joint ventures in the 1970s was predicated on the notion that African governments were predisposed to nationalizing foreign assets. A joint venture would then provide a multinational corporation with a measure of security against political risk. In order, to generate high profits, multinational corporations signed management contracts which provide them both with financial and management control and oversight on the enterprises. This way they ensure that hefty fees and expatriate wages are repatriated to the home countries.

Besides, many tourism businesses in Kenya are vertically integrated. International tour operation companies which take tourists to Kenya also own charter aircraft, have local subsidiary companies in Kenya with vehicles and personnel to take care of the ground operations, and also own accommodation facilities. This structural arrangement makes it possible for the Kenyan economy to lose much foreign exchange earnings. Moreover, prices paid by tourists are negotiated secretly abroad and paid there. Most of this money is never sent to Kenya. And in a vertically integrated operation it is difficult for anybody else to know how much money was received. Kenya spends enormous resources on tourism infrastructure. As most of the profits accrue to the private sector, the Kenya government spends more money on tourism than it gets from it (Bachmann, 1988: 196). In light of this fact, the country must re-examine its tourism strategy.

6

Change and challenge of unplanned tourism development

In this chapter I discuss the changes and challenges brought about by tourism development in the post-independence period. Another purpose is to analyse the critical issues in tourism in Kenya resulting from unplanned development. This also involves the response of local communities to tourism. In Chapter 2 the problems which come about when tourism development is done without the context of planning were outlined. This chapter builds on that information using the Kenya data.

As shown in Chapters 2 and 4, Kenya's tourism began almost spontaneously and expanded rapidly. This forced the government to do some reactive planning for areas in which tourism was already developing both in the national parks and reserves and at the coast. Such planning often attempts to rationalize what has been done on the ground by putting it on paper and does not consider the many likely impacts of the activity. Moreover, whereas planning was done to conform to the country's 5-year planning cycles, the special requirements of tourism planning were not considered. Unlike the conventional sectors of the economy, a 5-year planning cycle is considered too short in tourism. Tourism plans must take a longer time perspective, usually 10 to 15 years at a time (Inskeep, 1994). This is because tourism investments take a long time to mature.

This chapter might have been entitled 'problems of tourism development' or 'environmental and socio-cultural impacts of tourism development' in the fashion of many previous studies (for example Jackson, 1973; Mathieson and Wall, 1982). Whereas this might have captured the general thrust of the discussion below, it would have missed the essential complexity of visitor-guest interactions which is a two-way process. National governments and/or local authorities desire to encourage tourism development because of certain perceived benefits. This leads to the investment of resources to create a tourism infrastructure (airports, hotels, lodges, roads, vehicles, promotional materials and so on). There is therefore preparedness to receive visitors. Looking at this process merely as impacts of tourism is to oversimplify the picture to imply that causation is uni-directional and that the destination area (environment and people) is in some kind of static equilibrium only capable of disruption when the tourists begin coming in (see also Wall, 1996). This is not to claim that tourism does not cause disruption. Rather, it is to appreciate the complexity of the process which perhaps requires more sophisticated approaches to its inquiry.

In Chapter 4 it was shown that average per capita tourist receipts in Kenya has been declining since 1982 despite the growth of the absolute size of foreign exchange receipts. This problem of low foreign exchange earnings per tourist has persisted over the past three decades. Although there was a phenomenal increase in the number of tourists since independence and, with it, enormous national resource investments, the country has not done profitable business in tourism. As Kenya had not planned for the type of tourism it wanted, there was an influx of mass tourists. Unable to control it, Kenya decided to expand that market segment in the belief that foreign exchange earnings will grow with the numbers. Consequently, Kenya's tourism resources were stretched to the utmost and the quality of the tourism product began to decline. Since 1990 the tourist numbers began to go down dramatically as well when measured by the numbers of visitors to the parks and reserves. In fact, the contribution of tourism to the total value of exports of goods and services declined from 22 percent in 1990 to 18 percent in 1996 (Kenya, 1991a: 148; Kenya, 1998b: 18).

Despite tourism's contribution to the Kenyan economy, it is clear that it is not sustainable. In addition to the economic difficulties discussed in Chapter 4, Kenya's tourism faces a number of major challenges which must be solved if tourism is to remain a major export for the country in the new millennium. A discussion of the critical issues in tourism in Kenya follows.

Critical issues in Kenya's tourism

Kenya's tourism development is based on a number of objectives specified in the country's national development plans. Although the objectives spell out the desired economic outcomes of tourism development and the preservation of biodiversity aimed at making it sustainable, they in themselves do not meet the goals of planning. For example, it is not clear why tourism is desirable compared to alternative investment programmes or the costs versus benefits of tourism. What is the imperative of the tourism option?

The crisis facing Kenya's tourism may be summarized as breakdown of the physical infrastructure; environmental degradation of natural resources especially in protected areas; a narrow tourism product and source market for tourists; socio-cultural change and the uneven distribution of benefits especially to local communities; low foreign exchange earnings per capita and low retention rate; mass tourism, foreign ownership and management of tourism enterprises; a small domestic and regional tourism base; and political violence associated with the democratization process. Government response to the crisis facing tourism has been to offer national development objectives for tourism (Kenya, 1994c) and to commission a study on a proposed national tourism

masterplan (JICA and Kenya, 1995a; 1995b; 1995c; 1995d). The objectives themselves are:
1) conserving and managing Kenya's national parks and game reserves;
2) diversifying tourism products and markets as a means of encouraging local employment and broadening the distribution of tourism incomes to local communities;
3) ensuring a high level of retention of foreign exchange earnings;
4) encouraging up-market tourism based on "ecotourism-cum-wildlife safaris";
5) intensifying capacity building especially training of personnel so as to expand the participation, management and eventual ownership of tourism establishments by Kenyans; and
6) promoting international, regional and domestic tourism (Kenya, 1994c).

In the absence of a comprehensive tourism plan to guide the physical and institutional aspects of tourism development, further investments in the sector cannot be justified. Below, I discuss the main challenges facing Kenya's tourism at the eve of the 21st century.

Breakdown of the infrastructure

An editorial in a local newspaper perhaps accurately encapsulates the state of the country's physical infrastructure in 1998.

> Kenya's infrastructure is in a very bad state. So bad that locals (sic), let alone tourists, would not want to drive along Kenyan roads to enjoy the country's beauty (*Kenya Times*, June 16, 1998, p. 6).

Although flood water caused by heavy rains associated with the so-called El Niño phenomenon towards the end of 1997 washed away many roads and bridges, it is clear that Kenya's road network is poorly maintained and has collapsed after years of neglect. The Mombasa-Nairobi road, for example, and roads within national parks and reserves urgently need to be rehabilitated. Customer research shows that tourists are unhappily surprised by the condition of the roads which makes travelling uncomfortable and prolonged. As a result, the ambitious itineraries drawn up by tour operators are often unfulfilled. The railway system which was planned for different purposes is unsuited and too slow for tourism. At the coast, water is a persistent problem and electricity supply is irregular (Krhoda f.c.). Also, telecommunications services lag behind. The deterioration of the physical infrastructure is a strong contributing factor to the decline of Kenya's tourism in the 1990s. The situation must be reversed so as to improve the quality of Kenya's tourism experience.

Environmental change

Tourist numbers have exerted serious pressure on the environment, especially in the conservation areas. Over-exploitation of park resources has been observed in Nairobi, Amboseli and Lake Nakuru national parks, and Samburu and Maasai Mara national reserves (Muthee, 1992). As noted above, the tourist population is concentrated along the coast in Mombasa and Malindi and selected national parks. For example, 98 percent of the wildlife safari visitors go to only 7 of them namely Nairobi, Amboseli, Tsavo East, Tsavo West, and Lake Nakuru national parks; Maasai Mara national reserve, and the Nairobi animal orphanage. These are popular with visitors and each attracts more than 100,000 people a year (Chapter 4). In Amboseli and Maasai Mara, this popularity has led to the concentration of lodges and tented camps thereby affecting environmental quality. There are other problems: overcrowding of minibuses, fuelwood collection, problems of waste disposal, water pollution and loss of aesthetic quality (KWS, 1994).

Poor sewage and solid waste disposal from the lodges leads to the congregation of dangerous scavengers, especially birds. Beyond this, the sewage and solid waste dumps contain poisonous substances such as dry cell batteries which may threaten wildlife. As elsewhere in Africa, tourism accommodation and wildlife viewing facilities are established without local or regional masterplans (Homewood and Rodgers, 1991: 237).

In the Maasai Mara case, several lodges were constructed at the same time without much planning. Four lodges and camps, namely Olkurrut, Mara Safari Club, Mara Shikar, and Sekenani tented camp, all sprung up within one year between 1989 and 1990 (Koikai, 1992; Muthee, 1992). There is now a total of 17 lodges and built-up camps in the Mara with a bed capacity of 1492 (Koikai, 1992: 8) and several temporary camping sites. These facilities have led to a very large number of tourists into a relatively small national reserve with serious impact to the environment.

Many of the protected areas are located in semi-arid lands with delicate ecologies. Overcrowding has led to vegetation disturbance and erosion. Other problems are animal harassment by tourist vehicles. Despite existing regulations on park use, tour drivers chase selected wild animals, especially the predators such as lions, leopards, and cheetahs, by off-road driving so as to satisfy their visitors' desire for close-up photographic opportunities (Olindo, 1991).

Over 50 percent of visitor time is spent on only 5 animal species (Western, 1992b: 19). Also, visitor behaviour and demand to see the "big five" (lion, leopard, buffalo, elephant and rhino) make tour drivers to chase after only a few animals. The problem is particularly serious with tourists who choose the cheap beach holiday but visit Amboseli or Maasai Mara and want to see everything in one day before they leave the country (Western, 1992b). As a result, lions are unable to mate, and cheetahs which are diurnal hunters, cannot look for food; even those which have a kill are forced to abandon it. Besides, off-road driving tramples lion cubs. In general, the carrying capacities of a number of parks have been exceeded. In Maasai Mara, just like in a number of other conservation areas, tourism's impact has reduced wildness of scenery and is affecting the abundance of wildlife in their natural setting, the very virtues that the visitors are looking for in their gaze of the reserve (Henry, 1992; Henry, Waithaka and Gakahu, 1992).

The problem is equally serious at the coast (see Tole f.c.). Here, overcrowding by tourists and boats physically damage the coral reef whereas speed boats used for water sports including jet-skiing disturb marine life and cause oil spillage (Schoorl and Visser, 1991). Also, as noted in Chapter 3, many tourists collect shells and corals; and boat anchors destroy the coral reef. Further, many tourist hotels are clustered on the beaches without being connected to the municipal sewerage system or possessing their own treatment works. Except for a few hotels such as Severin Sea Lodge which has its own sewage treatment plant, many accommodation facilities drain raw sewage into open sea thereby contributing to water pollution and threatening sea life (Schoorl and Visser, 1991; Sinclair, 1990). In fact, of all the urban centres of the coast only Mombasa has a sewerage treatment plant although this appears to cover less than 20 percent of the town's population (Schoorl and Visser, 1991). The rest of the population uses septic tanks and pit latrines; however, without a storm drainage control system, dirt and garbage are washed to sea following heavy rainfall. Contamination from lack of sewerage systems is affecting wells and boreholes in Malindi and Lamu. These are crucial sources of water for domestic use for local populations.

The poor disposal of sewage at the Kenya coast not only contaminates the environment but will likely undermine the tourist industry because of the potential health risk. Also, the coast has an environmental problem with regard to solid waste disposal. Mombasa's solid waste is dumped in open field at Kibarani. This could pollute the neighbouring water systems. Besides, this is an eyesore on the bus ride from the Mombasa airport. Malindi's garbage is heaped near Casuarina Point, whereas Lamu's rubbish dump is located on tidal mud flats where it is easily washed to the sea. All this affects the environmental quality of the coast for tourism.

Finally, the beaches do not have any toilet facilities. As such, boat operators who take tourists into the marine parks and reserves, and the informal traders who sell curios help themselves in the bush. This affects the environmental quality of the beaches.

Wildlife-human conflicts

Wildlife-human conflicts are a problem of resource utilization in conservation areas. Increasing scholarly attention (Sindiga, 1984; 1995; Akama, no date; Akama, Lant and Burnett, 1995) and policy initiatives (KWS, 1990; 1994) attest to the seriousness of the problem. Recent studies show that the majority of the local people around protected areas have negative feelings about state policies and conservation programmes (Akama, no date; Akama et al., 1995). But how did these negative feelings develop?

Due to the carving out of land for the national parks and reserves, local communities lost invaluable herding resources and sometimes agricultural land. In this instance, local people bear the cost of conservation because of foregoing the opportunity to use their land in alternative ways. Further, the wild animals in the parks usually move in and out of neighbouring farms and ranches in response to spatial and temporal occurrence in the distribution of fodder and water. The lands outside the parks are crucial to wildlife; they serve as dispersal areas (Figure 6.1). These areas are threatened with

Figure 6.1

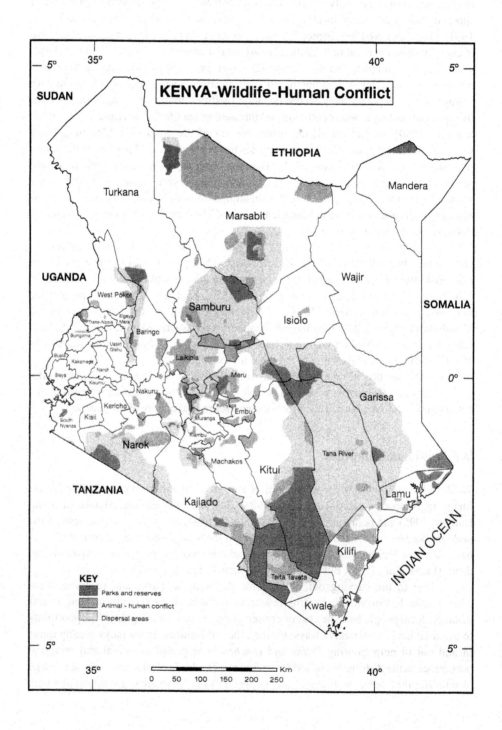

increasing "land sub-division, agricultural expansion and unplanned development of tourist accommodation, thus increasing human-wildlife conflicts" (Kenya, 1997: 88).

Besides, 70 percent of the wild animals live outside official parks in dispersal areas. The wildlife cause an enormous loss to the people by destroying property and killing humans because there are so many problem animals (Table 6.1). Between January 1989 and June 1994, wild animals in Kenya killed 230 people and injured 218 which provides an average of 42 deaths and 40 injuries per year (KWS, 1994). About 39 percent of these attacks were done by elephants. The losses incurred by local peoples may briefly be examined.

Potentially, all wild animals are pests and constitute a serious problem to African agriculture (Mascarenhas, 1971). The principal agricultural pests in Kenya include large herbivores such as elephants, buffaloes, hippos, zebras and elands. There are many others like wildebeests, baboons, monkeys, bush-pigs, porcupines, small rodents and birds (Table 6.1). Wild animals make it impossible to practice rotational grazing of live-stock which is the key to traditional pastoral systems (Sindiga, 1995). Further, wildlife carry many diseases which are dangerous to livestock. These diseases include malignant catarrh fever, a viral disease which kills livestock and is associated with the wildebeest; foot and mouth disease, a highly contagious viral disease which reduces milk supply and body weight; East Coast fever, a tick-borne disease caused by the protozoan parasite

Table 6.1
Problem wild animals in Kenya by district

Animals	District
Elephant	Laikipia, Nyeri, Meru, Samburu, Narok, Kajiado, Taita Taveta, Kwale
Buffalo	Laikipia, Nyeri, Meru, Samburu Narok, Kajiado, Taita Taveta, Machakos
Wildebeest	Narok, Kajiado
Hippopotamus, crocodile,	Narok
Lion, hyena, cheetah	Laikipia, Nyeri, Meru, Samburu, Narok, Kajiado, Taita Taveta, Machakos
Zebra, eland	Laikipia, Samburu, Narok, Kajiado, Taita Taveta, Machakos
Baboon, monkey	Laikipia, Nyeri, Meru, Samburu, Narok, Kajiado, Taita Taveta, Kwale, Machakos
Bush-pig, porcupine	Nyeri, Meru, Samburu, Kwale
Squirrel, mongoose	Laikipia, Nyeri, Meru, Samburu, Tatita Taveta, Kwale, Machakos
Quelea, other grain birds	Laikipia, Nyeri, Meru, Narok, Taita Taveta, Kwale, Machakos

Source: KWS, 1994: 34

Theileria parva and which attacks cattle thereby reducing the productivity of infected animals; and rinderpest, a contagious viral disease which kills cattle. Other diseases are pleuro-pneuro-pneumonia; nagana which is associated with wildlife-tsetse interactions; anthrax, sheep pox, entesitoxaemia and so on. The presence of wildlife which have a capacity to live with many of these diseases without serious impact to their populations is a constant source of frustration to local livestock-keeping. Also, wild animals make cultivation impossible by destroying crops in the fields.

The loss of income from death and injury and material losses is devastating to families. Wildlife-human conflicts are most intense where agricultural land borders national parks, for example Imenti, Nyeri, Trans-Mara, and Kwale and in pockets of agriculture surrounded by rangeland, for example, Kimana in Kajiado District, Leroghi in Laikipia, and Taita-Taveta (Figure 6.1; KWS, 1994). These losses escalate the cost of conservation. Unfortunately, only a few of the local communities obtain a small share of the tourism revenues through community projects such as piped or dammed water, schools, cattle dip structures, and health centres; however, these indirect benefits may not be felt at the household level (Sindiga, 1995; Chapter 7). Yet it is at this level where a conservation ethic needs to be cultivated in order to assure the survival of wildlife over the longer term.

In the case of marine parks and reserves, the problem is a conservation-human one rather than a wildlife-human conflict. It is a struggle by the local people to regain access and use of sea resources. Local economic activities such as collecting cowrie shells, fishing, harvesting forest products from the mangroves; and leisure pursuits associated with water have been restricted or curtailed (Sindiga, 1995). Further, the construction of tourist hotels in a strip development along the beaches has foreclosed the sea ethic of the local people and alienated them from tourism development. The ribbon development emerged from an unsupervised scramble by hotel developers to locate their facilities at the beach front. As there was no plan to go by, ecological and socio-cultural considerations were never taken into consideration.

Amboseli National Park, Kenya: A case study of wildlife-human conflict
Below, I present the case of Amboseli national park to illustrate the conflicts between wildlife conservation and local people. The case provides lessons not only on conflict resolution in conservation but also the necessity of local support for successful tourism-led conservation. The literature on Amboseli is extensive (Western, 1982a; 1982b; Smith, 1995; Talbot and Olindo, 1990). What follows is a highly summarized description to pinpoint the salient aspects of the Amboseli case.

Amboseli National Park, which measures 392 square kilometres, was established in 1974. It is located in the eastern Maasai district of Kajiado. Its history goes back to the 1909 game ordinance by which the entire Kenya Maasailand was declared a wildlife protection area known as Southern Game Reserve. On the 27,700 sq. km. of land, the Maasai were allowed to co-exist with wildlife. The purpose for the reserve was to stop the killing of elephants for ivory. Nevertheless, the new measure allowed the Maasai to live with the impressive diversity of wildlife as they had done for a long time. After all, the European view of the time was that the Maasai were themselves part of the wildlife scene (Knowles and Collett, 1989; Saitoti, 1978; Western 1982a; 1982b). Eliot (1966/1905: 143) appeared to emphasize this "wild" nature of the Maasai opposed to the "cultured" or "civilized" man when he described them as resembling the lion and the leopard.

In 1948 Amboseli was created as a national reserve measuring 3660 square km. Within its boundaries was Ol Tukai swamp which had always been invaluable to the Maasai and their livestock especially for dry season grazing. The decade of the 1950s was particularly good with plenty of grass and Maasai livestock multiplied quite rapidly. Wildlife in the national reserve increased as well. This attracted more tourists whose numbers increased from a few hundred a year to over 15,000 in 1960 (Western, 1982b).

The Kenya National Parks handed over Amboseli to Olkejuado County Council in 1961. The local authority managed the reserve; however, after a few years there was open evidence of severe resource destruction because of the pressure of wildlife and cattle. The Maasai insisted on utilizing the Ol Tukai swamp, which are fed by fresh water streams from Mount Kilimanjaro, for watering and grazing their livestock. They could not reconcile themselves to the idea of the reserve resources being used exclusively by wildlife. To ventilate their anger against wildlife and tourism, the Maasai began to kill rhinos and other wildlife (Talbot and Olindo, 1990). Some 30 rhinos were killed in 5 years and in nearly all the cases, the horns were not removed, suggesting that it was not the work of commercial poachers (Western, 1982b).

These problems came to a head and the government stood to lose about K£ 2.5 million which Amboseli generated annually from tourism by the late 1960s. In 1968, the government commissioned a study which proposed that 600 sq. km become a park with authority over it vested in Olkejuado County Council (Talbot and Olindo, 1990). The county council rejected the plan upon which it was agreed that Amboseli becomes a national park but with a reduced area of 488 sq. km.

In 1970 the Kenyan government declared Amboseli a national sanctuary and the Maasai would be provided with alternative water sources. But the Maasai were not satisfied. Wildlife would still roam on their lands and compete for herding resources. Besides, the Maasai had lost Ol Tukai swamp. The survival of wildlife required the cooperation and goodwill of the local Maasai community. They resumed spearing the rhinos. The rhino population declined from about 150 in the late 1950s to fewer than 30 in 1973 and only 8 in 1977 (Western, 1982b). The government decree was rendered impotent.

Following a severe drought in 1977 in which over half of the Maasai cattle died, the local people protested strongly that Ol Tukai swamp was their lifeline (Western, 1982b). This led to a number of concessions in which a section of Ol Tukai would be ceded to them in exchange for dry grazing territory thereby leaving the park with an area of 392 sq. km. In 1977 the Maasai were completely excluded from Amboseli which they had continued to use despite its declaration as a park in 1974 in exchange for piped water outside the park and financial benefits in form of a wildlife utilization fee. The water project was funded by the New York Zoological Society and the World Bank. The wildlife utilization fee was intended to compensate the Maasai for loss of access to grazing land and other costs related to sharing their land with wildlife. Other facilities, a school, dispensary, and community centre were created outside the park for use by park officials and the local Maasai. The Maasai would also receive direct financial compensation from campsites and lodges located on their land (Talbot and Olindo, 1990; Western, 1982b).

However, the water was piped to a fixed point and it is not accessible to all those who need it. The water point was sited on the assumption that the Maasai would become sedentary. This has not happened and the Maasai are beginning to take their livestock to park swamps. Also, the wildlife utilization fee appears to have been paid only up to 1981. In subsequent years, the Maasai have had to rely on campsite fees. However, conservationists look at Amboseli as a successful example on how a local community can participate in conservation and share in the benefits from it. But the larger lesson from the Amboseli case is clear. The Maasai strongly opposed the creation of a national park out of their grazing lands. When the Kenya government proceeded with its conservation programme without their participation, the local people protested by destroying wildlife, the very resource which the state intended to conserve primarily to serve the needs of the tourism industry. Not until the government conceded to providing tangible benefits such as piped water, schools, a dispensary and community centre did the local people agree to surrender the mythical Ol Tukai swamp which had always been crucial to their livestock management especially in the dry season.

Policies for resolving wildlife-human conflicts
In view of the significance of wildlife conservation on its own and its tourism value, wildlife-human conflicts will remain a permanent problem in the neighbourhoods of protected areas. As such, the role of policy is to reduce the conflicts to a tolerable level. This involves dealing with problem wildlife and devising mechanisms to allow local people to derive direct benefits from wildlife-based tourism. Such an approach is likely to encourage the residents of those areas to conserve the fauna and the flora.

The KWS has formulated policies to deal with wildlife-human conflicts according to the wildlife and tenure characteristics of land as follows (KWS, 1990: 41-45):
1) Priority wildlife areas adjacent to the parks. These are wildlife dispersal areas and corridors without which wildlife cannot survive in the parks (Sindiga, 1995). These areas have potential for wildlife-based economic activities, especially tourism. KWS focuses most of its attention on these lands.
2) Non-adjacent areas to protected areas but with high conservation value and/or great potential for economic activity based on wildlife.
3) Wildlife-human conflict areas whether adjacent to or far from a park. KWS policy is to separate wildlife from other land uses by means of a barrier where possible.
4) Non-adjacent areas, unconnected with any protected area or defined priority wildlife area, without severe conflicts but with at present only moderate or low potential for wildlife activity. These are marginal areas of wildlife habitation and are not national priority. However the KWS protects wildlife through education and extension services (KWS, 1990: 42).

The type of land ownership, size and ecological viability are important considerations in KWS policies. The main categories are as follows (KWS, 1990: 42-43):
1) Large ranches owned or leased by individuals, commercial companies or government organisations. The KWS policy is to allow the owners to utilize the wildlife on their land for their benefit.
2) Group ranches or other large ranches owned or leased by a group of residents. Such groups may include cooperatives, landowner associations or companies. The KWS grants user rights as in the privately owned ranches, to a body representing the membership of a communally owned ranch or ranches.
3) Trust land. KWS focuses assistance on the people who live on such land and who, therefore, bear the cost of maintaining wildlife.
4) Marine areas. KWS policy is to open access to marine areas for use by all. The utilization of wildlife, that is fish, corals, shells and so on, will be subject to licensing and control by the relevant government authority.
5) State land (especially forest reserves). KWS works with the Forest Department to conserve wildlife.

From the above categorization of land and policies, KWS approaches to mitigating wildlife-human conflicts may be summarized as follows: granting wildlife use rights to landowners; sharing park revenues with adjacent communities; seeking assurance that land use would include wildlife conservation; encouraging wildlife-based economic activities; erecting barriers; controlling problem animals; education and extension services on wildlife conservation; and law enforcement (KWS, 1990: 43). These approaches to management can be used singly or in combination depending on local circumstances. Some of these policies have been implemented and others remain only on paper. In the case of erecting barriers to stop problem animals from entering private land adjacent to parks, KWS has started a programme of electric fencing. This has been done or is being considered for Lake Nakuru National Park, Aberdares and Shimba Hills National Reserve. Such barriers may in the long term be ecologically devastating to wildlife. As no single protected area in Kenya is a viable ecological unit on its own, access to dispersal areas is crucial to the survival of wildlife in the parks. The implications of electric fencing of protected areas deserves a full ecological review before it is treated as a panacea to wildlife human conflicts. Fortunately, KWS policy of using a range of management approaches may assure the sustainability of wildlife conservation and tourism.

The KWS policies for private land adjacent to protected areas assume that the owners of the ranches are practising compatible land uses to wildlife utilization. As shown above, wildlife dispersal areas are places of increasing population pressure and a good amount of cultivation takes place. Crop cultivation is not compatible with wildlife conservation. The issue of population pressure and land use control appear to go beyond the purview of KWS. They must be addressed higher up in the government hierarchy. Finally, the resource conflicts between the local people and tourism-led conservation require to be addressed. This is because the goodwill of the local community is crucial to the success of any programme. Although the government is committed to opening up public access to the sea and beaches (Kenya, 1994b: 74), a comprehensive policy decision on land use within and surrounding national parks and reserves and the beach front would be a first step towards solving the problem of conflicts. It would ensure controlled tourism development.

Socio-cultural changes

Tourism leads to encounters between hosts and guests which may be productive to both sides. However, such contacts may also be negative to either party especially the African hosts. As a result there has been a lot of attention on socio-cultural impacts of Western tourism on Third World peoples (Mathieson and Wall, 1982; Wall, 1996; Harrison, 1992b; Lea, 1993). A number of critical reviews have dismissed tourism as a final form of colonialism in which Europeans subjugate Africans (Middleton, 1992). Their main argument is that international tourism is controlled by Euro-American entrepreneurs and that the benefits that trickle down to local communities are meagre. Local people are removed from the general operations of tourism business. Hotels are owned by investors from elsewhere and so are the tour operations. Some local inhabitants may obtain low level employment in tourism enterprises.

However, in a number of places local people have started to sell tourist art thereby making a little money. It appears that the revival of certain Kenyan art is associated with mass tourism. Such include the Akamba wood carvings (Horner, 1993), Kisii soapstone carvings which provide income to 5,000 people (Kenya, 1994j: 32), Kikuyu and Kamba baskets, Maasai and Okiek beads, necklaces and earrings (Klumpp and Kratz, 1993), Pokomo mats (Bachmann, 1988: 193) and arts and crafts produced by many other communities. Contrary to some claims that tourist arts and crafts are not authentic, there is no evidence to support this assertion (Harrison, 1992b).

The African arts and crafts build on traditional expertise (Soyinka, 1985) but may be modified to conform with the desires of customers (Schadler, 1979). Traditional art is then transformed into tourist art because of demand from Western tourists. "Tourist art is defined as any artistic object produced not for ritual or tribal purposes but for sale to traders or directly to tourists" (Schadler, 1979: 146).

In Kenya, the makers of curios and souvenirs lose money to middlemen who purchase the articles at throw-away prices and then sell them to the tourist market locally and abroad at handsome profits. But the scale of production of tourist art in Kenya is not yet known. Also, although certain aspects of Kenyan arts and crafts and dances have been encouraged, other forms of culture especially music and theatre have been curiously ignored, both by the Kenya government and foreign promoters of tourism (Bachmann, 1988: 194).

Tourist lifestyles in their isolated enclaves tend to accentuate the dramatic differences between foreign affluence and local poverty. Other objections relate to the superficial packaging of culture for tourist consumption, and cultural change. The development of mass tourism at the Kenyan coast, for example, created profound socio-economic change in the Muslim towns especially Mombasa and Malindi. Not surprisingly, a myriad social problems including a high drop-out rate from schools by male children, drug peddling, petty crimes, family disputes and prostitution have been blamed on tourism (Migot-Adholla, *et al.*, 1982; Beckerleg, 1995; Peake, 1989; Sindiga f.c.).

Although the relationship between tourism and prostitution is not linear, it is evident that sex is consistent with the motivation that underlies much of tourism (Ryan and Kinder, 1996). Such forms of relaxation may be socially disapproved in the West. The period of the visit therefore offers a temporary escape from the reality, norms and values which prevail in the western world (Smith, 1977; Graburn, 1977; Peake, 1989). This behaviour can, however, be disconcerting to the host community, especially among older people. At the Kenya coast, young boys are dropping out of school through the influence of tourists who are seen to consume alcohol, drugs and to engage in casual sex (Beckerleg, 1995; Sindiga 1996b). Such influence is so pervasive that traditional forms of parental control are breaking down (Beckerleg 1995). As these youths have no skills, they are not prepared for positions in surrounding tourism enterprises (Eastman, 1995). This leads to frustration, loitering, general delinquency and drug taking (Brule, 1988: 13; Beckerleg, 1995). Some of these youths end up as the so-called beach boys offering informal services ranging from "male prostitution for female and male clients, tour guiding and companionship" (Peake, 1989) to selling drugs and a host of other things. Although beach boys provide sex to "surprisingly numerous elderly women, who visit Malindi each year seeking companionship of young men", the boys do not take much pride in hustling old women; they hide away from home and acquaintances (Peake, 1989: 211-212). The beach boys engage in this behaviour so as to raise some money with which they would start a business.

Recent studies have noted that tourism at the coast has elicited only lukewarm response from the local Waswahili people (Eastman, 1995; Sindiga, 1996b). Save for some young men who work as clerks in the tourism industry (Peake, 1989), there have been few Waswahili willing to work at tourism enterprises partly because of the Islamic culture, low level of education, and an association of tourism with immorality (Sindiga 1996b). Consequently, large numbers of up-country Kenyans have gone there to participate in the tourism industry. Parallel to this has been a vibrant migration stream of Kamba, Kikuyu, Luhya, and Luo women to the coast to try to earn a living through female prostitution.

Some writers consider Kenya to be a "tourist paradise for Western hunters of sex" (Thiong'o, 1993: 173; Appendix 8). There is even a claim that the Kenya coast is perceived as a place where western tourists could buy African teenage girls "for the price of a ticket to a cheap cinema show" (Thiong'o, 1977: 175). Indeed, Kenya's beach holidays appear to have increasingly gained the image as "sex safari" (Migot-Adholla *et al.*, 1982). Although it is difficult to demonstrate the magnitude of girl children in sex tourism in Kenya, there appears to be a consensus even within the Kenya government that commercial sex involving them is rampant in pockets of civil society (Christian Aid, 1995; *Daily Nation*, October 25, 1995, p. 6; see statement on child prostitution in Kenya by the Minister for Home Affairs, F.P.L. Lotodo in *Daily Nation*, August 23, 1996 p. 20).

It is not being suggested that prostitution was unknown at the coast before the advent of mass tourism. In fact, for decades, Mombasa has received up-country workers at the port and city (Appendix 8). The selective movement of labour to the urban areas in favour of men led to a skewed sex-ratio. This was maintained this way because of the unavailability of urban housing for families whereby the men were forced to share tiny accommodation. Under the circumstances, the men sought sexual gratification with female prostitutes. This experience is typical of colonial Africa (Harrison, 1994). Migot-Adholla and his colleagues (1982) found that most hotel workers at the coast were single men living in rather poor conditions in villages around the tourist hotels thereby dramatizing the differences between guests and hosts in the tourist trade.

In general, women lack employment opportunities in tourist enterprises which appear to prefer men (Elkan, 1975). The predominance of men in the emerging tourist centres created a demand for female prostitutes. Despite local disapproval of prostitution, there are many lodging houses around beach hotels (Mwakisha, 1995; Migot-Adholla *et al.*, 1982). It is well known that these houses act as hideouts for prostitutes and drug peddlers. Also, the increasing numbers of clubs, discotheques, beach resorts and other tourist conveniences has provided a perfect umbrella for commercial sex workers.

Yet, there may be something in tourist behaviour that encourages prostitution and what the local host society sees as deviant behaviour especially among the youth. Male and female tourists walk around kissing in public hand in hand and dressed in swimming suits or shorts, behaviour that offends the local Muslim culture (Peake 1989; Sindiga 1996b). Ostensibly, to capture the imagination of their potential customers, sex workers go into discos "almost naked except for shapely beads or skimpy cloth over their loins. The faces are breached, the bodies slim and shapely" (Mwakisha, 1995). As Mwakisha adds, the prostitutes "wriggle and gyrate obscenely, attracting foot-thumping, claps, dollars, Deutsche marks and shillings from the floor." This scene, captured inside tourism facilities at Watamu near Malindi, confirms the intricate relationship between tourism and entertainment as mediated by the female prostitute.

As noted in Appendix 8, female prostitutes are not allowed into tourist-class hotels unaccompanied by a male partner. This practice has sometimes led to ugly and embarrassing harassment of bona fide female customers entering such premises. This is where the services of the beach boys come in handy. They assist to connect female prostitutes in neighbouring lodging houses to male tourist clients. As noted above, the beach boys themselves provide sexual services to female tourists (Peake, 1989). Sometimes, the beach boys accompany the prostitutes to bars, discos and other entertainment programmes in tourist hotels. Here, they conduct negotiations with tourists on behalf of their clients. Alternatively, the prostitutes make direct arrangements with willing male tourists with the beach boys monitoring the process and would provide protection where necessary.

Model African villages
In response to tourism, the Maasai have created model traditional villages where their culture is packaged for the consumption of the Western tourist. The "cultural manyatta", as the traditional Maasai model village is called, is created as a true Maasai home occupied

by families. Tourists pay a fee and tips for the experience. They can also purchase Maasai art. However, the cultural *manyatta* has been criticized on a number of grounds: (1) it adulterates Maasai cultural life; and (2) tour drivers and guides act as middlemen between the Maasai and tourist groups and take the highest share of tourist fees and tips (KWS, 1994). Because of these objections, others have suggested the creation of local cultural museums although this is only at idea stage. Tourism has thus led to the commoditization of culture. In addition, the cultural *manyatta* has received another form of objection: some tourists appear to pay some of the women to strip naked for photographs; others are said to be involved in casual sex with Maasai women (Naitore, 1995).

Also, Maasai *il murran* (warriors) perform traditional dances for tourists. Tourist hotels are well known for these performances. Maasai warriors are "tall, elegant, handsome" and "seemingly proud and indifferent to all but the most necessary external influences" (Kantai, 1971: vii). They wear their hair in plaited dreadlocks, apply red ochre to their heads and spot a colourful *shuka*, cloth wrapper on their bodies together with a club in hand. As such the Maasai remain the best example of the African noble savage or the authentic Africans in the minds of Western tourists. Although the view is inaccurate, it is claimed that the Maasai are completely oblivious to change (Spencer, 1988).[1] However, the perception persists and is reinforced by the traditional attire and the impressive physical adornment of the warriors.

In East African tourist gaze, there tends to be a preoccupation with the authentic, the true and the natural and the Maasai and wildlife represent these qualities. Without seeing the Maasai the tourist experience of East Africa appears incomplete. As a British tourist to the Maasai Mara National Reserve observes:

> Distant Masai (sic) tribesmen, banned from grazing their cattle within the parks, often appeared on our game drives, their traditional red tartan wraps giving them spectacular prominence on landscapes in which all other life forms had evolved to merge. *Their presence contributed to a truer African picture* (my emphasis). These people have been part of the savannah scene for hundreds of years (Seal, 1997: 19).

As can be noted, the association between the Maasai and nature are woven in these comments. Even in the post-tourist experience, that is, gazing geographically at distant landscapes and cultures through television and video in one's own home (Urry, 1991: 100) or through numerous coffee table books and tourist photography, the Maasai "stand in proud mute testimony to a vanishing African world" (Spear, 1993: 1). This appears to be a world much sought after by western tourists. As such it is played and replayed in tourist discourse.

The Maasai are very popular dancers as they fulfill the Western tourist's image of Africa as an exotic culture (Bruner and Kirshenblatt-Gimblett, 1994). Maasai dance is not a concoction for tourist gaze; it is true to Maasai cultural life. Ordinarily, singing and dancing are part of the daily culture of the Maasai in their homesteads (Smith, 1995: 100). It is recognized, however, that this alone cannot stop others, even the non-Maasai,

---

[1] A long string of authors has criticized the view that the Maasai are conservative and shown that they adapt to changes. However, some Western anthropologists (for example, Spencer, 1988) still see the Maasai as static. A critique of Spencer's work is Rigby (1996).

from impersonating Maasai garb, physical adornment and dance for the purpose of earning money from tourists.

Some of these male Maasai dancers are involved in what has been dubbed "romance tourism" (Pruitt and La Font, 1995: 423; Appendix 8) with female tourists who seek them out (Sommer, no date: 34). It is clear in the cases of the Gambia in West Africa and of Jamaica that middle-aged European and North American women specifically go for romantic tourism with local men (Pruitt and La Font, 1995; Harrell-Bond and Harrell-Bond, 1979: 88). In romance tourism, visiting Euro-American women seek a romantic and long-term interaction with the local men (Pruitt and La Font, 1995: 427). It is not clear why this happens; however, such women may seek greater attention and emotional involvement with men from different cultures in settings where they are unencumbered by western norms.

Tourism's negative socio-cultural consequences are most severe at the Kenya coast where tourist behaviour is at odds with the Islamic culture (Sindiga f.c.). The Swahili youths are particularly vulnerable to the "demonstration" effect of the "good" life associated with tourism. In Nairobi, another centre of Kenya's tourism, the population is quite sophisticated and the negative impacts of tourism are virtually unnoticed. Elsewhere in the national parks and reserves, the tourists go to the lodges which tend to be isolated from the local people. However, the efforts towards creating traditional model villages for the tourist gaze especially in Maasailand has potential for cultural conflict and may cause undesirable change such as begging and posing for photographs for money.

The commoditization of Maasai dance and cultural life through tourism may lead to cultural abuse. Accommodation establishments are too eager to fulfill the Western tourist stereotyped notions of authentic African culture by organizing traditional dances either by the Maasai or people dressed like the Maasai and presumably enacting Maasai traditional culture. This view of the Maasai as "authentic" African culture oversimplifies the reality and ignores the enormous variety of dancing routines among Kenya's multiplicity of cultures. Such a variety is for example represented at the Bomas of Kenya although even here there is room for greater diversity (Appendix 5).

Yet, as a marginalized community in Kenya's national life, the Maasai are looking at tourism as a possible source of income. As in the case of the Waswahili, few Maasai work directly in tourist enterprises especially hotels. This is partly because of lack of training which is itself an indication of the poor education standards in Maasai-land. Children of nomadic pastoral families are unable to enrol or continue with school because of the exigencies of pastoral life. Maasai direct participation in tourism has therefore been restricted to traditional model villages, dances, arts and crafts, and wildlife conservation efforts. Whereas Maasai participation in tourism via wildlife conservation is discussed in Chapter 7, it can be noted that Maasai women are beginning to do beadwork including necklaces, earrings and arm rings, and basketry for the tourist market. In addition, young men are making wooden clubs and spears for the tourist industry. Although traditionally the Maasai did not do iron work, they must now supplement their diminishing livestock herds with market goods as a means of survival. However, Maasai material culture is quite diverse and encompasses numerous categories as follows: clothing and body ornaments, for example, necklaces, wristlets, leather sandals, clothes from hides and skins, and leather bags; household equipment — gourds, calabashes, sleeping hide, bowls, stools, beer drinking horns, and pots; warfare, hunting and collecting — walking sticks, spears, bows and arrows, honey bags; animal husbandry-skin straps, cow bells; industry and manufacture — knives, pangas, axes, needles, hidescrapers; and other miscellaneous objects such as smoking pipes, snuff bottles and medicine horns (Odak, 1986: 216-241). Many of the material objects used in various aspects of Maasai life are of touristic interest. Women groups in particular are now increasingly engaged in basketry, bead-making, knitting and other traditional handicrafts for the tourist market in order to raise their standards of living.

Uneven distribution of tourism benefits

As discussed above, the international distribution of Kenya's tourism benefits is skewed to the advantage of multinational corporations. Kenya's tourism leakages are very high. Sometimes the leakages of total tourism revenues can be as high as 70 percent for beach-only tourism; however, the leakage falls substantially for safari visitors because of the element of local travel (Kenya, 1991a). The problem of leakage is exacerbated by the foreign ownership and management of the bulk of Kenya's tourism enterprises.

Green (1979) suggested that small African economies can mitigate against inequitable division of benefits from tourism through negotiated agreements. Such negotiations must be done in the knowledge of planned growth and development of the sector. There must also be skilled personnel to plan and manage tourism enterprises. Such people who should be educated to degree level (Kenya, 1991a) have been produced by Moi University since 1996 (Sindiga, 1994). These people can insure that tourism development contracts have specific measurable objectives and outcomes to the benefit of the host country. This will stop the tendency of signing agreements which are written in general terms which later provide multinational companies the opportunity to work in their own interest with little benefit to the host country. Graduates trained in tourism are expected to replace expatriate personnel and to start indigenously-owned tourism enterprises. Ultimately, controlling the ownership of the major subsectors of tourism will lead to a more equitable distribution of benefits (Lea, 1993: 79). But without policy resolution, this would be difficult to achieve in the short term because it involves competition with multi-national companies which are better-endowed with resources.

Competitiveness

As noted above, Kenya's tourism is meeting with stiff competition with other African destinations. To cope with the competition, Kenya needs to upgrade the quality of its tourism product, and conduct an aggressive promotional and marketing campaign overseas. Kenya's tourism promotion and marketing has benefitted from the work of private tour operators and travel agents and individual hotel chains both at home and overseas. The private sector contributes 60 percent of the promotional costs of participating in international fairs, exhibitions, seminars, workshops, and road shows and the government meets the balance. Also, Kenya's reputation as a tourism destination is passed on by word of mouth by people who have already visited the country. Kenya's varied environments, its wildlife and bird populations are also subject of many documentary films, books and magazine articles. These provide free publicity to the country's tourism. All these are no longer sufficient for the country to maintain a competitive edge.

Government promotion of tourism is done by the country's tourist offices abroad and by the Department of Tourism usually through its participation in international tourism fairs. However, the annual budgets of Kenya's seven offices abroad and two local ones is minuscule (Chapter 5). Lack of sufficient resources makes it impossible to market tourism. Three recent developments, however, hold promise in Kenya's tourism promotion and marketing. First, the Kenya Wildlife Service has started a tourism section within the organization (Chapter 4). This is a recognition of the crucial role of tourism income to wildlife conservation. The KWS is expected to take a more active part in tourism promotion. The idea of conservation qua conservation is changing to embrace a more management and utilitarian approach. Second, in 1996 the government established the long-awaited Kenya Tourism Board (KTB) (Chapter 5). The KTB is expected to take over the responsibility of packaging and marketing Kenya's tourism products from the Ministry of Tourism and Wildlife. In this regard, it is in the process of taking over the management of all tourist offices locally and overseas. Also, the KTB will be responsible for coordinating tourism promotion in general (Kenya, 1998a: 184). This way the marketing and promotion issue will be solved. In the first two years of its existence, the KTB mounted a vigorous promotional campaign of Kenya tourism overseas. For example, it placed advertisements in at least 35 travel magazines targeted to reach more than 45 million readers worldwide (Tagama, 1998: 31). This is likely to have a positive impact on potential tourists to Kenya. Third, the Kenya government has established a tourist police unit to attend to the special security and other needs of tourists. Initially, personnel from this unit have been deployed along the beaches at the Kenya coast where the so-called beach boys harass tourists. As noted above beach boys are informal hawkers of merchandise at the beach and provide several other services including drugs and female prostitutes. They are known to pester tourists to purchase their curios. In time, the tourist police unit will be expanded to cover all the major concentrations of tourist activity in the country. As the unit works specifically on tourist matters, it is expected that personal safety and security will be assured and the country's image will improve. However, a better assurance of security for tourists requires that the environment in which all Kenyans live is peaceful and stable. As indicated in Chapter 3 above, the instability, ethnic divisions and political power rivalries associated with the country's democratization process must be addressed satisfactorily in order to restore stability.

Kenya's international tourists come from a very narrow market in Western Europe and North America (Chapter 4). This market needs to be diversified to insure the stability of tourist flows. The Far Eastern market (Japan, Korea, Australia, New Zealand) and the

Middle East one, for example, have not yet been systematically exploited. Other potential markets are Canada, southern and eastern Europe, and South Africa.

Domestic tourism

Kenya's international tourism is highly seasonal. The high season for arrivals starts in September and lasts until March. This flow of tourists dries up during the period April to August. This seasonality is reflected in employment as workers must be laid off in the low season. The country established a domestic tourism policy in 1984 to encourage residents to travel locally, especially during the low season for international tourism. Although domestic tourism is supported for a variety of other reasons, the central objective is to even out the seasonality pattern thereby preserving jobs year round.

To give force to the new policy, the government established the Domestic Tourism Council (DTC) with membership drawn from the public and private sectors of tourism. As the secretariat is housed in the MTW, it is expected that the DTC would receive significant policy attention thereby improving coordination with all the participants. Indeed, the representation of the various tourism sub-sectors at the DTC is intended to provide travel incentives to the local people.

The other objectives of the DTC may be summarized as follows: promoting national unity and integration through knowledge and understanding of other areas; allowing local people to share in the government investment in tourism infrastructure; increasing investment from domestic tourism; redistributing income across the country; and conserving foreign currency by having Kenyans visiting their own country rather than travelling aborad (Sinclair, 1990). However, there are other reasons for developing domestic tourism. Kenya's international tourists come from a very narrow market in Western Europe and the United States (Chapter 4). An economic recession in these countries can lead to a dramatic reduction in the number of visitors and the associated foreign exchange earnings. Besides, international tourism is quite vulnerable to bad press publicity, internal security, threats to health and personal safety, poor tourism infrastructure (roads and communications), and accommodation facilities. Also, as shown in the preceding section, Kenya faces stiff competition for overseas tourists with other African nations especially Tanzania, Uganda, Zimbabwe and South Africa; and with the countries of Eastern Europe, especially since the collapse of communism in 1989.

It has been argued that a country must have a culture of domestic tourism as a basis for international tourism. As shown in Chapter 4, Kenya's beach tourism developed from a vibrant domestic tourism sector. This had led to the creation of a basic infrastructure using local resources and personnel upon which international tourism was established. This way the tourism industry can be sustained over a long period (Sindiga, 1996a). The point is often missed that the countries that generate international tourists also have a very strong domestic tourism industry.

Another advantage of domestic tourism is the absence of barriers such as language, currency, immigration procedures etc. that characterize foreign travel. Finally, domestic tourism can provide an opportunity for meeting the recreational needs of the citizens and supporting national resource conservation through public knowledge (Sindiga, 1996a).

Strategies for promoting domestic tourism

A number of strategies have been worked out for achieving the objectives of domestic tourism in Kenya. The DTC would organize annual workshops involving government and private sector participation to discuss ways of developing domestic tourism. A combination of incentives involving reduced tariff rates by hotels during the low season and discounted fares by Kenya Railways were put in place to encourage domestic travellers. Whereas large hotels would give discounts of 40 to 50 percent below normal charges in the low season, some budget hotels introduced reduced rates year round and Kenya Railways would provide a 10 percent reduction on the fares for groups of 10 people or more (Sinclair, 1990). Although some people have taken advantage of these, the majority of the Kenyans still cannot afford to pay the hotel bills for a holiday of a week or two because of low incomes and rather stiff tariffs of tourist-class hotels (Sindiga, 1996a). The railway system in the country has very low connectivity and does not cover many population centres. This leaves the internal traveller with no alternative other than the relatively expensive road transport.

Other strategies for promoting domestic tourism include lower entrance fees for local people into national parks and reserves, encouraging employers to provide incentive holidays for their good workers, using Agricultural Society of Kenya shows in various districts to provide information on internal travelling, using the mass media for promotion, and encouraging young people to become domestic tourists through schools and established organizations such as wildlife clubs (Sinclair, 1990). Although young people can be organized to take group tours through youth clubs and schools, it is not as easy to organize adults without a basis for such arrangements. Certain possibilities such as cooperative society membership, church groups and other civic bodies could provide a rationale for arranging group tours (Sindiga, 1996a). This suggestion is made on the presumption of shared interests among members of a group taking a tour.

An assessment by the UNDP and WTO (1993) claimed that

> Domestic tourism is beginning to develop with holiday visits made by some Kenyans to parks, reserves and the coast as well as elsewhere to visit friends and relatives. Many hotels and lodges offer low room rates for residents which encourage some domestic travel (UNDP and WTO, 1993: 1).

Perhaps this statement needs to be qualified with empirical data in order to test its veracity. Using hotel bednights data for the three years 1995 to 1997, Kenyan residents occupied some 13.6 percent, 15.5% and 15.8%, respectively of the total bednights in the country (Table 6.2). When the data are disaggregated according to tourism region for the three years, 20.6 percent of the bednights of the Kenyan residents were spent in Nairobi, 9.7 percent at the coast, and only 7.7 percent in the lodges. It is to be noted that Kenyan bednights in the "other category" — meaning unclassified hotels in different parts of the country and even in Nairobi and the coast (Chapter 5) — constituted 60.6

Table 6.2
Hotel bed-nights occupied by Kenyan residents, by region, 1995-97 ('000s)

Year	Nairobi	Coast	Lodges	Others	Total
1995					
Total	1,027.5	3,226.2	427.2	373.8	5,054.8
Kenya residents	161.6	332.8	33.5	161.4	689.3
% share (Kenya)	15.7	10.3	7.8	43.0	13.6
1996					
Total	1,087.2	3,215.8	493.2	265.0	5,061.2
Kenya residents	245.4	305.7	34.1	197.4	782.6
% share (Kenya)	22.6	9.5	6.9	74.5	15.5
1997					
Total	1,113.1	3,146.1	351.2	299.9	4,910.3
Kenya residents	262.3	291.8	29.8	192.9	776.8
% share (Kenya)	23.6	9.3	8.5	64.3	15.8

Sources: Kenya, 1996a: 178; 1997b: 183; 1998a: 181.

percent of the bednights for that category (Table 6.2). These data indicate that a relatively small proportion of Kenyan residents goes to the tourist lodges and to the coast. Some authors have interpreted this in racial categories and attributed domestic tourism to European and Asian residents and not Africans (for example Bachmann, 1988). This argument follows the now tired "racial overachievement explanations" for immigrant groups in Africa and not the Africans themselves (Chege, 1997). Others have claimed, contrary to all available empirical evidence, that Africans are not recreation-minded. It would be interesting to know for example the proportion of bednights spent by the immigrant communities out of the total figures for Kenyan residents represented in these data. Unfortunately the data are not disaggregated to that level.

It is clear nonetheless that many Kenyans may not be going to the international tourist hotels at the coast, and are not found in the same minibuses which carry foreign visitors to gaze at the wildlife landscapes. The majority of the Kenyans stay in small and medium sized hotels which are relatively inexpensive in terms of accommodation, food and beverage costs. Such facilities tend to be far from national parks and reserves. Game lodges have been developed specifically for the international tourist and the tariff structure reflects this bias.

Unfortunately, the central objective of the domestic tourism policy is to get Kenyans going to the same places and facilities used by the international tourists during the off-season. This policy is short-sighted and is not likely to lead to sustainable domestic tourism. This is not to say that Kenyans do not want to share in similar experiences as foreign tourists. Rather, it is to emphasize the relatively low incomes of most Kenyans against the cost of putting up at large hotels and lodges.

Also, international tourism is spatially concentrated at a few places. This is not necessarily suitable or interesting to the domestic tourist. Tourism could be diversified geographically and in terms of the product to cater for a large market segmentation based on income levels and interest. Such diversification is likely to create attractions closer to the centres of population, reduce the travel bill and encourage more people to participate in domestic tourism (Sindiga, 1996a: 26). The existing tourism infrastructure in the country including tour and travel operations is structured to serve international tourists. This is the case in most African countries. All tourism infrastructure including policy, planning, promotion and marketing are directed at foreigners, usually people from outside the continent. There are no facilities to cater for local visitors from the perspective of socio-economic circumstances and tourism infrastructure. On transport alone, there are no prescribed buses, either by the DTC or tour firms, to cater for domestic tourists who wish to visit national parks and reserves. Given that most Kenyans do not own personal cars and that tour safari vehicles are very expensive, domestic tourists have little means of visiting the protected areas.

Yet, there are a few examples of successful domestic tourism in the country. Organized farmers may spend time at an agricultural show or go for an educational tour of modern farming techniques in another area. Other kinds of civic groups also organize to go to visit counterparts in other regions of the country. Perhaps the best example of domestic tourism is the Wildlife Clubs of Kenya (WCK) which is discussed below.

Wildlife Clubs of Kenya (WCK)
WCK was established in 1966 as a charitable, non-profit organization. The funding in the form of aid and grants comes from government, non-governmental institutions and individuals. The objectives of WCK are (1) creating interest in and knowledge of wildlife, the environment and natural resources among the young people through conservation education; (2) sensitizing the youth and the public at large about the value of natural resources and; (3) developing a better understanding of wildlife conservation.

The WCK has more than 1,350 member clubs made up of about 80,000 members and 850 adult associate members. The members come from the student community in the secondary schools, colleges and universities. WCK is considered the most widespread conservation educational organization in the country (Berger, 1993: 15). It is recognised, however, that most of the clubs are urban-based or come from agriculturally-settled areas with little wildlife. This provides part of the raison d'etre for travel to the protected areas of the country. To assist the members to meet their objectives, WCK has centres in Nairobi, Nakuru, Nanyuki and Voi with hostel type accommodation. Members on safari can sleep in the hostels or pitch tent on centre grounds at subsidized prices. This way, they can visit neighbouring national parks where they are allowed free entry on account of their membership of the WCK. These incentives reduce the cost of domestic tourism considerably.

While they are travelling in various places of tourist interest WCK members are involved in many activities including field natural history studies, nature trails, animal field identification, and bird watching. It is expected that in future these young people would better appreciate the value of conservation and tourism and their complex interrelationships.

The growth of the so-called social tourism initially in Europe and then in the United States stimulated travel by the low income people. This is done by organizing children's camps, low cost accommodation in colleges and universities especially during vacations and through the creation of employee travel associations (Gunn, 1988: 64-65). Such innovations could be introduced in Kenya to complement the incentives already in place to encourage domestic tourism.

Regional development

One of the reasons for promoting tourism is the expectation that it will generate regional and national development through foreign exchange earnings, employment and revenues. Once tourism income increases, it stimulates the growth of other sectors of the economy through forward and backward linkages. This leads to a general rise in the standards of living of the local people.

International tourism in Kenya has rather weak backward linkages because of the predominance of foreign ownership and management of tourism enterprises. The country has invested heavily in expensive expansion of airports, protection of wildlife in dispersed locations, a linkage of the various tourist attractions with a road system, large hotels and lodges, telecommunications, and other infrastructure associated with tourism. Yet, Kenya has not received returns to this enormous investment. This is partly because of the emphasis on low spending mass tourists and the structure of international tourism with its heavy financial leakages in favour of multinational corporations based in developed countries (Chapters 4 and 5). As such, Kenya's international tourism has not played a major developmental role. The economic impact of tourism at the national level is only modest.

Although it is difficult to assess the impact of tourism at the regional level in the absence of regional plans, a number of observations can be made. Tourism is spatially concentrated in the two primate cities of Nairobi and Mombasa, at the coast and in a few national parks and reserves. Some 80 percent of the tourist accommodation is located in areas where only 10 percent of the country's population lives; in addition, most of the tour business are located in the two major cities. As shown in Chapter 5, about 50 percent of the tour operations businesses are based in Nairobi and some 43.5 percent are at the coast. The remaining 7 percent is distributed widely in various national parks and reserves around the country.

As tourism is spatially concentrated in a few areas, whatever forward and backward linkages with other sectors of the economy are restricted to those places. Also, employment and infrastructure development (water, electricity etc.) are confined to the areas of tourism development. The impact of tourism to the rest of the country is small or non-existent.

Political violence

Perhaps the most important factor explaining the decline of Kenya's tourism in the post-1990 period is local insecurity associated with political violence (Chapter 3). As noted above, ethnic clashes broke out in the country at the end of 1991 in the former 'White Highlands' where many ethnic communities had been resettled after independence. In subsequent years, ethnic violence flared up sporadically in one part of the country or other thereby seriously affecting tourism activities. Although the causes of the clashes are multi-dimensional and complex (Kenya, 1992), the main causes are related to the democratization process in the country. Traditional ethnic rivalries and competition over resources which had been suppressed in the post-independence period were activated by opposing political forces at the onset of multi-party politics.

Although tourists or tourist establishments were not targeted by the raiders, there was a drastic fall in tourist numbers. With the decline in tourist arrivals was tourist income. Many tourist hotels drastically reduced their tariff whereas others closed down for renovations. In the process, many tourism workers lost their employment. The efforts of individual tourism establishments to resuscitate tourist arrivals will, however, not bear fruit until political violence, ethnic tensions and general insecurity have been addressed by the government.

As part of the Kenya government solution to political violence, it established a judicial commission of inquiry into tribal clashes in the country on July 1st 1998 (Kenya, 1998c). The commission was created to investigate the ethnic clashes in Kenya between 1991 and 1998. Specifically, the commission must establish the origins, causes, and handling of the clashes by the law enforcement agencies. Although its establishment was somewhat belated, the commission's report may recommend prosecution or further criminal investigations of the perpetrators and ways, means and actions to be taken to prevent such happenings in the future (Kenya, 1998c). The fact that this commission was created indicates government determination to deal with the matter of political violence which has had serious consequences to the country's tourism industry.

Summary and conclusion

In this chapter I have shown that Kenya's tourism developed without a sectoral plan. With a number of strategic objectives, government support, and private sector initiative, and endowed with exceptional wildlife resources and sandy beaches, tourism picked a momentum which propelled it for three decades. Both in the protected areas and at the coast, tourism expanded before the necessary infrastructure was developed. This led to short term decisions and investments without a long term view of the industry's development. This area of expansion ended in 1990. To move forward, the country's tourism must be guided by comprehensive planning to provide the context and tools to resolve the critical issues which are facing the industry. This way, Kenya could avoid the Spanish example where unplanned construction, insufficient infrastructure, and pollution of the coastal areas forced the tourists to seek better facilities in other countries (Sinclair, 1990).

Kenya still lacks a coherent tourism policy to guide the development of the industry. As a result, government policy appears contradictory with regard to the choice between luxury and mass tourism.

> Luxury tourists spend more per day but require a very high level of inputs in terms of imported goods and the presence of far fewer other tourists. Mass tourism has

much greater potential to create more employment and generate foreign exchange but with the disadvantage of congestion in the parks and the beaches. Kenya will diversify and accommodate both types of tourism through land use planning while market forces will be allowed to ultimately determine the forms of tourism that develop in Kenya (Kenya, 1994b: 73).

It is not usual for a country to have both luxury and mass tourism. In the Kenya case, however, the government appears to leave questions of both policy and planning to market forces. Further, it is surprising that the government should imply that the country has too many tourists already when it has for many years targeted one million by the year 1990. This strengthens the view that the strategy of obtaining short run increases in foreign exchange earnings and employment from tourism can be stretched so far. Once a critical population has been reached, the quick-fix strategies can only keep an equilibrium visitor population for a limited amount of time because tourists are highly sensitive to the deterioration of the quality of a tourism product.

Kenya is in a dilemma of creating employment for its teeming population. The country's employment growth cannot absorb the increasing labour force. Faced with millions of unemployed people, government short term strategy is to create employment and increase incomes by market-driven mass tourism regardless of its impact on society and the environment. On the other hand, the country would like to redress the obvious environmental and socio-cultural effects of mass tourism by creating a market-targeted product-led type of tourism which promises higher per capita returns.

In the arena of policy and planning, a number of actions must be taken in order to improve the country's tourism product. For national parks and reserves, alternative policy must be sought to provide for a wider dispersal of the tourist traffic to currently underutilized parks and reserves. Such policies, however, should be backed by investments in physical and institutional infrastructure for handling visitors. Any such investments would require to be planned carefully to provide comparable attractions to those of the popular parks. Only then can visitor satisfaction be met.

At the coast, there is need to plan for tourist numbers within the perspective of general development in the area. Such facilities as water supply, sewage disposal, roads, and electricity must be considered carefully. Also, tourist numbers could be regulated to conform to the carrying capacity of the available resources.

Finally, peace, stability and security must be pursued in place of political violence. As the government itself has noted, insecurity in the country has scared away the tourists (Kenya, 1998b: 18).

Alternative tourism and sustainable development

In the wake of the changes and challenges posed by mass tourism to the resource base (environment), society and the economy, alternative or low impact forms of tourism have been suggested. This chapter discusses alternative tourism — or ecotourism — in Kenya and assesses its prospects for raising rural incomes and sustainable development. Another purpose is to examine community participation in tourism in the country. Alternative tourism is partly aimed at empowering local communities in managing their natural resources in ways which contribute to rural development. Rural people will have greater incentives to conserve the biological resources in their environment if the beneficial effects from tourism filter down to the individual families and households. This way, tourism could contribute immeasurably to African rural development where the majority of the population of the continent reside.

Tourism in the Western world is centuries-old; however, modern mass tourism started in 1958 when the first passenger jet service was inaugurated (Eadington and Smith, 1992: 5). During the intervening period there was rapid expansion of mass tourism assisted in great part by the development of resort infrastructure which could provide service and conveniences for many people. According to Eadington and Smith (1992: 6), "By the 1990s, there is a sense that the public has become 'tired' of the crowds, weary of jet lag, awakened to the evidences of pollution, and in search of something 'new'." Hence the yearning for alternatives that offer small scale, dispersed tourism development with fewer demands on investment and a higher level of local participation (Cater, 1994: 72). The alternative sought is not to all forms of tourism. Rather, it appears to be an alternative to the extreme forms of mass tourism (Butler, 1992).

Whereas an alternative to mass tourism is desired, there is no precise definition of the "new tourism". Alternative tourism is seen as "forms of tourism that are consistent with natural, social, and community values and which allow both hosts and guests to enjoy positive and worthwhile interaction and shared experiences" (Eadington and Smith,

1992: 3). The new tourism is known by many labels including ecotourism, nature tourism, sustainable tourism and so on (Boo, 1990; Lindberg and Hawkins, 1993). The 'alternatives' which have been developed include walking tours, bird safaris, camel safaris, guided nature walks, horse riding, barge and canal tours, bicycle tours, home and farm stays, youth tourism and an increase in domestic tourism (Eadington and Smith, 1991: 6; Western, 1993: 7). Some of these activities may be quite expensive to undertake and may not exactly fit into the definition of alternatives. Clearly, an increasing number of tourists is becoming aware of the ecological harm that conventional tourism causes, of the value of wilderness, and of the concerns for local people (Western, 1993). Ecotourists then are more than just a group of elite nature enthusiasts; they represent an amalgam of interests which cluster around environmental, social and economic concerns (Western, 1993: 7).

Definitions

Ecotourism

Although the term "ecotourism" is so much used in the literature and among tour operators, there is no agreement on the meaning of the concept (Commonwealth of Australia, 1994). This is partly because of the recent origin of the term. Ecotourism as a concept appears to have been brought into the literature only in 1983 by Hector Ceballos-Lascurain to mean

> Tourism that involves travelling to relatively undisturbed natural areas with the objective of admiring, studying, and enjoying the scenery and its wild plants and animals, as well as any cultural features found there. (quoted in Commonwealth of Australia, 1994: 15)

Since then, all the definitions of ecotourism embrace at least four basic elements:
- the natural environment is the primary attraction with the cultural environment playing a secondary role;
- sustainable use of the ecological and cultural environments;
- focus on education and interpretation of the resource; and
- provision of benefits to host communities.

The Ecotourism Society defines ecotourism as "responsible travel to natural areas which conserves the environment and improves the welfare of the local people" (Western, 1993: 8). The key ideas in this definition are responsible travel, natural areas, conservation and welfare of the local people. Others see ecotourism as being synonymous with nature tourism (Olindo, 1991; Boo, 1990). Olindo (1991) declared many years ago that Kenya is "the old man of nature tourism". In his view, Kenya's wildlife tourism which takes visitors to national parks and reserves to enjoy wildlife, is ecotourism. It has been argued, however, that nature tourism defined as the enjoyment of natural areas lacks a conservation element required to maintain natural ecosystems (Hvenegaard, 1994: 25). Thus, nature tourism does not necessarily mean ecotourism.

The Ecotourism Association of Australia (EAA) defines ecotourism as "ecologically sustainable tourism that fosters environmental and cultural understanding, appreciation, and conservation" (Weiler, 1995: 63). Based on this definition, the EAA developed the following mission statement:

> The Ecotourism Association of Australia aims to promote ecotourism, develop ethics and standards for ecotourism, promote understanding, appreciation and conservation of the natural and cultural environments visited, and facilitate interaction between tourists, host communities, the tourism industry, government and conservation groups (Weiler, 1995: 64).

On the basis of the above mission statement, EAA adopted a number of goals as follows (Weiler, 1995: 64):
1) all tourism must be ecologically sustainable;
2) ecotourism is to contribute to conservation both of destination areas and biodiversity;
3) ecotourism must provide benefits to host communities;
4) ecotourism should enhance environmental and cultural awareness; and
5) a broad range of ecotourism services should be available to cater for visitors from different socio-economic backgrounds.

Sustainable development
Ecotourism is seen as a catalyst for encouraging ecologically sustainable development. But what does sustainable development mean? Harris and Leiper (1995: xx) see sustainable development as a "form of managed economic growth that occurs within the context of sound environmental stewardship". Although there are numerous other definitional possibilities, this explanation serves the purpose of this discussion. Also, it is in keeping with the spirit of the United Nations Conference on Environment and Development meeting at Rio de Janeiro in June 1992. Popularly known as the Earth Summit, the Rio conference resolved that the needs of development at the present time must not jeopardise the ability of future generations to meet their needs.

Interest in ecotourism

Ecotourism has generated great interest from governments, tourism enterprises, tourists, conservation groups and other stakeholders in the industry (Boo, 1990; Hvenegaard, 1994; Lindberg and Hawkins, 1993). One of the reasons for this interest is the availability of pristine natural environments especially in Africa. These natural areas are attracting increasing numbers of tourists. Second, ecotourism emphasizes small scale, locally-owned infrastructure in contradistinction with the expensive infrastructure associated with mass tourism. On the basis of cost, use of local materials and indigenous operations of enterprises, ecotourism is particularly attractive (Cater, 1994: 71). Also, ecotourism is sensitive to the fragile nature of ecosystems and cultural systems. These qualities of ecotourism call for greater attention to destination planning, management of resources in line with consumer tastes, quality and price of tourism products

(Hvenegaard, 1994). The broad goals of ecotourism dovetail with ideas of sustainable development in the sense that nature resources are utilized for tourism according to local aspirations and local knowledge. However, there are few examples to demonstrate that the development of ecotourism destinations has gone according to plan (Hvenegaard, 1994).

Ecotourists are expected to have a harmonious relationship not just with nature but also the local communities which host them. As such they are expected to respect the host communities, their cultures and customs. This is not to assume that cultural attributes of such communities are readily known to the ecotourists. Rather, it is to emphasize that the tourists are sensitized to the local cultural circumstances. Ultimately, a kind of partnership should be developed with the result that cultural insensitivity and various forms of cultural abuse are minimised if not completely eliminated.

One of the favourite arguments put forward in support of ecotourism is that it attracts fewer tourists. Yet, numbers of tourists need not be a problem in all areas. Tour operators are intent on attracting more visitors. This may explain Western's (1993: 10) plea that the definition to ecotourism should shift from the narrow focus on small scale developments to principles applicable to nature-related tourism. In his view, "the principles applied to the mass market can do more good for conservation — and alleviate more harm — than a small elitist market". This perspective emphasizes the principles of creating and maintaining a balance of tourism, conservation and culture (Western, 1993: 10) rather than getting preoccupied with reducing the numbers of tourists. There appears to be a reversal of the long-held notion of ecotourism as an activity of a few up-market visitors as if the lower numbers in themselves would automatically lead to environmental conservation.

Initially, ecotourists were seen as an elite group of nature enthusiasts, ready to go to remote areas and who are comfortable with foreign cultures. Ecotourists are older, usually 30 to 50 years; well educated with a minimum of degree qualification; and with high incomes (Hvenegaard, 1994: 28; Whelan, 1991). Most of the US ecotourists would likely be professional or retired people who probably already have previous foreign travel experience (Whelan, 1991: 5). In general, ecotourists spend more money than conventional tourists in destination areas. Their preferred activities include trekking, hiking, bird watching, nature photography, wildlife safaris, mountain climbing, camping, fishing, river rafting, canoeing, kayaking, and botanical study (Whelan, 1991: 6). The argument here is that ecotourists need not be an exclusive band of people; it can be diverse groups of individuals from various socio-economic backgrounds but who are brought together by the principles underlying responsible tourism. Finally, supporters of ecotourism proceed on the belief that it achieves both conservation and development objectives (Lindberg, Enriquez and Sproule, 1996).

Although this assumption has not been tested empirically in Africa, it is clear that resource conservation encourages and supports tourism, and tourism in turn provides money to be ploughed into conservation efforts and local development initiatives. Indeed, tourism is at the heart of building support for wildlife conservation.

Community participation in ecotourism
The sustainability of nature-based tourism in Africa over the longer term depends on the support of local communities especially in wildlife areas. Sustainable development presumes the well-being of individuals and communities in a people-centred and conservation-based development (Gakahu, 1992: 117). This idea is based on the notion that local people have the greatest repertoire of knowledge on their ecology to be able to manage the resource system in a sustainable manner. As such, local populations must be involved in creative ways both in conservation and in direct tourism activities. Community-based conservation is a bottom-up approach to natural resources management. It is the reverse of the long-held top-down conservation strategies which tended to be technocratic and denied local people direct benefits of their participation in conservation (Western and Wright, 1994: 7; Murphy, 1985: 153).

> Tourism like no other industry, relies on the goodwill and cooperation of local people because they are part of its product. Where development and planning does not fit in with local aspirations and capacities, resistance and hostility can raise the cost of business or destroy the industry's potential altogether (Murphy, 1985: 153).

Such community involvement in wildlife conservation for tourism has worked with measurable success under the Communal Area Management Programme For Indigenous Resources (CAMPFIRE) in Zimbabwe (Murindagomo, 1990; Matzke and Nabane, 1996; Olthof, 1995; Hill, 1996). CAMPFIRE guidelines provide that 50 percent of the net revenues from wildlife utilization be applied to local projects in the areas in which the wildlife are located (Hill, 1996: 114). The key to wildlife conservation in Zimbabwe was the 1975 legislation which allowed landowners to derive direct benefits from wildlife. Rural communities earn the income mainly through hunting safaris. Some of the villagers have developed land use plans, provided access to primary education for children, created local employment and provided resources to cushion households against drought (Matzke and Nabane, 1996). Also, community-based tourism development is the stated policy of the Namibian government (Ashley and Garland, 1994; Ashley, 1995; Namibia, 1995); nevertheless it is too early to evaluate its success or otherwise.

Community participation in resource management for tourism has the potential capacity of increasing incomes and employment, and developing skills and institutions thereby empowering local people (Ashley and Garland, 1994). Ecotourism could thus fuel economic growth, equitable distribution of resources and in the process alleviate poverty. Africa's wildlife areas are characteristically inhabited by poverty-stricken communities to whom esoteric reasons for biodiversity conservation such as providing recreational, educational and research opportunities may not be meaningful (Magome, 1996). Only when rural communities share in the control and management of wildlife and derive economic benefits from sustainable use and management of wildlife do conflicts and competition for resources which threaten parks become minimised (Ashley, 1995; Magome, 1996). Brett (1996) has, however, cautioned against too much optimism in using participatory mechanisms in managing development. Unduly large community groups could hamper decision-making, generate greater social conflicts and reduce output (Brett, 1996). Besides, community organizations could become complex thereby requiring large outlays of resources to manage. However, some villagers in Zimbabwe have succeeded in decision-making on the distribution of revenues from safari hunters (Matzke and Nabane, 1996).

Another setback about community participation is the assumption that communities are homogenous groups. Nothing could be further from the truth. Every community is made up of diverse elements on the basis of defined criteria such as income, education, religious affiliation, gender, resource ownership and so on. This diversity in community composition can lead to problems of equity in access to resources and the sharing of benefits. Whatever procedures are used, planners must be sensitized to the fact that communities are made up of many segments and each should be given due attention.

Threats to sustainable ecotourism
As must have become clear in this analysis, one of the enduring problems of conventional tourism is the structural dependency of Third World destination countries on western multinational corporations. The latter control the organisation and management of international tourism. Is ecotourism any different? Ecotourists still come from the North. Although some may travel as independent ecotourists, most are handled by tour operators who nevertheless make claims of conducting eco-tours (Higgins, 1996). In this sense, ecotourism has the same foreign exchange leakages like mass tourism (Cater, 1994). Over the past decade, tour operators have assumed that they are involved in ecotourism merely by arranging nature-based tourism rather than low impact, conservation-minded tourism or ecotourism. As such, ecotourism tends to be seen more as a business propaganda tool to attract more clients than adhering to the principles embellished in the term. No doubt these claims have made ecotourism to become a high growth area in the travel industry (Higgins, 1996). And because ecotourists are generally rich people, tour operators scramble towards organizaing ecotourist travel and tour schedules. Many tour operators, however, look at ecotourism merely as a normal market segment.

Although ecotourism is formulated to encourage indigenous tourism enterprises, it is not clear what this means in reality. All the available evidence suggests that foreign investment in ecotourism in the Third World remains a lucrative business and is actually increasing in some countries (Cater, 1994: 73). This calls to question the idea of local participation in ecotourism. Such participation must include the ownership and control of tourism enterprises as a measure of enhancing local retention of foreign exchange earnings, the expansion of employment and also in the actual enjoyment of the ecotourism sites. Only this way can meaning be put into tourism-related conservation.

Ecotourism in Kenya

Kenya is one of the most popular ecotourist destinations in the Third World; the others are Nepal, Tanzania, China, Mexico, Costa Rica and Puerto Rico (Whelan, 1991: 6; Olindo, 1991: 23). The ecotourism industry is based on wildlife and also on coastal resources. It has been claimed, for example, that a Kenyan elephant is worth about US$

14,375 a year, or nearly US$ one million over its lifetime from tourist expenditures (Olindo, 1991: 23). Western and Henry's (1979) arithmetic put a lion's value in terms of generating tourism income to be US$ 27,000 per year whereas a herd of elephants was estimated to be worth US$ 610,000 per year (Sherman and Dixon, 1991: 121). Although it is not clear how these estimates were arrived at given the many wildlife species in any single national park, the estimates do point to the sustainability of non-consumptive forms of ecotourism.

Wildlife-based tourism in Kenya started towards the end of the nineteenth century and focused on consumptive uses such as sport hunting, bird shooting, and wild animal capture by American and European hunters (Chapter 4; Anderson and Grove, 1987). The participants were white tour hunters, resident white tour operators and guides assisted by Africans who worked as porters, gun bearers, and skinners (Olindo, 1991: 25). African subsistence hunting was outlawed in 1946 in order to preserve the animals for tourist hunters. However, conservation advocates won the day when after the Second World War, Kenya started the process of creating national parks. This was aimed at regulating hunting. By the 1970s, sport hunting had combined with poaching and subsistence hunting to threaten certain species of wildlife. This led to the government ban of sport hunting and the trade in game trophies in 1977 and 1978, respectively.[1]

Following the official banning of hunting, many Kenyans (tour guides, porters, skinners) lost their jobs. According to Olindo (1991: 25) it was from among this group of people that the practice of ecotourism evolved.[2] Kenya's tourism began to be

---

[1] Commercial poaching was a serious problem in Kenya during the 1970s and 1980s. The ban on both sport hunting and trade in game trophies went some way in curbing the problem of the decimation of certain animal species such as elephants, rhinos, lions, leopards and cheetahs. However, the ban was not sufficient to deal with many other problems faced by the Wildlife Conservation and Management Department (WCMD) such as poor working conditions, low staff morale, lack of vehicles and communications equipment, a broken-down park infrastructure (roads, housing etc.) and general insecurity because of the superior firepower of the poachers. These problems were substantially reversed when the KWS was created in 1989 from the ashes of the discredited WCMD. Under the first director, Richard Leakey, the KWS formulated a policy framework and development programme for the next six years (KWS, 1990) and gained significant public goodwill and donor support for its projects. This action assisted in winning back tourist confidence in Kenya as an important ecotourist destination. Leakey led a powerful effort which rehabilitated park infrastructure. For the first time after many years, roads were graded, communication facilities were improved, transport was once again available, mobility was improved and parks surveillance for poachers became possible. Staff morale was raised tremendously by a combination of better pay, training and improved working conditions.

A major problem with Leakey's plan was that it was almost exclusively based on donor funding. He was assisted in this campaign by his personal achievements but also by having one of the big names in African archaeology and anthropology. His person was therefore intricately intertwined with the success or otherwise of the KWS. Western donor organisations appeared to feel that Leakey was a guarantee to the resources which they gave to the KWS. As a result, when Leakey left the organisation in 1994, the money stopped coming. The new director, David Western, had to renegotiate some of the agreements. In this sense, Leakey was not an institution builder. Without Leakey, the KWS suffered a mild stroke; a testimony to the dependency which the man created. In an interesting turn of events, David Western was removed as KWS director in 1998 to give way to the re-appointment of Richard Leakey in September of that year. Although Leakey left the organisation in 1994 with surplus income, he returned to find the KWS in the red to the tune of hundreds of millions of shillings and low staff morale.

[2] Sport hunting is still banned in Kenya. As a result certain species of wildlife have increased tremendously and may be causing range degradation, e.g. elephants in Shimba Hills National Reserve. KWS may allow game cropping or the culling of certain animal species in order to

promoted in terms of shooting wildlife with the camera; and greater emphasis went into the promotion of natural landscapes of the country including biodiversity, wildlife, unique ecosystems, beautiful scenery including the Rift Valley and volcanic mountains, and the sandy beaches (Olindo, 1991). In addition, the country developed ornithological trips and botanical study tours and other such specialized tours. Within five years of the banning of sport hunting, Kenya was transformed into an important ecotourism destination with the total number of visitors increasing exponentially.

Although some authors think that ecotourism provides Kenya with much foreign exchange (Olindo, 1991: 26), such assessments are based on tourist numbers and gross foreign exchange earnings. Olindo (1991: 26) argues erroneously that "agriculture requires substantially greater capital investments than ecotourism".[3] As argued above, Kenya has made heavy financial investments in the tourism sector (airports, the park system, big hotels, training etc.). There is little evidence that the country has received full returns for its investment. The comparison of ecotourism is probably inappropriate in view of the fact that tourism is developed in a small part of Kenya, away from the majority of the population who do not depend on it for their livelihood. Further, ecotourism is susceptible to external factors and cannot be an assured source income. Despite the many problems of African agriculture it still provides for the subsistence and other needs to the bulk of the population. Perhaps the point can be made that tourism gross returns might be higher than traditional livestock-keeping on Kenya's rangelands. Thresher and Western's study estimated a tourism value of US$ 40 per hectare of wildlife to $ 0.80 per hectare from traditional livestock-keeping (Sherman and Dixon, 1991: 121). The net tourism returns per hectare are probably much lower.

Data from southern Africa show that "both the return on investment and the net revenue per acre is greater for wildlife than for cattle" (Magome, 1996: 12). Citing a study conducted by Collinson (1992) to evaluate land use options for the Madikwe Game Reserve in South Africa, Magome (1996) explains that wildlife tourism generates more jobs, pays higher wages per annum and provides greater net income and return on public investment than ranching. However, the capital cost to develop wildlife tourism both to government and private sector is much higher than for ranching.

---

preserve their populations. Commercial game cropping business is undertaken on ranches in Kajiado District and is supported by a profitable game meat market in Nairobi (KWS, 1990: 54). The number of operators in this business is limited because of the requirement for special skills, equipment and capital investment (KWS, 1990). There have been some representations over the past few years to allow limited sport hunting but this has been opposed by the relatively vocal ecotourism lobby and the conservation community in the country. It is feared that once some level of sport hunting is allowed, commercial poachers will get the opportunity to return to the country's parks and kill the wildlife for private gain. However, Kenya should learn from the example of Zimbabwe and Botswana where consumptive wildlife utilization has been used creatively and sustainably to the benefit of local communities. Insistence on the ban on sport hunting is a bad management strategy.

[3] As noted in Chapters 2, 4 and 5, there are many such misleading assessments which do not take into account the heavy leakages of the earnings from Kenya's tourism industry by virtue of foreign ownership and management of the tourism enterprises and the structural dominance by multinational corporations. Also, to substantiate such a claim requires cost-benefit analysis and a plan of investment. Since Kenya's tourism has proceeded without a plan (Sindiga and Kanunah, 1998), it is impossible to make statements about alternative investments.

Organised ecotourism

Although Kenya's nature tourism is many decades old, the ecotourism idea gained momentum in the 1980s following the falling standards of the management of the national parks and reserves. However, the first organized professional action on Ecotourism appears to be the Kenya ecotourism workshop which was held in September 1992 at the Lake Nakuru National Park. Appropriately entitled "Ecotourism and sustainable development: Potential benefits and constraints", the workshop which was organized by WCI, MTW, KWS, KATO and ACTS and supported by USAID, brought together professionals from a variety of backgrounds — ecologists, social scientists, planners and tourism professionals — to broach the subject for several days (Gakahu and Goode, 1992). The workshop explored several pertinent issues including policy, planning, marketing, visitor management and the impacts of ecotourism. Other subjects included the role of the tour operator and community involvement in ecotourism. At the end of their deliberations, workshop participants formulated a plan of action which provided for the formation of Ecotourist Society of Kenya (ESK). The ESK would fill a gap by providing a wider forum that could be a source of expertise, information and publicity and could become an independent body to oversee environmental standards of operation in the ecotourism industry (Gakahu and Goode, 1992). The representation in the ESK would cover all stakeholders including tourism enterprises, government, overseas operators and agents, conservationists, universities, experts, individual donors, and local communities. Among the roles of the ESK would be to issue green certification to authorize companies to promote themselves as being environmentally-responsible. An ESK certification is expected to differentiate truly ecotourism tour companies from the current fashion where even unregistered bodies tend to wear the ecotourism tag for the purpose of attracting tourists but deliver the conventional tourism product. The green certification will be issued to establishments, which meet certain ecotourism requirements under guidance from the ESK followed by inspection and certification. The ESK is in the process of defining appropriate standards and criteria (Gakahu and Goode, 1992; Appendix 6).

Both KATO and KAHC have shown a commitment to ecotourism. KATO, for example, conducts extensive training programmes for driver-guides who are the people who actually take Kenya's visitors to ecotourist sites. Also, it has courses for informing and educating visitors about ecotourism (Bisleth and Jensen, 1995). KATO's code of environmental conduct includes the following elements for both visitors and tour guides: keeping a distance from wild animals and respecting their habitats; adhering to park regulations; avoiding damaging the vegetation; avoiding collecting bones, skins, horns, shells and other wildlife items; respecting Kenyan customs and dressing decently; and avoiding unnecessary waste of energy and pollution (Bisleth and Jensen, 1995). In addition, KATO, which is one of the sponsors of ESK, is compiling a list of its members who are practising ecotourism ideals as a way of edging out unlicensed operators selling cheap trips, using untrained driver-guides and those who do not respect the ecotourism code.

On its part, the KAHC's ecotourism plan has the following elements: implementing energy-saving programmes, avoiding polluting the atmosphere with dangerous gases, creating environmental awareness among staff and visitors, waste reduction and its proper disposal, and keeping pollution out of the natural water systems. However, it is up to the individual institutional members of KAHC and KATO to choose to follow the guidelines provided by their umbrella organisations. And this is not being implemented without resistance because it costs money. Some tourism businesses have argued that ecotourism tours cost more money than the usual standard tours and this will reduce the willingness of the tourists to pay (Bisleth and Jensen, 1995). The extra cost for ecotourism development will go into developing park infrastructure in presently under-developed protected areas, developing other tourist attractions, implementing energy-saving measures and creating proper waste disposal systems in accommodation facilities. Other costs include staff education and extension services in local communities. All this will cost more and may cause a dramatic fall in the numbers of tourists, the lifeline of many tourism enterprises. A reduction in the number of visitors may translate to loss of jobs in the industry, a prospect pleasing to no one save for Kenya's tourism competitors.

Kenya's government policy on ecotourism
The Kenya government gives priority to environmental conservation and management in tourism development. It is committed to finding solutions to beach pollution and the deterioration of certain national parks through supporting the efforts of the KWS in wildlife conservation and management (Kenya, 1994b: 75). This is because the government recognises that

> tourism and wildlife development is a highly competitive industry and it is important that utilization of tourism resources and development of supporting physical infra-structure be carefully planned and conflicts between private gains and social costs of its development harmonised while ensuring preserving of the natural resources and promoting the aesthetic beauty of the country (Kenya, 1994c: 192).

Although the government announced a shift of emphasis from promotion of mass tourism to targeting upmarket ecotourist visitors (Kenya, 1994c: 194), this appears to be in conflict with the broad goal of maximizing on foreign exchange earnings, tax revenues and creating greater employment. This potential conflict is well appreciated by the country's planners (Kenya, 1994b: 73). The key might lie in spatial diversification of tourism because the country's nature reserves are widely dispersed over the nation's space (Chapter 4). This will require investments in the park infrastructure (hotels, roads and communications) and land use planning. Once this is done market forces will gradually determine the forms of tourism that the country develops (Kenya, 1994b: 73). Kenya's pragmatic approach appears to be rooted in the idea explored above of viewing ecotourism as a set of principles emphasizing responsible travel. The Kenya government sees ecotourism as having the potential

> of becoming a moderately useful tool for locally directed and participatory rural development based on a rational utilisation of environmental and cultural resources on which tourism is based. Efforts will be made towards ensuring community participation with a view to achieving commitment and motivation to the conservation and sustainable use of the ecologically delicate natural resources (Kenya, 1994c: 195).

A number of other policy measures will insure that tourism's impact on the environment is minimised. These are the proposals to require environmental impact assessment studies and green certification before approval of lodges and other large physical infrastructure development (Kenya, 1994c: 196).

Local communities and ecotourism in Kenya

A general criticism of ecotourism development is that local people tend to be excluded from the planning and implementation of projects (Whelan, 1991: 9). Also, local inhabitants are forced out of their traditional lands to give way to ecotourism projects such as parks. As a result of their exclusion from using protected area resources, they become disgruntled and begin to resent parks (Chapter 6; Olindo, 1991; Akama, no date; Akama et al., 1995). This was the case in Kenya where traditional lands held communally by pastoral nomadic peoples was alienated to give way to the park system.[4] Traditional livelihood systems were destabilized leading to severe resource degradation (Berger, 1993; Sindiga, 1984). As shown in Chapter 6, the wildlife-human conflicts threaten to undermine Kenya's ecotourism.

Prior to 1988, Kenyan authorities paid little attention to local communities in wildlife areas. In fact, there was no effort made to draw local attention to the economic benefits which could accrue from wildlife and natural resource management (Lusiola, 1992: 125; Berger, 1993: 14). Wildlife managers saw their role as revolving around the singular objective of policing the wildlife areas to insure that the animals were not harassed or killed. The relationship between protected areas, authorities and local people depended on the personality and individual skills of the warden in charge of a national park or reserve rather than institutional arrangements of collaboration (Western, 1982a; 1982b; Berger, 1993). Besides, there was hardly any collaborative relationship between park authorities and the people living in wildlife areas. Ordinarily, wardens are not trained in community extension work so that even at park education centres such as Nairobi, Tsavo East and Meru national parks, there was little reference to local community problems (Berger, 1993). Berger (1993: 15-16) identifies the key features of wildlife conservation in Kenya up to the late 1980s; among these are the following:
1) conservation programmes were preoccupied with wildlife protection;
2) negative attitudes of wildlife authorities to the public;
3) lack of a national strategy for working with people living with wildlife; and
4) uncontrolled tourism in parks.

The consequences of this policy approach which was predicated on the separation of people and wildlife were all too obvious on the society and the landscape. First, there was an increasing threat on wild animals due to human encroachment and resource extractions. The increasing human intolerance of wildlife is due to several changes including land tenure, land subdivision and fragmentation, expansion of cultivated land, political and economic liberalization, and awareness of property rights. Second, the

---

[4] This part should be read together with the section on wildlife-human conflicts in Chapter 6.

conflict between people and wildlife intensified leading to the expansion of poaching activities. Third, protected areas are inadequate because most of the wildlife live beyond their borders. Finally, there were large increases in the numbers of certain big mammals leading to resource degradation. These changes demanded a new broader policy perspective which would call for the conservation of biodiversity both inside and outside protected areas and the accommodation and co-existence between wildlife and the local populations. A new policy had to define the role of local people in tourism-led conservation. Without addressing the socio-economic benefits from conservation for communities living adjacent to the parks and reserves, wildlife and other natural resources could not be managed in a sustainable manner.

Gakahu (1992) reviewed grassroots involvement of local communities in tourism in Kenya and concluded that such participation was minimal and mainly confined to the supply of goods and services, sale of handicrafts and traditional dance entertainment.[5] But even in these activities, the local people must contend with competition by entrepreneurs from other parts of the country who are better prepared to do business and have access to credit.

Until recently the revenues from parks and reserves were shared between the government and the tourism industry. Of the two levels of government, the central authority provided a proportion of the gate fees from parks to the local government. Narok County Council, for example, earns 90 percent of its revenues from the Maasai Mara National Reserve but only a small proportion of the earnings reach the people living around the reserve (Berger, 1993: 15). Narok uses most of this revenue for payroll and general expenditure, leaving little money to support conservation. This raises doubt about the long-term sustainability of conservation. Local communities become indirect beneficiaries through development infrastructure financed from tourism incomes such as water, schools, health centres, veterinary services and so on (Chapter 6). These programmes, however, fall short of reaching individual people and households (Gakahu, 1992; Sindiga 1984; 1995; Berger, 1993; Talbot and Olindo, 1990). It is the individual families which bear the direct costs of wildlife conservation.

Before 1990 the government operated a compensation programme for loss and/or damage to crops, livestock and people. The programme was mismanaged, suffered from bureaucratic bottlenecks, fictitious claims, and was expensive. In 1989 alone, compensation claims amounted to Kshs 16.7 million (KWS, 1990: 180). In addition, the procedures for lodging claims were cumbersome and slow (Sindiga, 1984: 32). The government discontinued the programme in 1990 but without providing an alternative to ameliorating damage and loss from wildlife. This caused great resentment among the affected communities.[6] However, some form of compensation from serious damage and loss from wildlife appears essential in generating confidence in conservation. Perhaps legislative action is required to provide for a compensation insurance scheme (KWS,

---

[5] Although tourist arts and crafts have been developed among limited groups in Kenya most of the benefits from the sale of curios which is handled by middlemen do not go to the producers. Also, the size, extent and magnitude of the curio trade in Kenya is not known. It is probable, however, that most of Kenya's mass tourists especially those who go the coast have little money to spend on any extra's outside accommodation (Visser and Koyo, 1992: 79).

[6] Chapter 6 identifies the location of wildlife-human conflicts in various parts of the country.

1994). This will mitigate against local ill-will towards the KWS which is erroneously held responsible for the discontinued scheme.

In general, local dissatisfaction with tourism has evoked different responses among different communities in Kenya. Some communities are watching tourism developing all around them without engaging in it, such as the case of the Waswahili of the coast; others are organising to obtain greater benefits from tourism, as the case of the Maasai (Sindiga, 1995; 1996b). Recognition of the important role of community participation for the sustainable development of tourism has led to government encouragement of community-based projects (KWS, 1990). Such community participation must accommodate all local people as resource owners, users and partners in identifying, planning, negotiating and implementing ecotourism projects (Gakahu, 1992: 129). Community participation is expected to generate revenue thereby improving the standard of living of the local people; create employment opportunities; and make local people true partners in tourism enterprises development and management. In fact, such opportunities could encourage the people to move from subsistence herding and cultivating; in the process, damage to the land would be reduced.

On its establishment in 1989, the KWS sought to address the challenges facing natural resources management. Its goals are to manage protected areas on the basis of maintaining biological diversity and ecologic integrity. The inherent component of this policy is to form a "partnership" with governmental agencies, local authorities, private land owners and other competent authorities to mobilize support for biodiversity conservation (KWS, 1990). This partnership approach is created to provide an inegrated collaborative form of conservation and coordination. Furthermore, the KWS has placed high priority on ecotourism principles based on viewing wildlife. In doing this, the policy must deal with several constraints including limitations of land use and availability of technical and financial resources. Also, it must define conservation priorities with biological, economic and social criteria as well as resolve the human-wildlife conflicts which threaten to tear apart Kenya's biological diversity. This is the reason for a locally-driven grassroots approach to conservation through the formation of a partnership among legitimate stakeholders as opposed to the previous top-down preservationist approach to conservation.

Community participation in conservation through wildlife extension
The African Wildlife Foundation (AWF) inaugurated a programme of community participation in conservation through wildlife extension services in the mid-1980s. The programme involved developing cooperative relationships between park officials, local governments and rural communities which must co-exist with wildlife. The idea was to bring together the stakeholders in wildlife conservation so as to interact with one another and ultimately see each other's views, problems and expectations (Snelson and Lembuya, 1990). This way, common problems could be defined and solutions found through dialogue. Although the pilot project covered Nigeria, Rwanda, Tanzania and

Kenya, I here highlight the Kenyan project which was called the Tsavo Community Conservation Project (TCCP).[7]

The TCCP was started in 1988 with the intention of resolving a land use conflict between the local Maasai community and the authorities of Tsavo West National Park. Briefly, land in Loitokitok Division of Kajiado District was undergoing subdivision and registration either as individual ranches or group property. For years, individual ranchers and even members of group ranches in Loitokitok, like in other parts of Kenya Maasailand have divided their land and rented, leased or sold plots to immigrant farmers who then cultivate it (Sindiga, 1984: 34). Once a plot is cultivated, other land uses must be excluded. Consequently, the Maasai took their livestock into the park for pastures and water thereby threatening the sustainability of park resources, the basis of wildlife conservation.

The TCCP project was developed to establish community dialogue and partnership in conservation; in the process, the local community would remove its livestock from using park resources (Snelson and Lembuya, 1990: 108). This wildlife extension project was executed in Rombo and Kuku Group Ranches which are located adjacent to the Tsavo West National Park. But the local people insisted on obtaining tangible benefits from their participation in the wildlife extension programme. It was expected that the project would produce a number of beneficial outcomes, including employment opportunities, revenue from ecotourism and bird hunting, concessions and fees from tourist camp sites, and the creation of an indigenous tour operator service (Snelson and Lembuya, 1990: 109). The project proponents saw the TCCP as a mechanism of fostering ecotourism with the participation of the local community which would also benefit from conservation. Besides, community participation was seen as an empowerment process by which the local people would build up confidence in identifying and resolving local environmental problems (Berger, 1993: 48).

The wildlife extension project created an ongoing interaction with the local people through workshops, public meetings, surveys and fieldwork. The work was carried out by a group of extension workers and community members. Although wildlife conservation was the primary purpose of the project, the linkages with other elements of natural resources management such as soils, water, and forestry was inevitable (Berger, 1993).

The results of the TCCP show that it is possible to foster ecotourism and sustainable natural resources development with full local participation. The project achieved the following environmental outcomes: protecting water catchments in Rombo, Inkisanjani and Namelok; restoring irrigation areas through soil conservation, tree planting and agroforestry; controlling charcoal burning on Kimana Group Ranch; reporting of poachers on Kuku and Rombo group ranches; and incorporating wildlife as a productive resource through ecotourism activities on Group Ranch land (Berger, 1993: 153). However, Maasai incursions into the park never really stopped. The case study demonstrates nonetheless that wildlife conservation in Maasailand is increasingly seen as an economic resource (Berger, 1993: 157). Should the economic benefits not reach the

---

[7] For a detailed description of TCCP and wildlife extension in Loitokitok Division of Kajiado District, see Berger (1993) and Snelson and Lembuya (1990).

local people, the very basis of ecotourism will be put in jeopardy. This is becoming more urgent because of increasing population pressures on Kenyan rangelands. Human settlements are becoming dense and the cultivation frontier is expanding in areas of delicate ecologies. There is need to plan for the increasing population, expanding settlements and wildlife-based conservation to assure sustainable development.

Incentives for conservation

The implementation of the biodiversity strategy requires establishing conservation priorities, mobilizing and establishing partnerships, identifying biodiversity threats and benefits, and providing incentives to conserve. Such incentives include conflict mitigation through education, training and deterrence; and direct and indirect incentives for local communities to conserve. The indirect or non-consumptive incentives include ecotourism, recreation, adventure tourism, science, education and 'green hunting' (immobilizing or capturing animals for relocation or disease control). The direct or consumptive incentives include culling cropping, fee-paying hunting, game farming, game ranching and live animal capture. Another incentive could be cost coverage or benefit sharing programmes channelled in the form of community development programmes such as schools, bursaries for needy students, health clinics, water projects, road improvement projects, and livestock disease control infrastructure. The Wildlife Development Fund (WDF) established by the KWS covers a wide range of benefit sharing programmes including gate fees and in-kind services with communities, funds for wildlife associations, capacity building and enterprise development funds. However, the benefit-sharing programmes initiated by the KWS have evoked much controversy and require greater discussion.

The KWS started a revenue sharing programme with local communities using park entry fees only in 1990 (KWS, 1990). Regrettably, the government recognised this important ingredient in sustainable resource management somewhat late (KWS, 1994). It should have been built into the wildlife conservation programme from the outset. The main beneficiaries of the revenue-sharing scheme are landowners in wildlife dispersal areas. But it appears that landowners adjacent to fenced national parks receive no payment because of the view within the KWS that they do not incur any opportunity costs (KWS, 1990). This argument is unconvincing because many species of wildlife live outside protected areas on private farms and ranches. In order to conserve those animals, the KWS should formulate a more flexible policy to encourage the landowners to maintain the wildlife. KWS policy is to cede 25 percent of its park entry fees to local communities, usually through the local authority; in this case a county council.

In spite of the policy to share revenues with landowners, there is no fixed proportion of revenues from a park that a local community can expect. The KWS reserves the right to determine who receives what amount from revenue sharing (KWS, 1990: 51). In addition, nobody knows how the 25 percent figure was arrived at. As a review committee on wildlife-human conflicts in Kenya argued, the policy is silent about profit and loss and whether losses in any given year are to be shared with local communities as well (KWS, 1994: 51). Further, the idea of treating a county council as a stakeholder entitled to the share of benefits from conservation on a regular basis has generated much discussion. One view is that only landowners are the true stakeholders entitled to a share of benefits rather than the local authorities (KWS, 1994). This, of course, brings to the foreground the issue of local authorities competing with the KWS for the management of wildlife in the national and game reserves. The Kenyan law clearly invests the power of all wildlife management whether in protected areas or outside in the KWS. What rights then do county councils have on wildlife?

The Maasai Mara National Reserve provides the best example where the management conflicts between the KWS and Narok County Council are played out. The Maasai Mara, which is savanna grassland and an extension of Tanzania's Serengeti ecosystem, has one of the greatest wild animal concentrations in the world. The Maasai Mara has an estimated herbivore population of 237 per square kilometre (Sindiga, 1995: 51). As noted earlier, it is one of the most visited reserves and as a result, the quality of its attractiveness is deteriorating including the physical infrastructure. Yet, there has been little tourist planning and visitor management in the Mara (Western, 1992c: 69). Such planning would include identification of prime visitor attractions and diversifying these; attention to the infrastructure (roads, and lodges and especially their siting); routing and zoning; driver training and better trained interpreters and visitor guides; and using the pricing mechanism to reduce the number of vehicles in the reserve (Western, 1992c). The regulations covering off-road driving, minimum distances to animals and maximum number of vehicles around an attraction could also be used to conserve Mara's biodiversity and maintain its visitor appeal. But the KWS, which has the capacity to do the planning and infrastructure development, is not responsible for the Maasai Mara. Whereas the KWS is in charge of the wildlife, the local county council is in control of the lands (Western, 1992c). This institutional conflict could hamper the development and maintenance of the natural resources upon which tourism depends.

Since the ecotourism market demands a very high quality product, the stakeholders must come together and participate jointly in resource development. But this is not possible until the basic conflicts of compensation payments and revenue sharing have been sorted out. In December 1993, Maasai leaders in Narok led by the area's member of Parliament threatened to kill wildlife outside the Maasai Mara National Reserve if the policy on compensation and revenue sharing was not reviewed to their advantage (Sindiga, 1995: 51). It appears that the failure of the KWS in forging strong local community linkages for wildlife conservation and its insensitivity to resolving local problems led to the premature departure from office of Richard Leakey, the first director of KWS in 1994.

Residents in the neighbourhood of protected areas are clamouring for more equitable revenue sharing. The affected county councils also complain about non-remittance of the 25 percent gate fees. In addition, the KWS is accused of inaccessibility and lack of accountability to local communities. One of the grievances of the local people is that they are not represented on the board of KWS (Sindiga, 1995). This is seen as insensitivity to local problems related to wildlife and tourism. Because of the status of the Mara as a popular ecotourism site, it might become necessary to create a management board to guide its affairs (Western, 1992c). Such a board would comprise of professional people in wildlife management and tourism and representative local leadership to take care of community interest (Sindiga, 1995: 52).

The Narok County Council collects gate fees from the Mara and pays landowners in dispersal areas as part of revenue-sharing. From 1989, the council has been levying Ksh. 50 on each visitor to the reserve. This money is paid to the neighbouring group ranches through a trust fund established for the purpose (Sindiyo, 1992). The proportion of money set aside for the landowners is 20 percent of the gate fees. It is used in implementing community projects such as schools, health centres, cattle dips and other services. However, the Maasai Mara dispersal area covers an area of 3,400 sq. km., an expansive territory, with many landowners. This increases the potential for future conflict on revenue sharing among them. But revenue sharing has caused a number of problems. First, the Kshs.50 fee levied on a tourist visiting the Maasai Mara is probably too low to meet a landowner's costs of conserving wildlife. Second, the revenue from the reserve is not paid to landowners directly but serves as a tax waiver to the community (Sindiga, 1995).[8]

Community initiatives in wildlife-based tourism

Although directing greater economic benefits from parks to local communities is an expressed goal of the Kenya government (Kenya, 1975; 1979; KWS, 1990), the pilot programmes of sharing revenues at Amboseli and Maasai Mara have fallen short of local expectations (Gakahu, 1992). The major principles underlying revenue sharing are that local people bear the cost of wildlife conservation by absorbing crop and livestock losses, and foregoing potential income from alternative land uses; and that local communities will continue to support parks and reserves if they are seen to assist in people's development efforts (KWS, 1990). This means that wildlife-based economic incentives should provide for conservation in a sustainable manner (Chapter 6). The current revenue-sharing programme has failed to compensate the producer, that is, the individual landowner in the dispersal areas. This has led to community efforts aimed at direct participation in tourism activities with a view to earning greater incomes.

With KWS support, local people have organised themselves to create income generating activities including providing camping concessions and exclusive camp sites; public camp sites and other low-cost accommodation; leases or partnerships with lodge and hotel operators; guiding tours; and supplies and services to lodges (Kenya, 1990; see also Chapter 6). The KWS seeks to encourage landowners to develop tourist infrastructure outside protected areas. This is intended to make landowners plan the best use of utilizing wildlife on their lands subject to KWS regulations. Other activities undertaken by local people include organising for tourists, visits on private ranches and farms to view wildlife for a fee. Ostrich farms, for example, are very popular in Kajiado District.

---

[8] In Amboseli National Park which the KWS handles directly, the government collects gate fees and then shares out the revenue with Olkejuado County Council which would then finance community projects just like the case of Maasai Mara National Reserve. This has caused discontent among the local people. See chapter 6 for additional information on Amboseli.

Some of these activities have been developed in areas adjacent to the national parks and reserves. It is expected that these initiatives will increase incomes to rural people by spreading ecotourism benefits. At the Maasai Mara reserve, for example, ten of the developed lodges or camps are located on private ranches outside the borders of the protected area (Tuya, 1992).

Group ranch wildlife associations
Both in Kajiado and Narok districts, members of some group ranches in the dispersal areas have organised themselves to form wildlife associations. These associations are seen as indigenous conservation groups acting as management groups for their communally held land. The associations collect wildlife viewing fees from tourists and distribute the proceeds to the membership. Initial reports indicate that these associations are making a substantial amount of money from ecotourism (Sindiga, 1995: 52).

Although many more associations are being planned, Ol Choro Oirouia and Koyaki-Lemek have been formed in Narok. Other group ranches around the Amboseli park such as Olulului Ololorashi, Mbirikana, Kimana and Kelengei and those close to the Tsavo West National Park — Rombo and Kuku — are planning to draw up agreements with the KWS in order to protect their rights and be compensated for protecting wildlife. The emergence of indigenous organisations to participate in biodiversity conservation and ecotourism is to be encouraged. These wildlife associations are employing teams of trained scouts to provide security for wildlife. Also, as organisations representing grass-roots mobilization of people and resources, they are likely to attract outside investment.

Framework for community-based tourism development

Although the KWS has recognised the role of local communities in ecotourism, community development has not received as much attention as biological conservation. Reid *et al.* (1998) have noted that community development should be the primary goal with tourism serving as a means to achieving the goal and enhanced biodiversity would become the positive outcome of goal achievement. This way, local people would appreciate the importance of wildlife to their welfare and therefore become much more involved in conservation.

By adopting a "partnership" progamme, the KWS has demonstrated its sensibility to the goal of community development. However, the KWS puts too much emphasis on biodiversity to the detriment of community development. Without community development activities of the same size and attention as biodiversity, the whole programme could fail. The local people in the neighbourhoods of protected areas will need to see meaningful improvement in their standards of living and economic fortunes if they are to continue participating in biodiversity conservation, the basis of Kenya's ecotourism. As McNeeley (1995: 211) has recognised, community support in biological conservation can only be achieved through participation. Such participation is assured when the benefits are clear, unambiguous and direct; the community is involved in the conservation planning process and proposed tourism activities; and the community understands the costs and benefits of its involvement. Besides, financial and logistical support must be provided and local people need education and training to achieve skills required in participating in both conservation and ecotourism (Reid *et al.*, 1998; McNeeley, 1995; Appendix 6).

Training and education of the rural people is important especially in tourism development. Indeed, human resource development problems have been identified as a major impediment to upgrading the standards of service in the tourism industry (Dieke, 1997; Appendix 4). Besides basic literacy and numeracy, training should include business, management, accounting, cross-cultural skills and tourism. Such training should be done at the community level. Despite the presence of formal tourism and hotel schools in Kenya, most residents from the areas with tourist attractions in the country have hardly received such training (Eastman, 1995). This means that a mix of the on-the-job training, inservice courses and refresher courses must be undertaken for the benefit of the communities. In the end, the people who have direct contact with tourists, for example curio sellers and private wildlife ranch owners, will find an avenue for training.

Also, it is important that community training for ecotourism be conducted by people from the same community. In a study conducted in Maasailand, it was found that there were retired teachers, employees of non-governmental organisations and middle level employees in lodges and hotels who could perform the training role (Reid *et al.*, 1998). Such community people who are educated and enjoy respect and trust within the community, are best suited for the function. Once identified, however, these individuals should be given trainers' training before filling their role.

Yet, community-based tourism development cannot succeed without attention to the product which a given region is marketing. Each region should develop its own attractions to achieve an identity of its own. This calls for community groups to organize themselves for the purpose of selling its tourism product to the visitors. But product development is not a single stop affair; it must be continuous and in step with changing tourist tastes. Only this way can a destination keep a competitive edge against similar destinations elsewhere. So far, wildlife is the primary attraction for most East African destinations. However, the tourist is now looking for a unique experience. This requires more imaginative packaging and tourism product development. There is no doubt that Africa is well endowed in supplying many different products from its rich tourism resources apart from wildlife. These include the varied natural environments, physical landforms, beaches and the myriad cultural resources.

It may be concluded therefore that notwithstanding the recognition of the primary role of local people and communities in ecotourism development in Kenya, this policy objective has not smoothly proceeded with implementation. This discussion of community-based tourism development shows clearly that there are many impediments to making community groups real partners in ecotourism development. Among the issues to be resolved include the ownership of wild animals and lack of appropriate skills among local people. The true economic empowerment of local people and communities must address the ownership, control and management of ecotourism enterprises.

Summary and conclusion

Kenya's tourism is nature-based. In order to be sustainable, tourism requires conservation. Similarly, tourism provides badly needed revenues for conservation programmes. For Kenya, ecotourism is not exactly an alternative form of tourism. Rather, it represents observance of certain underlying principles including minimum environmental impact through dispersing visitors, keeping the environment clean through proper waste disposal systems, and saving energy. In addition, ecotourism must provide jobs for the local people, a market for local products, and encourage cultural sensitivity in guest-host relations.

However, ecotourism in Kenya is still managed and controlled by multinational corporations from the developed countries. As such, the foreign exchange leakages which characterise conventional tourism are also present in ecotourism. Significantly, Kenya's ecotourism enterprises are still predominantly owned by foreign companies. The structural organization of international tourism remains intact. Benefit-sharing from ecotourism has proved to be troublesome. So far, direct benefits to landowners have been minimal. This has led certain communities to form wildlife associations so that they can participate directly in ecotourism development and the benefits accruing from it. Although this grassroots mobilization of landowners is beginning to bear some fruit, local wildlife conservation associations are characteristically elite groups which monopolise the benefits from tourism (Sindiga, 1995). The authorities should ensure that such groups have majority participation and that the distribution of benefits is equitable both across socio-economic groups and gender categories. Also, participation in ecotourism development inevitably draws the Maasai herders into a global system on which they have little control (Britton, 1982). Such a system may require more sophisticated management. Local people have little expertise in contemporary wildlife conservation and tourism management (Dieke, 1993c).

There is also the issue of planning which should be done to integrate national tourism objectives with local needs. Ultimately, it will enhance wildlife conservation and the sharing of benefits of ecotourism in an equitable manner. Such planning is required to address the issues of ownership, management and coordination of national reserves. Currently, a local authority can levy whatever fees it wishes to allow tourists to enter a national reserve. Also, local wildlife management associations operating on private lands adjacent to protected areas impose their own fee rates. This is likely to cause a problem as such associations proliferate and each begins to erect barriers to levy charges on tourists. Too many fees collection centres might trigger negative reactions among visitors and tour operators. Planning should identify the body that bears responsibility for the development of all categories of protected ares. This includes planning for new lodges and camp sites, notably the number and siting of such facilities.

Regional cooperation in tourism

One of the strategies for increasing the competitiveness of African tourism is regional cooperation within the continent. For Kenya, this means fostering cooperation within the eastern Africa sub-region. Such cooperation in tourism can be a component of the numerous regional groupings designed to bring about economic integration and faster development in Africa. Regional cooperation is intended to encourage the easy movement of tourists across common borders and to establish joint packages for multi-destination travellers. Such packages which would market tourism on an East African basis, are in demand. Prior to the mid-1970s East Africa was successfully marketed as a tourism region. Afterwards, each country established administrative barriers which made it impossible to make cross-border trips.

This chapter examines the issue of regional cooperation in tourism in Africa. What are the merits of regional cooperation in tourism? How can regional cooperation in tourism contribute to development on the continent? What are the problems which hinder such cooperation? These are the questions around which the following discussion is constructed. It is assumed that regional cooperation in tourism can become an element in the attempts to form economically integrated country groupings. As such the general problems of economic integration in Africa will be the same ones which hamper cooperation in tourism development. The final part of the chapter discusses intra-Africa tourism. The focus is on the potentials and limitations of developing intra-Africa tourism to complement non-African tourism on the continent.

Basis for regional cooperation in tourism

Regional cooperation has been suggested as a viable way of obtaining the greatest benefits from African tourism through increasing its competitiveness. The clearest statement on this matter was put forward by African leaders in the 1980 Lagos Plan of

Action (LPA) (World Bank, 1989; Dieke, 1995). LPA drew attention to the notion that the current structure, organization and management of African tourism which emphasizes foreign ownership and management of tourist enterprises should be reversed. Instead of the current trend where African tourism is dominated by Western multinational companies, LPA espoused the view that tourism on the continent should be promoted, controlled and managed by the Africans themselves. Specifically, the LPA put forward the following goals for African tourism: (1) development of intra-African tourism; (2) providing technical training for African staff to gain competence to manage tourism enterprises; (3) creating interstate or intra-regional tourist circuits; and (4) regional cooperation so as to utilize Africa's varied tourism resources in an efficient manner (Dieke, 1995: 88). The idea of regional cooperation in tourism is part of wider thinking of pulling together Africa's vast resources in order to reverse the continent's economic decline and put it back on the road to development. This approach emphasizes Africa's self-reliance through the promotion of regional groupings of states and encouraging trade and economic development within the region (World Bank, 1989; Nyong'o, 1990; UNECA, 1989). It identifies one of Africa's development problems to be small economies which characteristically have low levels of income and small population sizes. Ndiaye (1990: 36) has argued that

> the problem of small economies is a widespread phenomenon in the continent. Today some thirty countries accounting for about one-half of independent Africa's total population have income per head of less than 350 United States dollars per year. Only seven countries, with less than 10 percent of Africa's population have income per capita of 1,000 US dollars or more.

About half of Africa's countries have a population of less than five million each; 13 countries have an area of less than 50,000 sq. km. each while 13 are landlocked (UNECA, 1989: 5; Chapter 2, Table 2.1). Within individual countries, population centres are unevenly distributed and this makes it difficult to develop transport networks and to supply basic services such as water and electricity. This is particularly so for geographically large countries. As such the majority of Africa's national economies are poorly integrated. This is partly inherited from the colonial period when transport networks in many countries were created to assist in the outward expropriation of resources rather than serving indigenous populations. Africa's fragmentation is a major constraint on exploiting the continent's vast resources. The rather low personal incomes add to the small size of the markets to make it difficult for single countries to support modern enterprises.

Tourism is one of the sectors which can benefit from market integration and increased cooperation within Africa. Indeed, regionalism is seen to be one of the critical considerations of tourism development in Africa; the other is multiple destination marketing (Teye, 1991: 288). Regional development of tourism in Africa is supported by a number of arguments. The continent has a great diversity of attractions ranging from historical and archaeological monuments to physical landscapes, cultural pluralism and very rich flora and fauna. However, the tourism industry as currently established yields inequitable benefits to the disadvantage of Africa. If Africa was united, different countries would be able to pool their attractions into an integrated whole and cooperate in terms of capital, infrastructure and human resources to serve the needs of tourism (Teye, 1991; Dieke, 1995). Tourism activities have substantial economies of scale when planned on a regional basis (Mitchell, 1970: 12; Popovic, 1972: 50). In addition, joint infrastructure development, planning, marketing research, and training could be done at less cost to the advantage of the cooperating member countries. Also, regional cooperation could reduce competition for tourists by neighbouring states in the same region and enhance gains from the tourism industry. Further, removing administrative obstacles which make tourism costly to the tourists could increase tourist flows (Mitchell, 1970: 13). In terms of promotion, it is more effective to market a region with its varied tourism resources than a single country (Popovic, 1972). However, joint promotion does not mean that the unique features of individual countries are not highlighted. Rather, it is to promote each country as part of a region with many things to see thereby providing the tourist with a choice on whether to go to one country or several of them within the region. Further, tropical Africa is far away from the traditional tourist sourcing countries in Western Europe, North America and the Far East. The long-haul trip is expensive. This locational disadvantage provides a rational basis for regional cooperation. This way, Africa could market its tourism product at a lower cost for each country, overcome the prevailing negative perceptions about the continent and gain better leverage in dealing with large tourism institutions in the West (Dieke, 1995; Teye, 1991). In short, regional cooperation must provide meaning to an African identity. Such identity goes beyond policy actions, infrastructure development and the creation of institutions to "a more fundamental need to mobilize the media and educational and cultural institutions to promote the concept that cooperation within Africa is likely to enhance the progress of all African societies" (World Bank, 1989: 161). This approach calls for changes in attitudes among Africans and the engendering of small-scale cooperative relationships among people of different countries.

> A systematic program to achieve this could include organizing seminars, workshops, and exchange visits for African journalists; establishing a regional information center to produce and distribute feature articles, pamphlets, videos, and films; and incorporating courses on African history, culture, and economics into school curriculums, especially at the university and postgraduate levels (sic). In addition relaxing travel restrictions and residence requirements would encourage increased contacts within Africa at the personal level (World Bank, 1989: 161).

Multiple destination marketing of tourism is likely to be achieved under circumstances of regional cooperation among countries. This is because it allows possibilities of diversifying the tourism product (Teye, 1991) and provides the visitor with a wide variety of attractions in one trip. Multi-destination tourism is recognised as an important component of travel among southern African countries. The promotion of regional and international cooperation in tourism is a policy objective of the Namibian government (Namibia, n.d.: 228).

Regional cooperation in Africa

Perhaps no other developing area has such a proliferation of regional cooperation organisations as sub-Saharan Africa. Africa has more than 200 such organisations of which 160 are intergovernmental and the rest are non-governmental (World Bank, 1989: 149). Although many of these regional bodies have been formed after independence, a number of them trace their history to the colonial period. These regional groupings have the greatest potential for fostering tourism within their areas.

Concepts in regional cooperation

There are two basic concepts underlying regional cooperation, namely customs union approach and functional approach (Zehender, 1988). The customs union approach focuses on market integration. The approach is motivated by the desire to create a larger market thereby achieving economies of scale for industrial development. In the literature, integration efforts aim at expanding intra-regional trade through the reduction or removal of tariffs to trade in goods and services whereas regional cooperation takes a broader meaning to refer to any joint activity across country borders in economic matters (McCarthy, 1996: 213). Both the LPA and UNECA (1989) have identified Africa's fragmentation as an economic constraint which must be overcome. By dividing Africa into three sub-regions — west, central, and east and southern Africa — the LPA expected that each grouping would become a free trade area, then form a customs union and end up with an economic community (World Bank, 1989; UNECA, 1989).

Although many regional organisations have been formed, they have experienced several problems. Many of the governments do not pay their membership fees and many countries tend to be pre-occupied with their internal affairs rather than regional matters (World Bank, 1989). Others complain of uneven distribution of costs and benefits, and smaller countries believe that their powerful partners are making higher gains from economic integration. As a result "progress toward market integration has been disappointing, with the share of intraregional trade in total trade still at the level it was 20 or more years ago" (World Bank, 1989: 149). Nearly all the assessments of regional cooperation in Africa paint a bleak picture.

> There has been hardly any really worthwhile progress toward increasing trade within Africa. In the individual subregions of the continent, cross-border transport of goods and people is now considerably more difficult than in the colonial period; every general declaration of intent to change this regrettable situation falls foul of all kinds of apparently immovable obstacles (Hofmeier, 1988: 54).

The following examples will highlight the problems and prospects of regional cooperation in Africa.

Examples of regional cooperation

Economic Community of West African States (ECOWAS)
ECOWAS was established in 1975 and comprises of 16 countries covering 150 million people (Asante, 1990; Zehender, 1988). The primary objectives of ECOWAS is to promote economic development through cooperation. This is to be achieved through the removal of tariff and non-tariff barriers between members and the creation of a customs union, that is a common external tariff (Asante, 1990). ECOWAS has four specialized commissions intended to promote its central objective. These are trade, customs, immigration, monetary and payments; industry, agriculture and natural resources; transport, communications and energy; and social and cultural affairs (Teye, 1991: 290). Almost each of these commissions has an implication on tourism development. Immigration and customs procedures hamper free movement of tourists across national borders. Financial remittances from country to country are the heart of regional tourism development. And so are transport and communications.

However, ECOWAS has not made much headway in economic integration and policy harmonization. The grouping is dominated by Nigeria and Côte d'Ivoire. Nigeria, for example, accounts for 55 percent of the population and 60 percent of the GDP (Zehender, 1988). Institutionally, ECOWAS is an elitist group without links to the important sectors of the economies of member states. For example, ECOWAS has no mechanism of interacting with the private sector, chambers of commerce or even trade unions of member countries (Asante, 1990: 106). This means that ECOWAS encourages interaction merely among government officials and relevant bureaucrats. Consequently, there has been little regional trade and movement of capital among member states because of national administrative barriers such as import licenses. Also, capital markets are underdeveloped (World Bank, 1989). In fact, recorded regional trade within ECOWAS is small and represents only about four percent of the member countries total exports (Zehender, 1988: 52). ECOWAS has not made much headway in its declared objectives of regional integration.

Communauté Economique de l'Afrique de l'Ouest (CEAO)
CEAO was established in 1974 by six francophone countries which are also members of ECOWAS. This West African economic community which was joined by Benin in 1984 has a total population of about 40 million. All the members of CEAO except Mauritania belong to the West African monetary union, share the CFA franc which is pegged to the French franc, and have a common central bank (World Bank, 1989). Côte d'Ivoire and Senegal are the leading members of CEAO.

CEAO has done better in all areas than ECOWAS and represents the best example of market integration. CEAO

> has achieved a high degree of integration that supports economic specialization and facilitates the flow of labour from the poor Sahelian countries ... to the richer, coastal countries ... while supplying goods in the opposite direction. By reducing non-tariff barriers and establishing a satisfactory compensation mechanism, trade within CEAO has expanded significantly and is now around ten percent of total trade (World Bank, 1989: 149).

Union Douanière et Economique de l'Afrique Centrale (UDEAC)
The Central African Customs and Economic Union (UDEAC) is another disappointing example of regional integration. Although UDEAC members use a common currency, the CFA franc, trade within the group has declined instead of improving. About half of UDEAC's African trade is with ECOWAS compared with less than 45 percent within the UDEAC group (World Bank, 1989: 150).

Communauté Economique des Etats de l'Afrique Centrale (CEEAC)
The Economic Community of Central African States was established in 1983 as a ten-member country regional grouping with 55 million people. Its members include Gabon, Cameroon, Congo (Brazzavile), and Congo (Kinshasa). The CEEAC is another disappointing example of market integration. It had problems getting started and despite declared intentions of striving towards a common market, internal trade is limited due to tariff barriers.

Preferential Trade Area for Eastern and Southern Africa (PTA)
The PTA was formed in 1981 by 15 countries in eastern and southern Africa holding a population of 165 million people. Its establishment was probably a response to the collapse of the East African Community (EAC) in 1977. The PTA was created to promote trade by reducing tariff and non-tariff barriers and preferential treatment for certain products produced by member countries. The PTA was conceived initially as a free trade area which would be the first step towards the establishment of a customs union, followed by a common market and ultimately developing into an economic community. The PTA's objectives include the promotion of cooperation and development in various fields such as trade, customs, industry, transport, communications, agriculture, natural resources and monetary affairs (Martin, 1990).

In the transport and communications sector which has implications on tourism development the PTA programme calls for constructing and upgrading interstate roads and railway systems so as to improve accessibility among member states. Also, a harmonized customs control transit system would facilitate free crossborder travel. Further, a PTA insurance scheme would eliminate the slow and costly process of taking out an insurance cover for a motor vehicle each time a traveller crosses a border. In the area of air travel, flight schedules of PTA airlines would also be harmonized to make it possible to operate easily. Other areas to be harmonized include inland water and maritime transport and establishing direct communication links between member states.

The PTA has faced its share of problems which has made it difficult to meet its stated objectives. Tariff reduction has been slow and consequently, trade within the PTA is weak (World Bank, 1989; Martin, 1990). This is partly because of the application of the 51 percent ownership rule. Briefly, to qualify for preferential treatment, a commodity's producing firm must be at least 51 percent locally owned and no more than 60 percent of its components should come from outside the PTA membership. Some countries have complained about this rule. Also, countries such as Comoros and Djibouti continue to charge certain taxes on all imported goods. Finally, there is fear among the smaller country members of being dominated by the economically more advanced partners especially Kenya and Zimbabwe. The latter two countries have positive balances of trade with the PTA subregion (Martin, 1990: 171).

To encourage regional tourism within the PTA — so that nationals of member states could interact with one another — and to promote trade through business contacts, the organisation issued travellers cheques in 1988. Although some countries including Kenya and Djibouti were slow in implementing the decision, the launching of the instrument was considered successful (Martin, 1990: 173). However, without the removal of other travel restrictions, this step alone could not ensure large-scale tourist flows among member countries. In fact, the PTA travellers cheques facility was said to be underutilized (Martin, 1990) and got suspended.

The PTA moves forward, be it slowly. Its other problems have been summarized by Martin (1990: 175-178). They include differences in political ideologies among member states and membership in several subregional groupings leading to conflicts of allegiance and divided loyalties. For example, many PTA states also belong to other organisations such as SADCC, IGADD, ECCAS and so on (Courier, 1988). Another problem is that certain states in the region including Angola, Botswana, Seychelles and Madagascar are not members. Finally the problem of uneven distribution of benefits persists. Incidentally, the two economically powerful members, Kenya and Zimbabwe are anglophone whereas the smaller states including Djibouti, Mauritius, Comoros, Rwanda and Burundi are francophone. This has created some rivalry and generated a level of animosity. Overall, the PTA has been adjudged moderately successful (Green, 1994: ix).

In December 1994, the PTA became the Common Market for Eastern and Southern Africa (COMESA) with 23 member countries covering an area of 13.3 million sq. km. and 314 million people as of 1995 (Schweickert, 1996). The members are Ethiopia, Eritrea, Djibouti, Somalia, Sudan, Kenya, Uganda, Tanzania, Seychelles, Rwanda, Burundi, Comoros, Madagascar, Mozambique, Malawi, Zaire, Zambia, Angola, Zimbabwe, Namibia, Swaziland, Lesotho and Mauritius.

Southern African Development Coordination Conference (SADCC)
SADCC represents a strategy for regional cooperation which Zehender (1988) termed the functional approach. Unlike the market integration approach of all other examples discussed here, SADCC adopted an incremental, project-oriented regional cooperation strategy (World Bank, 1989). One of the goals of SADCC was to reduce the economic dominance of South Africa in the economies of member states. Other goals were to create equitable regional integration, mobilization of resources and to secure international assistance within a framework of economic liberation for the region (Boyd, 1985). It was thus both a political and economic regional grouping. The initial members of SADCC were Angola, Botswana, Lesotho, Malawi, Mozambique, Zimbabwe, Zambia, Swaziland and Tanzania.

SADCC has a tourism sectoral commission which is located in Lesotho. It is intended to foster cooperation in tourism development in the SADCC region. Also, SADCC invested in large transport and regional industrial projects. As Teye (1990) notes, transport projects have a great impact on tourism development. In general, member governments are responsible for sectoral programmes allocated to them. Although SADCC has been applauded as a successful organization (for example, World Bank, 1989), others have claimed that it has been too dependent on donor funding to be a viable regional cooperation organisation (Mandaza, 1990). Besides, regional integration under SADCC has been hampered by differing economic and political ideologies and ways by which each member country organizes its political structures and infrastructure development.

Regional cooperation in tourism in East Africa

Since the mid 1970s, there has been little regional cooperation in tourism in East Africa. Of the three East African countries, only Kenya has cooperation packages involving tourism marketing and promotion with the Indian Ocean islands of the Seychelles and Mauritius. Comprehensive regional tourism packages among the three East African countries of Kenya, Uganda and Tanzania are hampered by immigration and customs regulations which make it difficult to move people and vehicles between countries. Clearance procedures are long, tedious and cumbersome. In particular, it is difficult to move automobiles from one country to another. Further, tour operators cannot remit their proceeds from one country to another (Kenya, 1994b). It would be greatly attractive to develop and market tourism on an East Africa basis because of the demand for multi-destination tourism in this region (Kenya, 1994b: 73).

This section examines the history of regional cooperation in tourism within the East African Community (EAC) which collapsed in 1977. The primary purpose is to bring out the advantages which Kenya, Uganda and Tanzania enjoyed in offering an East African regional tourism product rather than the individual countries and to examine the problems which bedevilled this arrangement. Perhaps this historical experience can provide lessons for planned regional cooperation not only in East Africa but the African continent as a whole.

The history of the EAC goes back to the British colonial period when, in 1948, the East African High Commission (EAHC) was formed. As a de jure regional arrangement, the EAHC brought together civil servants from the three colonies. There was also a legislative council made up of representatives from Kenya, Uganda and Tanganyika. At the head of the EAHC was the Governors Council. The primary role of the EAHC was to foster regional development in public services, finance, defence, industrial promotion and research. As a result, a single currency was created for the whole of East Africa. Public services such as posts and telecommunications, railways and harbours, customs, medical, agricultural and social research, and institutions of higher learning were administered jointly as East African organisations.

In 1961 when one of the East African countries, Tanganyika, became independent, the EAHC was transformed into the East African Common Services Organisation (EACSO). The latter ultimately became the EAC after all the three countries had gained their independence from British overrule. The EAC became the most promising economic community in sub-Saharan Africa and boasted a common currency, a regionally coordinated infrastructure, harmonized economic policies, a system of common institutions and labour mobility within the region (World Bank, 1989). Among the very successful ventures was the railway system and the common airline, East African Airways, both of which assisted in intra-regional trade flows and movement of tourist traffic. The airline in particular, had become a smooth-running, profit-making venture capable of competing with world class airlines (Tibazarwa, 1988).

In the decade of the 1960s, several conflicts arose within the EAC and this foreshadowed its future. In 1966, the common currency which had previously facilitated the movement of goods, services and people across the borders, was abandoned in favour of national currencies. Also, conflicts of interest among the partner states and sharing benefits pushed the EAC to the brink. As will be shown below in the case of regional tourism cooperation, the sharing of benefits from cooperation fuelled the fire of disintegration. Further, different member countries adopted different political ideologies and this led to conflict. Whereas Kenya followed capitalist tenets of development, Tanzania adopted *Ujamaa*, African socialism. Increasingly, Tanzania's socialist government saw Kenya as a "man-eat-man" country and these charges were later openly aired on Radio Tanzania. In the meantime, Uganda had a political crisis in 1966 related to the role of the monarchs of the kingdoms of that country, especially Buganda. The government of the day suppressed the royalist elements, consolidated the republican status and announced its intention to move to the left. In 1969, Uganda published a blue print for socialism, the "Common Man's Charter". The members of the EAC were slowly moving away from one another. The case of tourism below will further clarify the problems of East African cooperation under the auspices of the community.

Cooperation in tourism within the East African Community
The history of tourism in East Africa goes back to 1938 when tourism policy in the region began to emerge. Following the world economic depression of the 1930s, there were attempts to create official travel organisations. As noted in Chapter 4 above, in East Africa this led to the formation of the East African Publicity Association (EAPA), but the intervening war years provided it with little opportunity to do tourism work in the region. Tourism was emerging as an important industry and the matter was taken up by the East African Governor's conference leading to a tourism conference in Nairobi in 1947. This conference formed a representative committee of the EAHC to oversee the matter and set up an interim office of EATTA (East African Tourist Travel Association). The latter was incorporated in 1948 as a semi-official organisation with a central role of developing and promoting tourism in East Africa as a whole. EATTA prepared a document on tourist attractions in East Africa and the road travel conditions. This was the first document of its kind in the world and was published both in English and French in 1951 (Ouma, 1970: 10). The association then opened tourist offices in Nairobi, Kampala, Dar es Salaam and Mombasa. In subsequent years, EATTA launched a carefully prepared publicity campaign for East African tourism at home, in the rest of Africa and the world by the use of published material, mass media, and through conferences and representations (Ouma, 1970).

On the operational side, tour operators based in one country could take tourists to any of the other countries. Apart from EATTA which handled all the promotional matters, trade associations, including hotel keepers, tour operators, travel agents, and professional hunters also worked jointly on a regional basis. This was possible because the EACSO had removed all administrative obstacles which could make such cooperation difficult.

It did not take a long time after the independence of the East African states before cracks began to appear on regional cooperation in tourism. Uganda and Tanzania felt that the cooperation was benefitting Kenya at their expense. Mitchell (1970: 4) estimated that of all the tourism receipts in East Africa in 1967, for example, about 59-64 percent went to Kenya, 22-33 percent to Tanzania and 13-19 percent to Uganda. This distribution of benefits appears to have been the underlying element in the complaints lodged by Uganda and Tanzania.

Uganda abandoned EATTA in 1963 arguing that the benefits it derived from regional tourism cooperation relative to its subscription was less than the same ratio for the other members (Mitchell, 1970). The country saw itself in a disadvantageous position and had always tended to remain at the backwaters of East African tourism activity. Most tourists started their journeys in Nairobi and then moved to Tanzania and later to Uganda, if at all. Lacking in firm support from the member states, EATTA collapsed in 1965.

The story hereafter is well known. Individual countries imposed administrative barriers which made the free flow of people impossible. Immigration controls were set up at the borders of each country in 1966 and 1967. This made tourism movement from one country to another somewhat cumbersome and impeded tourist flow. Uganda then imposed sales tax and a requirement for local registration of vehicles in that country if there was more than one visit in a year. The immediate impact of this was the raising of the cost of conducting tour operations business. Also, Tanzania required tour firms taking tourists to that country to be registered there and imposed stiff penalties for those that did not meet the conditions. Most tourists from Kenya flew into Tanzania on chartered aircraft for one or two days and then returned to Nairobi. The new requirement was clearly intended to undermine Kenya's leading position in tourism business in the region. It was a matter of time before regional tourism in East Africa collapsed. This came in 1977 when Tanzanian president Julius Nyerere sealed the Kenya-Tanzania border. The EAC broke up and with it most of its organs including the sub-committee on tourism.

In 1971 Uganda's government passed into the hands of Idi Amin Dada, a semi-literate soldier whose reign of terror for about a decade remains unparalleled in black Africa for its brutality against and murder of innocent people. Tourism in Uganda virtually collapsed during that period. In Tanzania, the contradictions between tourism and that country's version of socialist development pushed tourism out of the development agenda. After a wide ranging debate on the merits and pitfalls of tourism initiated by some members of the then ruling party, Tanganyika African National Union (TANU) Youth League of the University of Dar es Salaam in 1970, tourism was seen to contradict the country's aspirations to become a socialist state (Shivji, 1975; Kahama, 1995: 155). More importantly, the tourism sector was put into the hands of an inefficient public sector body called the Tanzania Tourist Corporation. With only lukewarm support, investment into tourist enterprises had stopped in the early 1970s. Facility maintenance was poor and quality of service deteriorated. The introduction of stricter bureaucratic procedures and controls at airports and other points of entry told a sad story of political malaise. Visitors were subjected to body searches, and numerous written declarations before being allowed entry (Kahama, 1995). In addition, the physical infrastructure collapsed. Roads to the beach hotels and to the wildlife conservation areas became virtually unmotorable. In the 1980s, the 500 km trip from Dar es Salaam to Arusha, at the vicinity of the famous Serengeti and Ngorongoro took up to 24 hours (Kahama, 1995: 155). Given the circumstances of Tanzania's tourism, many visitors preferred to spend their holidays in Kenya. They could reach the wildlife areas of northern Tanzania if they could cross the border by car or charter aircraft. However, this option of a short visit to Tanzania was becoming increasingly difficult because of administrative barriers before the border was finally closed in 1977.

Table 8.1
East-African tourism, international arrivals and receipts[*]

	Kenya Arrivals (000s)	Kenya Receipts (US$ m.)	Uganda Arrivals (000s)	Uganda Receipts (US$ m.)	Tanzania Arrivals (000s)	Tanzania Receipts (US$ m.)
1987	661	354	37	5	131	31
1988	695	394	40	8	130	40
1989	735	420	41	9	138	60
1990	814	466	69	10	153	65
1991	805	432	69	15	187	95
1992	782	442	92	38	202	120
1993	826	413	115	50	230	147
1994	863	421	149	61	262	192
1995	691	454	189	79	295	259
1996	907	493	240	100	326	322

* The figures for receipts exclude international transport.
Source: WTO, Personal communication, 2 April 1997

Recent developments in East African tourism
Tourism in East Africa is healthy and growing. In 1993 tourism's contribution to the GNP was 6.1 percent in Kenya, 5.3 percent in Tanzania, and 1.4 percent in Uganda (Fair, 1996: 156). Ever since, the volume of tourist traffic and receipts from tourism have increased rapidly both in Uganda and Tanzania (Table 8.1; Homewood and Rodgers, 1991). As Kenya's tourism underwent a relative decline in the early 1990s (Chapter 6), tourism in Uganda and Tanzania began to recover. In 1992, the Tanzanian government launched an ambitious programme to reverse its earlier image; it established a tourism board and started a publicity campaign as well as liberalizing and privatising its economy and especially the tourism sector (Fair, 1996). With the assistance of the World Bank,

Tanzania has upgraded the tourism infrastructure including accommodation in the protected areas, access roads and passenger facilities at harbours and airports. Fair (1996) notes that as a result of new investments, Sheraton Hotel was opened in Dar es Salaam in 1995 and three luxury lodges and a tented camp were constructed by the Serena Hotel group in the northern part of the country.

In Uganda, relative political stability under Yoweri Museveni since 1986 led to the rehabilitation of the tourism infrastructure and provided the impetus for a revitalized tourism sector. In an effort to encourage tourism, Uganda abolished visa requirements for citizens of 33 countries and is encouraging direct air links to the country (Fair, 1996).

The revitalization of the tourism industry in East Africa is an excellent sign for the region. It offers a basis for regional cooperation in the sector. While an impression might be created that the East African neighbours are benefiting from Kenya's tourism decline in the early 1990s, "Experience has shown that well-established tourist countries have nothing to fear from development of tourism in neighbouring countries" (Popovic, 1972: 55). Only vibrant and competitive tourism sectors in the three East African countries could become a basis for viable future cooperation. A positive image of the region can attract greater numbers of tourists, who will have greater flexibility on the countries and places to visit. Ultimately, this should remove the fear that one country will take a larger portion of tourism proceeds and encourage cooperation. Besides, the East African Community experience provides important lessons for the proposed cooperation in the region. Individual states must make certain political concessions and subdue national interests in order to foster regional cooperation (Dieke, 1998: 43). This should inform the new East African cooperation arrangement under the auspices of the East African Cooperation Agreement which was signed by the three heads of state of Kenya, Uganda and Tanzania on November 30, 1993.

Future East African cooperation
A draft treaty on the relaunched East African cooperation was published in 1998. The aim of the treaty is the gradual integration through the creation of a common market, monetary union and ultimately political federation for the three East African countries. By establishing a common market in the region, customs duties and other restrictions imposed on goods manufactured in East Africa will be eliminated; however, common external tariffs for foreign goods will be maintained. The East African countries have already agreed to implement zero tariff for intra-cooperation trade (Kenya, 1998b). This removal of tariff barriers will facilitate trade within the East African cooperation region. In preparation for establishing a monetary union, the three countries are expected to have convertible currencies and harmonize their fiscal and monetary policies (Kenya, 1998b: 19). The partner states will accord each other most favoured nation treatment with regard to trade. With reference to tourism, the draft treaty calls for cooperation in the promotion of tourism and wildlife management.

Specifically, the treaty provides for a coordinated approach to the promotion of quality tourism and wildlife management. This will allow for a framework of cooperation in tourism by insuring that the benefits from the industry are equitably distributed. Other provisions of the relevant article of the treaty provide for:

- establishing a common code of conduct for tour and travel operators;
- standardizing hotel classifications
- harmonizing the professional standards of agents in the tourism and travel industry; and
- developing a regional strategy for tourism promotion whereby individual efforts are reinforced by regional action (*East African*, June 1-7, 1998: 15).

Also, the draft treaty provides for coordinated policy for the conservation and sustainable use of wildlife, the basis of East Africa's tourism industry. Among the strategies for achieving this goal are: adopting common policies for wildlife conservation both inside and outside protected areas; exchanging information on wildlife management and development with a view to adopting common policies; coordinating efforts in controlling poaching; encouraging the joint use of training and research facilities and developing common management plans for transborder protected areas; and adopting common policies for the conservation of national antiquities, historical sites and museums and preventing illegal trade in cultural property (*East African*, June 1-7, 1998: 15).

Once the East African cooperation agreement becomes operational, the administrative barriers to cross-border tourism activities will be reduced or eliminated. This will be aided a great deal by the simplification of immigration procedures and the evolution of coordinated and complementary transport and communication policies. The treaty provides for the improvement and expansion of the existing transport and communication links and the establishment of new ones with the aim of facilitating the movement of traffic and the promotion of greater movement of people, goods and services. Tourism activity will be a crucial beneficiary of this arrangement.

Despite this commitment, the Bologonja tourist gate which joins Maasai Mara National Reserve in Kenya and Serengeti National Park in Tanzania, remains closed since 1977. Although the two countries agreed to opening the land border for all tourist traffic in 1985, the Bologonja gate has never been opened ostensibly because Tanzania fears losing revenue as most tourist trips will be based in Nairobi (Ubwani, 1998: 18). This case exemplifies the field realities of competition in tourism business within East Africa. Some of the problems of East African tourism in the 1960s and 1970s may rear their head again in the relaunched East African cooperation in the late 1990s and in the 21st century.

Prospects for regional cooperation

Economic integration efforts through regional groupings in sub-Saharan Africa have failed to achieve their goals. Cooperation among poor countries suffers from many shortcomings among which are low income, low level of industrialization, inadequate transport and communications, and a low level of trade. Besides, many African countries suffer from lack of foreign exchange and credit. These make it very difficult to produce competitive goods at a reasonable price. However, over the longer term

Progress toward market integration and increased cooperation in a whole range of areas — economic, technical, environmental, food security, educational and research — is central to Africa's long-term development strategy (World Bank, 1989: 162).

In tourism, greater benefits can be achieved through regional cooperation and market integration. Perhaps the key to all this will be the political stabilization of the African state. Africa's chronic political instability and regional conflicts make it almost impossible to attract tourists. Despite the huge potential for regional tourism development, the political problems and suspicions among countries in a given region tend to negate its growth. Also, the major African tourist destinations have worked closely with overseas companies in hotel development, tour and travel operations (Chapter 5). These overseas connections are crucial to marketing and promoting African destinations. The relationships already forged between African countries and foreign enterprise are likely to suffer should Africans push too hard with the regional development idea. Foreign tourism enterprises perhaps feel better served with the maintenance of the status quo (Dieke, 1998: 43). Should Africa press too hard with regionalism, the international tour operators are likely to shift to other tourism regions of the world. With this development will go the relatively small proportion of tourists to Africa.

Intra-Africa tourism

The above discussion focused on inter-African tourism initiatives. But this analysis would be incomplete without reviewing the status of intra-African tourism activity. Africa depends on tourists from the developed countries rather than on intra-regional and domestic sources (Dieke, 1995; Teye, 1991). Table 8.2 shows the origins of the tourist arrivals in Africa as recorded in 1995. However, tourist statistics in Africa must be read with caution. There is no accurate information especially on intra-Africa tourism. Intra-Africa tourism like domestic tourism largely remains an informal activity; it goes on across the borders but remains either poorly recorded or unrecorded just like other informal economic activities in the continent (Ellis and MacGaffey, 1996). With this caveat in mind, it appears from Table 8.2 that only 46.2 percent of the tourist arrivals in African countries came from within Africa; the majority came from outside the continent. But as can be noted, the data are highly variable according to sub-region and require further explanation. Whereas southern Africa recorded huge intra-Africa tourism flows accounting for 84.7 percent of the total, North Africa received most of its tourists from other regions of the world. This means that there is a lot of intra-regional movement in the southern Africa region especially the Republic of South Africa and Botswana. This is probably a result of South Africa's enormous economic strength. Many people move into South Africa from neighbouring countries for jobs of a few months in the mines and docks and then return to their home. Others are probably business people who visit South Africa for the purpose. In 1993, 60.8 percent of the tourist arrivals in Namibia were from South Africa; intra-Africa tourism accounted for 77 percent of the arrivals (Namibia, n.d.: 226). Overall, visitor and tour operator surveys indicate that visitors to Namibia combine

Table 8.2
Origin of tourists to Africa, 1995

Destination	Total arrivals ('000)	Africa (Percent)	Outside Africa (Percent)
Africa	19,045	46.2	53.8
Eastern Africa	3,968	46.4	53.6
Middle Africa	335	10.0	90.0
North Africa	7,252	16.0	84.0
South Africa	5,932	84.7	15.3
Western Africa	1,558	46.9	53.1

Source: WTO, Personal communication, 28 February 1997

trips to South Africa, Zimbabwe and Botswana (Namibia, n.d.: 225) showing the importance of multi-destination tourism.

Table 8.3 shows a somewhat detailed picture of the origins of tourists in selected African countries in 1995. Except for Zimbabwe and Swaziland, the other countries are heavily dependent on visitors from outside the continent. Many of the tourists into these countries are South Africans who visit over weekends or for a few days and generally spend little money. Although Zimbabwe recorded the largest number of arrivals, its tourism receipts are only modest suggesting that intra-Africa tourists are generally low-spending. This is also the case with Swaziland. Perhaps for this reason, many countries tend to promote tourists from the developed countries. This is not merely an effort to earn foreign exchange required for investment and development purposes; it is also because holiday tourism is a product of Western affluence, materialism, and lifestyle. Some

Table 8.3
Origin of tourists for selected African countries, 1995

	Total arrivals ('000)	Receipts (US$ million)	ORIGIN Africa (Percent)	Outside Africa (Percent)
Kenya	691	454	26.5	73.5
Uganda	189	79	--	--
Tanzania	295	259	39.0	61.0
Zimbabwe	1,363	154	85.4	14.6
Mauritius	422	430	34.0	66.0
Botswana	644	162	--	--
Namibia	399	263	--	--
Ghana	286	233	34.0	66.0
Senegal	280	130	20.2	79.8
Cote d'Ivoire	188	72	55.7	44.3
Swaziland	300	35	84.5	15.5

Source: WTO, Personal communication, 28 February 1997

authors have noted that pleasure tourism tends to be limited in Africa (Teye, 1991; Dieke, 1995). Dieke has summarized the situation as follows:

> ... indigenous African's demand for travel is penalized by their low income per capita and extended family commitments and therefore their modest purchasing power. In this sense, it is not leisure but visiting-friends-and-relatives (VFR) tourism — mainly for family reasons — that predominates in much of Africa. Even the African elites who have the means to engage in tourist activities generally tend to vacation outside Africa or to retain vertical allegiances with erstwhile European mother countries (1995: 76).

Since intra-Africa tourists tend to stay with friends and relatives, it is argued that the need for hotel accommodation is diminished (Dieke, 1998: 42). It follows then that this market segment does not contribute much to the African economy.

Summary and conclusion

This chapter has discussed the twin issues of regional cooperation in tourism and intra-Africa tourism. Clearly, there are several benefits to be gained from regional cooperation in tourism activity. A regional destination offers varied attractions thereby allowing the tourist the opportunity to choose what he or she would like to see. Besides, the contemporary trend in tourism emphasizes multi-destination travelling. A region made up of three or more countries is likely to offer the diversity of tourism resources which are in demand among tourists. For the host countries it is cheaper and more cost-effective to promote and market a region rather than a single country.

Regional cooperation in tourism can be done within the framework of Africa's many sub-regional groupings. Despite the proliferation of such economic communities, there has been relatively little market integration in Africa. Borders of African countries are difficult to cross because of a myriad administrative barriers all of which hinder regional tourism development.

Tourism is well developed in only a few countries in Africa. Such tourism attracts visitors mainly from developed countries. Except perhaps in southern Africa, intra-Africa tourism remains poorly developed. Yet, intra-Africa tourism could be enhanced by a more positive attitude and pride of the African peoples about their own continent. Intra-Africa tourism could be achieved with greater interaction of the African peoples at the personal, professional, trade and other levels. Despite short term impediments, long-term regional cooperation must be realised in Africa. With it will be a boom in intra-African tourism.

9

Tourism and African development: Conclusion

The goal of this study was to assess the viability of tourism as a development strategy for sub-Saharan Africa. This was pursued using the Kenyan example with the specific objectives of assessing the contributions of tourism to development and examining the outcomes of tourism development. Intertwined in these objectives are at least three issues. Does tourism provide benefits to the African economy? Is it an acceptable form of development especially among the local peoples? Is tourism an appropriate tool of African development?

There is little doubt that tourism may be the best way of utilizing certain remote areas, particularly Kenya's rangelands where it generates resources which would otherwise not come to the region. Although some studies have shown that tourism provides greater resources per unit of land than say traditional livestock-keeping, tourism as an alternative investment option is less well understood. This is because there are no cost-benefit studies to assist in assessing the relative role of tourism in development compared to other alternatives such as agriculture and manufacturing. The few available scholarly opinions on this matter are quite divergent. Some lend support for tourism as a more efficient and cost-effective investment option while others are completely opposed to this view. Although a number of studies tend to favour tourism, few have persuasively made the case for tourism as a less costly investment option (Coppock, 1977: 5). Indeed, the matter is more complex than this because there are many types of tourism, each requiring different levels of investment. Conventional tourism absorbs large investments to develop infrastructure. Such infrastructure — which include large airports, roads, national park systems, lodges and large hotels — all need substantial national financial outlays. These capital developments absorb large amounts of scarce foreign exchange earnings through the importation of materials, vehicles and spare parts. Besides, additional sources must go into developing piped water systems, electricity, communications, and sanitation. Without general development in a country where these services are available, they must be put in place to serve the tourism industry. As a result of this, African countries have spent large amounts of national resources to create tourism enclaves which are supplied with basic services generally unavailable at the local population centres. The local people pay the opportunity costs of services developed with the use of tax money and foreign loans which they are enjoined to repay. In addition, the spatially segregated tourism resorts tend to perpetuate inequality in which tourists lead an affluent lifestyle while the hosts remain in poverty without basic services. This undermines the basis for positive cultural interactions between hosts and guests and local goodwill for tourism.

Developing tourism as a tool of African development presumes that there is conscious choice and selection of tourism in order to yield defined optimal results. This also assumes that there is ability and willingness to control the volume of tourist flows so as to reach a defined optimal level (Middleton, 1977: 100). Throughout sub-Saharan Africa, tourism has developed without much planning. In the few countries in which there is substantial tourism development, none had an initial blue-print on the type of tourism desired, growth rate control and even consent by local communities. Even Kenya with a relatively well developed tourism industry, has had no long-term planning perspective for tourism. A number of factors explain this planning weakness, among which are understaffing and lack of staff with expertise in tourism planning. This is because tourism is not a conventional planning sector. Besides, tourism suffers from the image of being a luxury export completely based on external demand on which local planners have relatively little control. Tourism is dependent on political stability, perceptions of personal safety, security and health. Any of these factors can influence tourist numbers and hence revenues and thus paralyse planning strategies. Also, planning in tourism suffers from lack of detailed data on length and location of visits, visitor expenditure patterns and related information. In Kenya, tourism statistics are based on tourism regions which are not related to any of the planning units of the country. In Africa in general only a few countries have attempted tourism planning including Tunisia and Uganda. Kenya is beginning to formulate a tourism master-plan as is Tanzania.

Lack of tourism planning leads to serious environmental and socio-cultural problems and a deterioration of the tourism product. However, planning is not a panacea for all the problems associated with tourism. By providing goals and objectives of tourism planning, and comparing these with national development goals and objectives, it may become possible to work out whether the expectation of tourism as a tool of development are being met. Without defining the type of tourism desired and controlling the tourist numbers to bring about planned outcomes, it is difficult for tourism to become a tool for African development. There are other reasons which raise doubts about tourism's ability to become a development strategy for Africa.

Compared to other world regions in terms of geographical area and population, Africa receives a very small share of global tourism both in terms of arrivals and in monetary receipts. In fact, tourism is poorly developed in most of sub-Saharan Africa. The middle Africa region (Angola, Cameroon, Central African Republic, Chad, Congo (Kinshasa), Congo (Brazzaville), Gabon, and Sao Thomé and Principe) receives very little tourist traffic. And, save for Senegal, Ghana and Cote d'Ivoire, this is also the case in western Africa. For these sub-regions, tourism does not even exist as a viable foreign exchange earning option. This situation could, however, be turned around with planning, marketing, political stability and investments in the sector.

Another problem in Africa is the relatively little-developed intra-Africa tourism. Because of the very widely-held perception that indigenous Africans are not leisure-minded, it is said that the continent lacks "an organic source of tourists" and this makes the prospects of intra-African tourism quite bleak (Dieke, 1995: 89). This probably misses the point for two reasons: large numbers of African residents travel outside Africa to other world regions; and the majority of Africans do not make enough money to allow paying for a holiday in another country. Unlike in Western Europe and North America where responsibilities for the unemployed and senior citizens are taken up by the welfare state systems, in sub-Saharan Africa, this burden remains on the shoulders of a small productive sector of the population. This is the group that should be travelling in pursuit of leisure.

African countries assiduously cultivate tourists from developed countries so that they can obtain hard currency required for development. This fact alone discourages the development of intra-African tourism. Most African currencies are not convertible. As such, there is lack of a currency medium through which regional tourism could be conducted within the continent and denies Africa the opportunity to raise revenues through intra-Africa tourism.

Although African countries focus on international tourism from other continents, they do not get full benefits because of the heavy leakages associated with it. International tourism is structured in a way that the ownership of enterprises, management and control are in the hands of Western multinational corporations. In Kenya, multinational corporations either outrightly or jointly with Kenyan investors own the majority of the tourist class hotels and tour operations businesses. Such arrangements have in-built expatriate management staff who control the running of the businesses. Foreign exchange leakages occur in the form of repatriation of profits, management fees, franchise payments, and wages by expatriate managers. Besides, Kenya obtains very low earnings from package tourists. Much of the leakage occurs with chartered and scheduled airlines and international tour operators who retain most of the foreign exchange abroad. This is especially so for beach-only mass tourists at the coast who are subsidized by the Kenyan tax-payer. This situation must be reversed if tourism has to play a crucial role in the country's development.

Dealing with foreign exchange leakages is a difficult problem. This is because of the structure of ownership within the tourism industry and the fact that many tourism subsectors tend to be vertically integrated. Also, multinational companies wield power and clout because they are the ones which source the tourists. This brings the fear that if they are pushed hard for greater openness in their dealings, they are likely to divert the tourists to another country or another part of the world altogether. Certainly, greater indigenous ownership and participation in various tourism enterprises including hotels, local charter airlines, and tour companies is one of the solutions. The other is encouraging Kenya Airways to increase its share of the international travel market. But this is easier said than done because foreign airlines are already deeply entrenched in the more lucrative routes. Also, the pricing structure of the tourism product must be done in such way that leakages are minimized. This requires the maintenance of a high quality product to encourage tourists to pay to have the experience. There must also be sensitivity to changing tastes and individual requirements of the tourists.

The challenge of tourism in Kenya since the beginning of the 20th century has been changes related to the kind of tourism product desired at different time periods. Up to 1960, Kenya's wildlife-based tourism focused on consumptive utilization. European aristocrats and the American rich went for sport hunting not just in Kenya but in sub-Saharan Africa in general. Hunting in the African 'jungle' was considered manliness (Anderson and Grove, 1987) although African subsistence hunters were seen as poachers. The creation of national parks in the immediate post World War II period was intended to maintain and preserve "Eden" for continued European psychological enjoyment rather than to maintain the African ecosystem complex (Anderson and Grove, 1987).

Kenyan tourism became somewhat diversified in the 1960s when beach tourism started to attract large numbers of foreign visitors. This was developed upon a base of domestic tourism started by resident European populations in the colonial period. However, the influx of international all-inclusive package tourists posed a special challenge to the tourist industry in the country. The few family hotel businesses established in the colonial period could not cope with large numbers of tourists. Joint ventures were created between the state, resident entrepreneurs, international finance, and multinational corporations to develop tourism enterprises. This process was assisted a great deal by the country's capitalist economic policies.

Kenya's emphasis on numbers of tourists rather than per capita foreign exchange earnings partly led to the overexploitation of the tourism resources especially national parks and reserves. Consequently, a number of critical issues stand on the way of Kenya's tourism in the 1990s leading to the deterioration of the tourism product. Although government explanation for the decline of the tourism industry tends to emphasize external factors such as competition with other countries and adverse publicity on the security situation, it is recognised that the problem is largely internal. The internal factors are the breakdown of the physical infrastructure, especially roads, and a deterioration of the attractions including the beaches because of overcrowding, and fears about personal security.

Kenya's lack of a tourism plan suggests that the change and challenge that the tourism industry has been undergoing, was not anticipated. This situation has caused some paralysis and even panic among the stakeholders of the industry. In the wake of tourism's decline, there are attempts to encourage ecotourism so as to contain the worst effects to mass tourism. Despite ecotourism's formulation emphasizing small scale enterprises owned and managed by the local people, this has not happened in Africa. The structure of international tourism with the control of western multinational corporations remains intact. And with this, the hope for revolutionary change in the management of tourism and equitable sharing of the benefits remains an elusive dream. This tends to undermine the role of tourism as a leading component of the African economy.

Appendices

Appendix 1: Sub-Saharan African countries: basic indicators

	Population mid-1992 (millions)	Area (000s. of sq. km)	GNP per capita U.S. dollars 1992	GNP per capita Av. annual Percentage growth 1985-92	Life expectancy at birth (years) 1992
SUB-SAHARAN AFRICA	541.4	23,632	530	-0.8	52
excluding South Africa	501.7	22,411	340	-0.2	51
excl.S.Africa & Nigeria	399.8	21,500	352	-1.1	51
Angola	9.7	1,247	-	-0.9	46
Benin	5.0	111	410	-1.5	51
Botswana	1.4	567	2,450	6.6	68
Burkina Faso	9.5	274	310	0.3	48
Burundi	5.8	26	210	1.0	48
Cameroon	12.2	465	830	-6.9	56
Cape Verde	0.4	4	840	2.3	68
Central African Republic	3.2	623	410	-2.6	47
Chad	6.0	1,259	220	1.3	47
Comoros	0.5	2	530	-2.2	56
Congo	2.4	342	1,110	-1.8	51
Cote d'Ivoire	12.9	318	680	-5.2	56
Djibouti	0.5	23	...	-7.3	49
Equatorial Guinea	0.4	28	340	0.6	48
Ethiopia	54.8	1,101	110	-2.0	49
Gabon	1.2	258	4,220	-1.6	54
Gambia, The	1.0	10	370	1.0	45
Ghana	15.8	228	460	1.2	56
Guinea	6.1	246	490	1.3	44
Guinea-Bassau	1.0	28	220	1.7	39
Kenya	24.7	570	330	0.9	59
Lesotho	1.9	30	610	0.9	60
Liberia	2.4	97	...	...	53
Madagascar	12.4	582	230	-1.7	51
Malawi	9.1	94	230	0.7	44
Mali	9.0	1,220	310	-4.5	48
Mauritania	2.1	1,025	540	-0.1	48
Mauritius	1.1	2	2,800	6.1	70
Mozambique	16.5	784	70	1.3	44
Namibia	1.5	823	1,670	2.5	59
Niger	8.2	1,267	290	-1.8	46
Nigeria	101.9	911	330	3.4	52
Rwanda	7.3	25	250	-2.8	46
Sao Tome and Principe	0.1	1	370	-1.7	68
Senegal	7.8	193	780	0.1	49
Seychelles	0.1	0	5,750	4.1	71
Sierra Leone	4.4	72	160	-0.2	43
Somalia	8.3	627	...	-2.3	49
South Africa	39.8	1,221	2,828	-1.3	63
Sudan	26.5	2,376	300	-0.2	52
Swaziland	0.9	17	1,080	5.1	57
Tanzania	25.9	886	110	1.9	51
Togo	3.9	54	400	-1.9	55
Uganda	17.5	200	170	2.0	43
Zaire	39.8	2,268	...	-0.8	52
Zambia	8.3	743	370	2.2	48
Zimbabwe	10.1	387	580	-0.7	60

cont.>>>>

Appendix 1, cont.

	Population mid-1992 (millions)	Area (000s. of square km)	GNP per capita U.S. dollars 1992	GNP per capita Av. annual Percentage growth 1985-92	Life expectancy at birth (years) 1992
SUB-SAHARAN AFRICA	541.4	23,632	530	-0.8	52
excluding South Africa	501.7	22,411	340	-0.2	51
excl.S.Africa & Nigeria	399.8	21,500	352	-1.1	51
NORTH AFRICA	120.4	5,738	1,218	-0.9	67
Algeria	26.3	2,382	1,850	-2.2	67
Egypt, Arab Republic	54.7	995	650	0.8	62
Libya	4.9	1,760	...	-5.5	63
Morocco	26.2	446	1,050	1.3	63
Tunisia	8.4	155	1,760	2.1	68
ALL AFRICA	661.8	29,371	657	-0.9	54

Source: World Bank, 1995: 6

Appendix 2: Kenya population 1979 and 1989 by province and district[1]

Province/District	Population 1979 (thousands)	Population 1989 (thousands)	Land (sq. km.)	Density
Nairobi	**828**	**1,325**	**693**	**1,911**
Central Province				
Kiambu	686	914	2,587	353
Kirinyaga	291	392	1,485	264
Muranga	648	858	2,525	340
Nyandarua	233	345	3,373	102
Nyeri	486	607	3,266	186
Central	**2,344**	**3,116**	**13,236**	**235**
Coast Province				
Kilifi	431	592	13,006	46
Kwale	288	383	8,260	46
Lamu	42	57	6,818	8
Mombasa	341	462	282	1,637
Taita Taveta	148	207	16,965	12
Tana River	92	128	38,782	3
Coast	**1,342**	**1,829**	**84,113**	**22**
Eastern Province				
Embu	263	370	2,805	132
Isiolo	42	70	25,604	3
Kitui	464	653	29,803	22
Machakos	1,023	1,402	13,968	100
Marsabit	96	129	72,290	2
Meru	830	1,145	9,884	116
Eastern	**2,719**	**3,769**	**154,354**	**24**
North Eastern Province				
Garissa	129	125	43,392	3
Mandera	106	124	25,871	5
Wajir	139	123	56,923	2
North Eastern	**374**	**372**	**126,186**	**3**
Nyanza Province				
Kisii	870	1,137	2,198	517
Kisumu	482	664	2,077	320
Siaya	475	639	2,524	253
South Nyanza	818	1,067	5,708	187
Nyanza	**2,645**	**3,507**	**12,507**	**280**
Rift Valley Province				
Baringo	204	348	10,954	32
Elgeyo Marakwet	149	216	3,049	71
Kajiado	149	259	21,756	12
Kericho	633	901	4,940	182
Laikipia	135	219	9,162	24

cont.>>>>

---

[1] Although the provinces have remained the same number, most of the districts have since been subdivided into smaller ones. These data reflect the old district boundaries because the sizes of some of the new districts do not appear to have been determined. The population figures for 1989 have been rounded off and the tally may not be identical with the original.

Appendix 2: cont.

Province/District	Population 1979 (thousands)	Population 1989 (thousands)	Land (sq. km.)	Density
Nakuru	523	849	7,190	118
Nandi	299	434	2,784	156
Narok	210	398	18,002	22
Samburu	77	109	20,808	5
Trans-Nzoia	260	394	2,467	160
Turkana	143	184	69,146	3
Uasin Gishu	301	446	3,218	138
West Pokot	159	225	8,937	25
Rift Valley	**2,242**	**4,982**	**182,413**	**27**
Western Province				
Bungoma	504	679	3,072	221
Busia	298	402	1,652	243
Kakamega	1,031	1,464	3,561	411
Western	**1,833**	**2,544**	**8,285**	**307**
Kenya	**15,327**	**21,444**	**581,787**	**37**

Sources: Kenya, 1994a: 11-1 to 1-2; Kenya, 1991b: 32.

Appendix 3: Kenya national and marine parks and reserves

	Area (km^2)	Year gazetted	District
National Parks			
1. Sibiloi	1,570	1973	Marsabit
2. Central Island	5	1983	Turkana/Marsabit
3. South Island	39	1983	Marsabit
4. Malka Mari	876	1989	Mandera
5. Marsabit	360	-	Marsabit
6. Mount Elgon	169	1968	Trans Nzoia
7. Saiwa Swamp	2	1974	Trans Nzoia
8. Meru	870	1966	Meru
9. Kora	1,787	1989	Tana River
10. Mount Kenya	715	1989	Nyeri/Meru
11. Ndere Island	4	1986	Kisumu
12. Mau*	-	-	-
13. Lake Nakuru	188	1967	Nakuru
14. Aberdares	715	1950	Nyeri
15. Ruma	120	1983	Homa Bay
16. Hell's Gate	68	1984	Nakuru
17. Longonot	52	1983	Nakuru
18. Fourteen Falls*	-	-	-
19. Ol Donyo Sabuk	18	1967	Machakos
20. Nairobi	117	1946	Nairobi
21. Amboseli	392	1974	Kajiado
22. Tsavo West	9,056	1948	Taita-Taveta
23. Tsavo East	11,747	1948	Taita Taveta/Kitui
24. Arabuko Sokoke	6	1991	Kilifi
25. Chyulu	471	1983	Machakos
Marine Parks			
26. Malindi	6	1968	Kilifi
27. Watamu	10	1968	Kilifi
28. Mombasa	10	1968	Mombasa
29. Kisite	28	1978	Kwale
National Reserves			
30. Marsabit	1,198	1962	Marsabit
31. Nasolot	92	1979	West Pokot
32. South Turkana	1,091	1979	Turkana
33. Losai	1,806	1976	Marsabit
34. Kerio Valley*	-	-	-
35. Kamnarok	88	1983	Baringo
36. Kakamega	4	1985	Kakamega
37. Lake Bogoria	107	1970	Baringo
38. Samburu	165	1963	Samburu
39. Shaba	239	1974	Isiolo
40. Buffalo Springs	131	1963	Isiolo
41. Bisanadi	606	1978	Isiolo
42. Rahole	1,270	1976	Garissa
43. North Kitui	745	1979	Kitui
44. Mwea	68	1976	Embu
45. Maasai Mara	1,510	1974	Narok
46. South Kitui	1,833	1979	Kitui
47. Arawale	533	1974	Garissa
48. Boni	1,339	1976	Lamu

cont.>>>>

Appendix 3, cont.

	Area (km^2)	Year gazetted	District
49. Dodori	877	1976	Lamu
50. Tana River Primate	169	1976	Tana River
51. Shimba Hills	192	1968	Kwale
Marine Reserves			
52. Kiunga	250	1979	Lamu
53. Malindi	213	1968	Kilifi
54. Mombasa	200	1986	Mombasa
55. Watamu	32	1968	Kilifi
56. Mpunguti	11	1968	Kwale
National Sanctuary			
57. Maralal	6	1968	Samburu

* In process of gazettement.
Source: Sindiga, 1995: 46-47.

Appendix 4: Tourism education in Kenya

This appendix discusses the status of training and education in tourism in Kenya. Training provides specialized skills required by personnel working in an increasingly complex sector. Tourism is especially susceptible to the sensitivities and characteristics of the personnel who handle travellers. The demand for tourism itself reflects tastes and trends in personal consumption, factors which the personnel of tourism enterprises must be aware about and be able to deal with.

Training is the transition between formal education and the needs of occupation and employment (Sindiga, 1994). Training prepares individuals with certain skills, attitudes and work habits which improves the quality of their productivity and provides job satisfaction. However, tourism education must be life-long. This is because technology and attitudes change and workers must have an opportunity to periodically upgrade their skills in order to cope with the requirements of an ever-changing world.

As already noted in this study, the management of various sectors of the tourism industry in Africa remains largely in the hands of expatriate personnel. Yet, the standards of service in tourism cannot be upgraded without training (Dieke, 1997). In Kenya, ninety percent of the personnel in the hotel and tourism industry is untrained (Sindiga, 1996c). This is partly because of Kenya's phenomenal expansion of the tourism industry since the mid-1960s. It is also because many small and medium-sized hotels and other tourism enterprises which tend to be family businesses prefer to engage untrained people so that they can pay less in personal emoluments. In addition, they see their businesses as a source of employment for family members.

Up to the 1960s there was no training policy in tourism in Kenya. The industry was managed by expatriate personnel working for foreign companies. Kenyans worked in subordinate positions and were given hardly any training (Ouma, 1970). This situation led to the opening of a hotel management course at the Kenya Polytechnic in Nairobi in 1969. This programme absorbed secondary school leavers and gave them training for four years with the goal of working as hotel managers.

With its focus on the hotel management aspect only, the Kenya Polytechnic programme proved somewhat narrow. Singly, it could not improve the quality of service even in the accommodation sector. The need for broader training led to the establishment of the Kenya Utalii College (UC) in 1973 as a joint project of the Swiss and Kenya governments. UC — and the Utalii Hotel which serves as a teaching facility — offers certificate and diploma courses in food production, food and beverages service, front office operations, house-keeping and laundry, hotel management; and travel operations and tour guiding (Appendix 5).

UC's present problems are outlined in Appendix 5. However, for the more than two decades that UC dominated middle level training in the tourism sector, its training capacity was restricted. The college admitted Kenyans as well as foreigners from many other countries. By the mid-1990s, UC had trained only 11,000 Kenyans and hundreds of students from 40 different countries including Ethiopia, Botswana, Mauritius, Malawi, Tanzania, India, Senegal and Grenada (Sindiga, 1994). The need for more training opportunities had led to the establishment of a number of middle level institutions both private and public. It is expected that the private colleges in particular will be required to be registered with the Ministry of Tourism and Wildlife as a guarantee to the quality of their curricula and also as an effort to ensure that training is harmonized by centralizing curricula, testing, and certification (Kenya, 1994b: 74). The Kenya Institute of Education has already responded to the need by drawing up a diploma tourism programme initially to be used by the Coast Institute of Technology and other institutions which are keen on teaching the subject in order to alleviate the shortage of trained personnel.

Training in the tourism industry is seen as an incremental means of indigenizing the management and ultimately the ownership of the tourism industry. This will then trigger higher employment in the country by reducing the level of foreign exchange leakages (Chapters 4 and 5). The strategy is to proceed with indigenization while maintaining high standards and quality of service.

Continuing Vocational Training and Education (CVTE)
Despite Kenya's training efforts in tourism-related fields, the majority of the personnel in the industry have not received appropriate training. The training programme must then cater for both pre-service personnel and those already working in the industry. In the latter case, training is conducted through extension services involving in-service and refresher courses for short periods. CVTE is seen as any professional education or training activity involving on the job training for serving employees. As noted above, CVTE enables workers to adapt to new circumstances and obtain skills and qualifications which allow them to deliver quality service associated with the tourism industry. Another purpose of CVTE is to enable workers to improve their qualifications.

There are hardly any studies on CVTE in tourism in Kenya. But UC organizes extension courses for employees of tourism organisations usually in April when Kenya's international tourism is in low season. These courses are generally successful; however, few enterprises are willing to pay for their workers to obtain CVTE and many of them have no training budgets (Sindiga, 1996c). This is especially so for small- and medium-sized hotels which cater for domestic tourism and account for the largest number of employees.

Several categories of jobs in the tourism industry require training. These include tour leaders, telephonists, accountants, reception staff, drivers, tour managers and camp assistants (Munyori, 1992). Besides, few employers in tourism have in-house training programmes for their workers. For example, Munyori (1992) found that among the 160 member companies of KATO, less than 25 percent had a training budget. Only three firms in-house training programmes. Yet a survey of KATO members revealed a need for CVTE among various categories of staff including driver-guides, security, first aid, sales, client-staff relations, local tourism and client expectations. Many tour firms, however, are unwilling to release their workers for more than a week and they will not pay more than Kshs.1000 per person per week. This behaviour forecloses the ability of staff to increase their productivity and to innovate in their daily functions.

A survey conducted among tourists by Henry, Waithaka and Gakahu (1992) in the Maasai Mara National Reserve in 1990 found drivers to be good at their job, courteous to clients and able to provide basic wildlife information. However, the driver-guides did not volunteer much information or offer interpretation. This is a serious problem in Kenya's tourism industry. Most driver-guides are drop-outs from Kenya's school system and few of them are trained. Many tour companies use them instead of qualified tour guides (who are available) because they attract less pay. Their knowledge tends to be limited and they merely regurgitate the script they have been given with little understanding of why things occur in the way they do. Perhaps, CVTE could assist this group of workers in their handling of visitors to the country. Tour drivers are the first-line contact between visitors and the country. This primary role in tourism requires well-informed and knowledgeable people who can read and interpret all the landscapes of the tourist gaze. This has become more urgent because of Kenya's focus on ecotourism. All the people who handle tourists should be given training in the basic tenets of environmental conservation and cultural studies and be sensitized to guest-host relationships.

University training and research
Kenya's middle level colleges provide tourism training in specific skills for the operatives in various sub-sectors. Training tends to be segmented and it is difficult for the individuals so trained to conceptualize the tourism industry as a whole (Sindiga, 1996c). Several aspects of the tourism industry including promotion, marketing, planning and management have received little attention. And so has tourism research. It is in the backdrop of these limitations that the presidential committee on employment saw a need for training of tourism officers at university level (Kenya, 1991a: 151). Moi University responded to this call and established the Department of Tourism (MUDOT) in 1991 (Sindiga, 1994; 1996c). Until MUDOT was established, there were no university level programmes in tourism education in Kenya. This became necessary as a way of achieving Kenya government policy objectives regarding the tourism industry. These objectives include the following: creating and expanding employment opportunities in the tourism sector, providing local management skills and facilitating Kenyanization, improving the quality of service offered by tourism enterprises, and restructuring the tourism industry in order to achieve sustainable development. The creation of the MUDOT was intended to upgrade training in tourism in Kenya and to pay particular attention to tourism research. MUDOT initially introduced a four-year B.Sc degree programme. In addition, postgraduate programmes which would emphasise problems of African tourism, are planned.

Moi University's B.Sc tourism programme equips graduates with skills to plan, design, implement and manage touristic resources in ways that enhance sustainable development (Box A.1). The goal of the programme is to produce highly but broadly trained individuals in the sciences; planning, management and administration; and sensitized to the variety of the ecological and cultural habitats of the world. The main features of the curriculum are exposure to the basic sciences including ecology and geography; an additional foreign language; skills in computing; tourism studies; economics, finance and planning. The programme emphasizes practical work, field courses and hands-on experience. For a period of three months at the end of the third year, each student must participate in a field attachment programme to gain practical experience in a tourism enterprise as part of the degree requirements. In the final year of study, students focus on tourism promotion and two additional clusters of courses from tourism management systems, hospitality and recreation services management, and travel and transport management. Although tourism and hospitality are frequently handled separately, MUDOT takes a wholistic view of the entire tourism sector. Accommodation facilities and food service are essential to tourism and a student of tourism policy and planning needs to know the basic functioning of hospitality services. This curriculum should be reviewed periodically in line with local tourism industry needs and world-wide trends in tourism education.

MUDOT graduates first entered the job market in 1996. They are expected to play a leading role in tourism management in the country. This will alleviate the local shortage of personnel with appropriate skills to plan, implement and manage tourism projects in line with national development objectives and needs. Because the domination of expatriate personnel in tourism in Kenya is related to the ownership of the enterprises, it is expected that a pool of competitive local skills will in future force the owners to indigenise the supervisory and management positions. In addition, the graduates can themselves start indigenous businesses which can then work in partnership with foreign firms involved in the tourism industry to the advantage of Kenyans. So far, MUDOT has taken up its twin mandates of tourism education and research quite seriously even in the face of lack of adequate infrastructure and a very heavy undergraduate teaching workload. MUDOT staff research programme has addressed various critical issues in Kenya's tourism including local communities and state conservation programmes (Akama, n.d; Akama, Lant and Burnett, 1995; Akama, 1996; Sindiga, 1995), training and employment (Sindiga, 1994; 1996c), domestic tourism (Sindiga, 1996a), local participation in tourism (Sindiga, 1996b), and tourism planning in Africa (Sindiga and Kanunah, 1998). Also, MUDOT staff have been actively involved in field research in community participation in tourism (Reid, Sindiga, Evans and Ongaro, 1998), urban tourism (Ondimu, forthcoming) and related areas. In time, MUDOT will become the centre of tourism research in Africa. It will be engaged in contributing to the solution of the social, economic and environmental problems confronting the Kenyan tourism industry (Chapter 6) and to provide timely data required for decision making.

Training in allied fields

Tourism training in Kenya's middle-level colleges focuses on the hospitality sector and tour operations and travel. A number of other institutions supply personnel to various subsectors of the industry. The MTW runs the Wildlife and Fisheries Institute at Naivasha to train rangers who undertake security duties in the country's protected areas. Also, the institute offers short courses for service officers of the ministry. Although the focus of the institute is conservation, wildlife, fisheries and natural resources management, paramilitary skills are taught as well. As such, the personnel not only appreciate the multiple roles of protected areas and especially for the vital nature tourism in the country but also learn to use arms against poachers and other unauthorized hunters.

A few hundreds of wildlife personnel in Kenya are trained at the College of African Wildlife Management at Mweka near Moshi in Tanzania. Established in 1963, the Mweka college offers courses in wildlife management, natural sciences, estate management, and

Box A.1 Moi University B.Sc Tourism Degree Programme Objectives

Curriculum objectives
At the end of their training the graduates will be expected to be able to:
1. plan, design and develop touristic facilities taking into account the variety of Eastern Africa's ecological and cultural environment;
2. plan and effectively manage for the optimal utilization of touristic resources including parks and museums;
3. conserve and enhance ecological, social, cultural and technological heritage;
4. enhance standards of management in the tourism industry and related areas.

Specific objectives
Knowledge
The student is expected to have a knowledge of:
i) geographical, ecological, and cultural diversity of the world
ii) basic sciences
iii) natural resources management
iv) the tourism industry including automated management system, tourism promotion, travel and transport, and hospitality and recreation services.
v) sound environmental management

Skills
The student should be able to:
i) interpret the human environment
ii) design travel schedules
iii) be effective in oral and written communication
iv) relate to and get along with other people always working to promote interpersonal relations.
v) solve problems related to customer service and satisfaction.

Attitudes
i) a positive and accommodative attitude to the needs of tourists
ii) the work and professional ethics of managers
iii) a positive attitude to changing needs of tourists
iv) a positive attitude to develop and exploit touristic resources while at the same time considering long-term sustainability.

recreation and conservation education (Ankomah, 1991). The latter includes courses in park planning interpretation and management; land use planning; and tourism.

To upgrade the standards of wildlife management and biological conservation, Moi University started the Department of Wildlife Management in 1985 within the Faculty of Forest Resources and Wildlife Management. The Department offers undergraduate and postgraduate degree programmes in wildlife management, a recognition of this important resource for the country. This department teaches courses in biological conservation, park planning, design and management. It complements the role of MUDOT on the nexus between nature conservation and tourism. In addition, students of the two departments share certain courses such as ecotourism, tourism policy and planning, park management and wildlife management.

Further, other programmes in Kenyan universities produce graduates with skills to work in the accommodation and food areas of tourism. Such programmes include home economics at Kenyatta University, home science and technology at Moi University and Maseno University College, and food technology and applied nutrition at the University of Nairobi. The personnel from these cognate disciplines complement those from tourism programmes and apply their skills for the benefit of the tourism industry.

Conclusion

Although the majority of the workers in Kenya's tourism industry are untrained, the country has taken important steps in personnel training. In this, Kenya is probably better-endowed than many sub-Saharan African countries that have no training facilities in the tourism and hospitality fields. Most of the hotels which handle international tourists have trained personnel; however, the small- and medium-sized establishments which cater mainly for internal tourists are run by untrained people. Many such establishments tend to be family concerns and are run as such. These enterprises could benefit from tourism extension work which emphasizes the importance of high quality and efficient services in the service sector. In fact, trained people could improve the quality and quantity of services thereby allowing an enterprise to attract more clients. In the end there are greater profits to be made with the use of trained personnel.

Appendix 5: Public sector organisations in Kenya's tourism industry

Bomas of Kenya

Bomas of Kenya is a cultural facility created in the 1960s to promote African culture, music, dance and architecture in Kenya. Bomas, which derives its name from the Kiswahili word *boma*, a homestead with a stockade, is fully owned by the government through the KTDC. Bomas is located at Langata, Nairobi on an 83 acre leasehold land. When it was set up it had a resident theatre, with a capacity for 4000 people, and dance companies. The purpose of Bomas is to foster African traditional dances, arts and crafts and traditional housing types from various Kenyan ethnic communities including the Kikuyu, Luo, Kamba, and Turkana. The facility is an entertainment outfit for tourists, both domestic and foreign, and for the enjoyment of the residents of Nairobi. Bomas is visited frequently by school parties during the week and serves as a family entertainment arena in the weekends. Besides, it is a neighbourhood bar for an evening drink for Nairobians.

So far, Bomas has not been run on commercial principles. The facility is hardly marketed or promoted. Bomas has had very weak linkages with other facilities which cater for tourists. As such, Bomas has tended to be excluded from most tourist itineraries. This is probably because public corporations are not always good at business. Frequently, personnel remuneration is paid from public coffers and need not be tied to any performance criteria or indicators. Also, the financial system may be inflexible thereby frustrating ongoing programmes with a serious impact on staff morale. But the problem at Bomas appears to be corruption, mismanagement and very low staff salaries (Gachamba, 1994).

In the past, the 84 Bomas dancers used to stage major outdoor performances and even overseas ones (Gachamba, 1994). This has, however, fizzled out largely because of mismanagement. Bomas must diversify its activities and be run profitably. Such could include a hotel and leisure complex. Bomas sits in Nairobi as a national cultural icon which could be reinvigorated with a little imagination, planning and funding. It is for this reason that the public investments committee of Parliament recommended that Bomas be retained as a restructured institution rather than being privatized (Gachamba, 1994).

Catering Levy Trustees (CLT)

The CLT was created to marshal resources from hotels and restaurants so as to pay for training tourism and hospitality workers. The catering and accommodation establishments are required by law to remit a proportion of their receipts to CLT.

The trustees control and administer the fund; establish, equip and control institutions which train future hotel and restaurant staff; and may pay for the maintenance of such institutions and training fees for people under training. It appears that the CLT has focused on Utalii College to the exclusion of other institutions. This practice requires to be reviewed to the advantage of tourism and hospitality education in general. It is to be noted that the government has now agreed to convert the catering levy into a catering training and tourist development levy which will also provide reliable financing for the activities of the Kenya Tourism Board (*Weekly Review*, May 22, 1998, p.17).

Kenya Utalii College

Utalii college was established in 1973 to provide trained personnel in tourism. With a total capacity of 600 students, Utalii runs full-time courses in hotel management, food production, travel operations and tour guiding at certificate, associate diploma and diploma levels (Table A.5.1). In addition, Utalii organizes short in-service and refresher courses for personnel in industry, usually in the month of April each year when Kenya's international tourism is off-season.

As noted above, training expenses at Utalii are funded from a two percent levy charged on the incomes of hotels and restaurants. Although the Utalii programmes have contributed significantly to capacity building in the hotel accommodation section (Kenya, 1993), Utalii has been criticized as providing training for international tourist hotel service and management and ignoring small budget hotels which cater for domestic tourism (Kenya, 1983: 145; Sindiga, 1996c).

Table A.5.1
Tourism courses at Kenya Utalii College

Course	Duration (years)	Award
1. Hotel management	4	Diploma
2. Food production	2	Certificate
3. Food and beverages service and sales (basic)	1	Certificate
4. Food and beverages service and sales (advanced)	1	Certificate
5. Front office operations	2	Certificate
6. House-keeping and laundry	2	Certificate
7. Travel operations	2	Associate Diploma
8. Tour guide	2	Associate Diploma

Source: Kenya Utalii College, 1991

Yet it is the small and medium-sized hotels which offer the greatest promise in generating greater employment (Sindiga, 1994). Also, despite Utalii's efforts, 90 percent of the personnel in the tourism industry in Kenya are untrained (Sindiga, 1996c; Appendix 4). Further, except for the hotel management course which offers skills in management theory, most of Utalii's courses provide operational skills required in various departments of an accommodation facility and in travel and tour guiding. For example, the food production course trains cooks whereas the service and sales courses prepare waiters for restaurants; others are trained for house-keeping, laundry, reception and ticketing. This segmented training produces good operators in single departments; however, the graduates are unable to conceptualise the tourism industry as a whole (Sindiga, 1996c).

It appears that Utalii College, with the modern Utalii Hotel which acts as a training ground, are undergoing severe difficulties of lack of adequate accommodation for staff and students (JICA and Kenya, 1995d). Enrolment is far beyond the planned capacity and the teaching staff complement is very thin. The hotel is said to be in dire need of refurbishment (JICA and Kenya, 1995d).

African Tours and Hotels (AT&H)

AT&H was established as a private company in 1947. In the 1960s its board of directors comprised of two local Europeans and two Africans. It owned a number of hotel-related properties including Stag's Head Hotel, Nakuru, Namanga River Hotel, Hunters Lodge, College Inn in Nairobi and leased Kilaguni Lodge in Tsavo (NCCK, 1968: 70-71). Later, KTDC bought equity shares in the outfit and became the majority owner. Other shareholders are Kenya Airways and the Industrial Development Bank.

In the 1970s, AT&H owned up to 22 hotels and lodges in various parts of the country including areas where tourism was relatively underdeveloped (Sinclair, 1990). During the mid-1970s, AT&H expanded to provide both tours and accommodation. The future of the company is unclear as KTDC is divesting from many of the tourism enterprises. It is possible that AT&H which has accumulated expertise in hotel management and tour operations over the years, could itself be sold to private investors. It may be noted that AT&H is the only indigenously owned company in the tourism business with the capacity to manage hotels and tour operations.

Appendix 6: Private sector bodies in Kenya tourism

Kenya Association of Tour Operators (KATO)
KATO is a private organisation which represents the interests of tour operators in the country. The members are companies involved in the tour operations business. The organisation provides a forum for licensed operators, acts as a representative of tour operators, and promotes Kenya's tourism. Other objectives of KATO are to improve the standards of service by member companies, uphold the business ethics of the membership, and negotiate and make agreements aimed at improving tourism in Kenya.

KATO is run by a full time chief executive assisted by an executive committee of 10 members. In addition, it has 10 subcommittees representing various areas of interest to the organisation. These are marketing; security of tourists; transport; education, environment and ecotourism; regional facilitation and airport; tented safari operators; hotels and lodges; coast branch; and domestic tourism. KATO is concerned with various issues which affect tourism in Kenya. These include promotion and marketing, security of tourists, improvement of facilities and services, road conditions, involvement of local people in tourism, streamlining of formalities and clearance procedures at airports, standardisation of facilities and pricing, payments and cancellations, environmental problems, and social problems related to tourism (JICA and Kenya, 1995d; Sinclair, 1990). In its efforts to tackle these issues, KATO keeps regular contacts with government departments and especially the Ministry of Tourism and Wildlife (MTW).

Kenya Association of Travel Agents (KATA)
KATA is a voluntary association of travel agents in Kenya. Their role is to sell holiday packages and other services including car hire and excursions to tourists. Travel agents also sell airline tickets on behalf of various airlines represented in the country. It works closely with Kenya Airways. KATA represents the interests of its members and cooperates with various bodies including KATO, KAHC, MTW, Central Bank, Civil Aviation Board and Board of Airline Representatives.

Kenya Association of Hotel Keepers and Caterers (KAHC)
KAHC aims to encourage, promote and protect the interests of the proprietors and owners of hotels and restaurants. It brings together hotels and catering institutions, especially the large ones. The association is the representative of its members and as such acts as spokesperson, provides an information exchange network, promotes and protects good industrial relations and fosters good working relations between itself and workers' unions (JICA and Kenya, 1995d). The association takes up various issues affecting the tourism industry with government departments and allied bodies.

Kenya Budget Hotels Association (KBHA)
This body comprises of small and medium-size hotel establishments in Kenya. These hotels handle up to 70 percent of all domestic tourism business (Sindiga, 1996a). KBHA was formed as an expression of dissatisfaction of the behaviour of the big hotels in

fostering domestic tourism. The large hotels tended to work to promote their individual businesses rather than focusing on domestic tourism as a whole.

The KBHA aims to protect its members' interests and plays a major role in promoting domestic tourism (Kenya, 1994b: 74).

Mombasa and Coast Hotelkeepers Association (MCHA)
MCHA is a regional association based at the coast. Its aims and objectives are similar to those of KAHC.

Ecotourism Society of Kenya (ESK)[1]
ESK was formed in 1996 following several years of preparation work on the issue of sustainable tourism (for example, Gakahu and Goode, 1992). It is a not-for-profit organisation with the goal of achieving sustainable tourism through promoting environmental awareness and assisting community projects related to ecotourism, developing a standardized environmental audit to evaluate the tourism industry's commitment to environmental conservation and management, and publishing eco-tourism regulations and a code of conduct. The society was formed in the wake of environmental degradation in protected areas and at the coast and negative cultural influences associated with tourism. The ESK is expected to raise the level of awareness in conservation issues thereby minimizing the impact of tourism (Chapters 6 and 7). In addition, ESK is providing professional leadership and guidance in natural resources management. It is also leading the way in drawing up guidelines on the environmental impacts of tourism development.

The ESK has recently formed the "Ecotourism Partnership" as a commercial agency for promoting and implementing community-based wildlife tourism. A team of tourism industry and development professionals will provide investment, management and marketing skills to tourism projects in the country. Among the elements in ecotourism partners mission statement are the following:
- to offer a professional management and marketing service for ecotourism facilities in East Africa;
- to develop and promote innovative products at a profit according to ecotourism principles through a network of associates and partners;
- to focus on the following values in their work: satisfaction of guests, high quality products, a respect for the culture of host communities, social and economic development of host communities, promotion of Kenya as a high quality destination, sound financial management, giving fair returns to shareholders and other stake-holders, and integrity in dealings with various partners and associates (Reid *et al.*, 1998).

---

[1] Unless otherwise indicated, this section is drawn from unpublished documents of the ESK including conference notes of an ecotourism conference held in Nairobi, 27 October to 3 November 1997 under the title "Ecotourism at a Crossroads; Charting the way Forward", and ESK briefing notes prepared in 1997 and recorded in Reid *et al.* (1998).

In 1997, the ecotourism partnership programme was negotiating three projects which reflect its commitment to community-based tourism projects and sound natural resources management. These projects are as follows:

1. Northern Mara Conservation — to construct a luxury tented camp to provide revenue to the neighbouring communities to conserve the forest along the Mara river.
2. Shaba National Reserve — to develop a cultural centre, a museum and a tented camp to bring tourists in one of Kenya's most scenic areas.
3. Magadi Conservation Area — to work with community representatives to develop, manage and market this unique and undeveloped area for tourism.

The ESK recognises the role of the private sector in its work. As such it is taking a vital coordinating role in facilitating a working partnership between communities, conservationists, operators and financiers. In order for community-based ecotourism to be successful, it must be sustainable. Their definition of a successful community-based ecotourism enterprise is as follows: a sound business, commercially viable and with properly managed operations. The ESK encourages all partners to pursue profit making if ecotourism enterprises are to succeed.

The ESK has identified a number of obstacles to ecotourism development in Kenya. These include the absence of product development and lack of serious destination marketing; lack of key business skills, relating to marketing; management; and product design (Chapter 7). As part solution to these problems, the ESK is creating a partnership between communities, the conservation world and the private sector using new models of cooperation and development to encourage growth in viable ecotourism enterprises.

Appendix 7: Criteria for hotel classification in Kenya

	One star hotel	Two star hotel	Three star hotel	Four star hotel	Five star hotel
Location & building Site & environment	The building, its entrance and its location should be suitable for a hotel.	As for one star	The locality and environment including the outlook shall be suitable for a hotel.	The locality and environment including the outlook shall be suitable for a hotel of international standard.	The locality and environment including the outlook shall be suitable for a hotel of high international standard.
Capacity	The hotel should have at least 10 lettable bedrooms.	As for one star	As for one star	As for one star	As for one star
Lobby, lounge & other public area; Minimum size of public rooms	Minimum size of lobby/lounge, meeting rooms, bars and covered terrace should not be less than 1/2 sq.m per guest bed.	As for one star	Minimum size should be 1 sq.m per guest bed.	Minimum size should be 1 1/2 sq.m per guest bed.	Minimum size should be 2 sq.m per guest bed.
Conference & banquet rooms	Not required	One small meeting room with furniture to match the general standard of the hotel.	One large room with comfortable furniture and well maintained.	One large room and two small ones both carpeted, well lighted and maintained. furniture, furnishing and fittings to be of very good quality and P.A. system for the large room. High quality decoration except of vacation hotels which should be as for three stars.	One large room and two small rooms all carpeted, well lighted and maintained. Highest quality of furniture, furnishing, fittings and decoration. P.A. system for the larger room.
Restaurant features and facilities	One restaurant well furnished maintained, ventilated and lighted.	As for one star	As for one star not with a coffee shop or a snack bar in addition. Size of restaurant to be in proportion to the size of the hotels.	At least two restaurants including a grill room plus a coffee shop. Total seating capacity for town hotels and 100% for vacation hotels.	As for four stars but all high quality equipment. Where a la carte is applied, a gueridon service must be provided.

cont.>>>>

Appendix 7: Criteria for hotel classification in Kenya, cont.

	One star hotel	Two star hotel	Three star hotel	Four star hotel	Five star hotel
Guest room minimum size	Minimum size of bedrooms should be 12 sq.m.	Minimum size to be 15 sq.m.	Minimum size to be 15 sq.m.	Minimum size to be 18 sq.m.	Minimum size to be 18 sq.m.
Suites	Not required	Not required	At least 2% of town hotel or 1% of vacation rooms should be suites equipped with high quality furniture and fittings, wall-to-wall carpeting.	At least 3% of town hotel rooms and 2% of vacation hotel rooms should be suites in permanent set up. Very high quality furniture and fittings. Wall-to-wall carpeting, telephone extension should be provided in both sitting and bedrooms. Refrigerator should be provided. At least one executive suite.	At least 5% of town hotel rooms and 3% of vacation hotel rooms should be suites with the highest quality furniture fittings and furnishings. The suites must be in permanent set up with telephone extension in sitting and bedrooms. Refrigerator to be provided. At least two executive suites.
Bathroom Ratio of Rooms with private bathrooms	At least 75% of all the rooms should have private bathrooms and common bathrooms should be one for every three guest rooms.	At least 90% of all the rooms should have private bathrooms and common bathrooms should be one for every two guest rooms.	As two star	As two star	As two star
Size of bathrooms	Every bathroom should not be less than 3.5 sq.m.	As for one star	Size should not be less than 5 sq.m.	Size should not be less than 6 sq.m.	As for four stars
Hygiene & sanitation Refuse disposal	There should be refuse disposal system which meets the local health standards.	As for one star	As for one star	As for one star	As for one star
Sewage	All drainage must be connected to the sewage system of the town where applicable; where there is sewage system, it should be connected to septic tank of an approved size and soakage pit or any other approved form of effluent disposal.	As for one star	As for one star	As for one star	As for one star

cont.>>>>

Appendix 7: Criteria for hotel classification in Kenya, cont.

	One star hotel	Two star hotel	Three star hotel	Four star hotel	Five star hotel
Water supply	Drinking water must be properly treated if not from any an approved source.	As for one star	As for one star	As for one star	As for one star
Water storage	There should be enough storage capacity to last at least one day in case of a breakdown in supply.	The storage capacity should be for three days.	The storage capacity should be for five days.	The storage capacity should be for week.	As for four star
Telex facility	Not required	Not required	Telex facility available	As for three star	As for three star
Personnel ratio of staff to bed capacity	The ratio of staff to number of beds should be 0.6 to one.	The ratio should be 0.8 to one.	The ratio should be 0.9 to one for town, hotel, and 1.0 for vacation hotel.	The ratio should be 1.0 for town hotel, 1.2 for vacation hotel.	The ratio should be 1.2 for town hotel, 1.5 for vacation hotel.
Swimming pool	Not required	A swimming pool of adequate size should be provided for vacation hotel. Must be well maintained.	A swimming pool of adequate size should be provided for all categories. Must be well maintained.	Large swimming pool of not less than 100 sq.m for all categories. Must be well maintained. Should be of high standard of finishing.	As for four star
Health club	Not required	Not required	Not required	Well equipped sauna and gymnasium, steam bath whirlpool, Turkish bath and massage.	As for four stars but of high quality and an instructor for gymnasium.

Source: JICA and Kenya, 1995d: A-138

Appendix 8: Tourism and commercial sex in Kenya

As demonstrated in this study, tourism has a number of beneficial effects including foreign exchange earnings, government revenues through taxes, and employment of the local people. It is expected as well that tourism would proceed "without compromising cultural values or destroying the environment" (Kenya, 1985c: 140). Whereas studies have been undertaken to determine the impact of tourism on the environment especially in the national parks and the beaches (for example, Visser and Koyo, 1992; Gakahu, 1992), there is little systematic work on the effect of tourism on culture in Kenya. This is partly because data on the social dimensions of tourism are difficult to obtain. Moreover, government officials talk about the "dark side" or negative cultural impact of tourism in broad generalities, the aim being the preservation of tourist numbers by promoting the positive aspects and down-playing the negative ones. One so-called dark side is tourism-related female prostitution. Areas of tourism concentration in Kenya such as the coast appear to have attracted large numbers of prostitutes not only from the up-country regions, but also Uganda, Tanzania and other neighbouring countries (Wilson, 1980).

This appendix examines the relationship between tourism and commercial sex in Kenya with particular reference to the coast region. It discusses the landscapes of prostitution at the Kenya coast and considers the possible relationship between tourism and the incidence of sexually transmitted diseases (STDs) especially AIDS. Ultimately, it outlines proposals for further research in the areas of tourism and prostitution with a view to contributing to informed policy interventions. This analysis is necessary because prostitutes have been implicated to be major sources of the human immune deficiency syndrome or HIV/AIDS virus (Podhisita *et al.*, 1994). Indeed, female prostitutes in Africa suffer a high rate of and are more likely to contract various types of STDs than the general women population both because of unprotected sex and having multiple partners (Ngugi, 1995).

Context

Spatial population movement in human history, for whatever purpose, has long been associated with disease expansion (Prothero, 1961). Migrant labourers to areas of plantation agriculture and/or urban places in tropical Africa have been singled out for spreading malaria and STDs from their places of origin to destinations and vice versa. Long-distance truck drivers appear to be responsible for the spread of STDs especially AIDS along their routes of operation (Bwayo *et al.*, 1991b).

Before the onset of the AIDS pandemic there were few interdisciplinary studies on female prostitution in Africa. Over the past decade, however, there has been a plethora of research on prostitution and sexual networking. The purpose of such studies is to guide policy and behavioural interventions to arrest the rapid expansion of the HIV/AIDS virus.

Tourism provides ideal conditions for the spread of certain diseases. For example, in Thailand where large numbers of European and Japanese tourists go to seek commercial sex, STDs have reached epidemic proportions and the general population has a universal risk of infection regardless of age, sex, residence and occupation (Podhisita et al., 1994: 297). In general, men who travel without their wives for either a holiday, business, a conference, or to sell their labour may be tempted to purchase commercial sex from prostitutes (Bakwesegha, 1982: 96). For many tourists who go to developing countries, however, sex on its own is an important attraction (Leheny, 1995; Ryan and Kinder, 1996; Lea, 1993). As noted in Chapter 6, Kenya is considered a paradise for sex hunters. On their part, young women in search of money tend to migrate to those regions where there is a concentration of urban workers and tourists (Archavanitkul and Guest, 1994; Anarfi, 1993). In Kenya, both the coast and Nairobi have the largest concentrations of female prostitutes. They are also the major areas for HIV/AIDS infection. Are tourism and the spread of AIDS inter-linked?

Problems of data
The problems of data gathering on various aspects of prostitution including estimating the number at a given place have long been noted (Wilson, 1980). The Kenyan case is somewhat complex because commercial sex is officially disapproved and legally proscribed. This is not to say that prostitution does not take place. Rather, it is to recognize the difficulty of obtaining data on the extent and magnitude of prostitution and tourism-related commercial sex. This analysis is based on the available literature. It does not purport to provide definitive answers to the problem. The purpose is to offer pointers to further research in an important area. Throughout the study, the term tourist is seen in its widest sense and includes truck drivers.

Prostitutes/commercial sex workers: the definitional problem
Although many people can recognise prostitution, few can meaningfully describe the phenomenon. To some people, a prostitute is regarded as a man or a woman who has multiple sex partners. Such a definition may not, however, be defended in Africa and elsewhere where polygyny is accepted. There are many people, for example students, soldiers, truck drivers and others in society who habitually keep many sex partners but are not regarded as prostitutes (Sindiga and Lukhando, 1993).

Different writers on prostitution define their subject in varied ways (Muga, 1980: 7). Many authors agree that prostitution involves the exchange of sexual services with money or some other material gain over the short term at a given place (Muga, 1980; Harrison, 1994). A prostitute may be taken to be a person (male or female) with certain characteristics. These are as follows: a desire for immediate or delayed monetary and/or other material payments in exchange for a sexual experience; and a tendency to discriminate among prospective clients in order to maximize on benefits (Bakwesegha, 1982: 5). Thus a prostitute will pick the highest paying client at a given time. Although some tourists choose to interact with their hosts through commercial sex, prostitution and tourism need not go together (Harrison, 1994: 36).

There is no doubt that the pecuniary consideration is the primary motive for prostitution. Few commercial sex workers want to create enduring relationships with their clients. Generally, there is no emotional involvement between the parties in commercial sex (Pruitt and La Font, 1995: 423). This might appear ironic to those who are familiar with the behaviour of many Kenyan prostitutes at the coast. A number of them have created liaisons especially with their white clients which end up in "marriage" and an airticket to Europe. It is clear from interviews with female prostitutes at the coast that the women who go to Europe are motivated by the image of the affluent Western world where they can make quick money, part of which they can remit to support their families in Kenya (Mwakisha, 1995). To their chagrin, many of those who land in Germany or Italy are quickly "divorced".[1] Disowned and penniless, these women are said to be sexually abused by gangs of men; some of them are trapped in brothels abroad as commercial sex workers (Mwakisha, 1995).

Although prostitution is recognised as a social problem, it does not appear to be outlawed in Kenya. As such there is no legal definition of the term prostitution. According to Chapter 63, Section 154 of the Laws of Kenya, prostitution per se is not illegal; however, living off earnings from prostitution is a crime. The relevant provision of the law reads as follows:

> Every woman who knowingly lives wholly or in part on the earnings of prostitution, or who is proved to have, for the purposes of gain, exercised control, direction or influence over the movements of a prostitute in such a manner as to show that she is aiding, abetting or compelling her prostitution with any person or generally, is guilty of a misdemeanor.

Unfortunately, the Kenya law holds only women to be prostitutes. This is inequitable. However, the Laws of Kenya also prohibit men from soliciting or living on such earnings in the same terms as women. It is not clear why there is secondary application of the law to men. As homosexuality is considered an unnatural act under the laws of Kenya, this probably means that pimping is punishable under that law as a misdemeanor.

Those familiar with the Kenyan mass media will, however, be surprised to learn that prostitution is not illegal in the country. There are frequent reports of police swooping of alleged prostitutes in the major urban areas. Such individuals are usually arraigned before courts of law; however these women are never accused of practising prostitution. Rather, they are charged with vagrancy. Sometimes they are taken to medical laboratories to undergo tests for STDs. This reflects a lacuna in the law on this matter. Similar to Kenya, the laws of Uganda have no clear provisions on prostitution (Bakwesegha, 1982). The Ugandan statute is written in virtually the same words as the Kenya one, a relic of the two countries' colonial past under British hegemony.

Perhaps an intriguing observation to be made about criminalizing earnings from prostitution is the fact that such resources both in Kenya and abroad may be critical for the survival of a prostitute's family. Many Kenyan female prostitutes already have children by the time they enter the trade. Such children are left with their families to whom periodic remittances are made to support them. Archavanitkul and Guest (1994) show that in Thailand, sex workers make relatively high incomes and remit large proportions to their families thereby improving the standards of living. For such women, prostitution is an economic strategy for earning a decent living.

---

[1] As noted in Chapter 4, the preponderant number of tourists to the Kenya coast are Germans and Italians, among other groups.

The fact that there is no clear official definition of prostitution in Kenya means that there are no statistics on commercial sex workers. Yet prostitution and even commercial homosexuality and lesbianism are said to be practised by tourists (Mwangi 1995). With these limitations, the present study is an attempt to focus on an increasingly important problem.

Landscapes of prostitution at the coast

As noted in Chapter 6, female prostitution appears to be a problem at the coast and up-country centres of tourism activity. By nightfall, Kenya's large towns see the movement of female prostitutes from their hide-outs into the streets, bars, and hotels where tourists and the well-to-do in society go for a drink. Many female bar attendants are seen, rightly or wrongly, as part-time hawkers of sex to supplement their small incomes. Western tourists tend to be prime targets of the prostitutes because they are believed to pay more for sexual services. The local geography of tourism then reflects that of female prostitutes. Although quantitative data are unavailable, a qualitative rendering of the landscapes of prostitution may be provided. The centres of commercial sex workers can be viewed along a continuum from areas of least to most prostitution. The areas with least prostitution are Diani Beach hotels to the south of Mombasa and Lamu whereas the most prostitution is in Mombasa and Malindi-Watamu (Bachmann, 1988; Migot-Adholla et al., 1982). What is the accounting for these differences?

Areas of least prostitution
A mix of factors including type of tourism, distance from the main centres of the population and social geography may explain the pattern of prostitution. In the south coast, particularly Diani, hotel accommodation is expensive. This is a quiet area which attracts British, German and Italian tourists who prefer to relax on the beach with some swimming and in-house entertainment. Diani is also a relatively crime-free area partly because it is located some 30 kilometres from Mombasa. In addition, hotel development in Diani is relatively recent and goes back less than thirty years. As such the developers were able to discourage the construction of lodging houses around their properties. The absence of slum development discouraged the settlement of up-country people and hence the prostitute population (Migot-Adholla et al., 1982). Further, the local population in the Diani neighbourhood is the Muslim Digo. The gender roles and social segmentation of the coast societies largely excludes women from economic, political and religious realms (Guennec-Coppens, 1984: 15). Islamic tenets do not allow women to work directly with tourists. Also, the traditions of the coast people, both Muslim and non-Muslim impose restrictions on teenage girls. Writing on Lamu women, Guennec-Coppens (1994: 29) notes as follows:

> The status of young girls is ... demanding with numerous restrictions and constraints, numerous domestic tasks aimed at preparing them for married life. On the other hand, taking into account the virginity cult and the severe, even jealous control the elders exercise over the young girls, it is easier to understand why young girls wish to marry, this being the only access to some degree of liberty.

Women are "free" to participate in community activities only after marriage. Most girl children are not taken to school. The few who go to school tend to drop out even before completing eight years of basic education and get married. This removes them from potential prostitution. The apparent void in commercial sex workers has tended to attract up-country women to the coast.

This is, however, not to suggest that Swahili women are not involved in prostitution; they are. The high level of marriage instability among the Waswahili women as shown by the high rate of divorce provides a recipe for personal economic instability. Data from about a decade and a half ago showed an average figure of seventy three divorces for every one hundred marriages every year suggesting a very high rate of conjugal instability (Guennec-Coppens, 1984: 21). However, this provides the women with partial escape from male control and greater physical mobility. At a further remove, marriage instability may provide a pool of women, some of whom may go into prostitution. Nevertheless, there are unmarried Waswahili women in the trade as well (Beckerleg, 1995).

Lamu is a Muslim town with Islamic traditions going back to the 8th century A.D. Lamu long remained the seat of Islamic conservatism and orthodoxy (Salim, 1973: 152). It is still considered to be the centre of Islamic teachings at the coast. Each year, Muslim pilgrims from Kenya and other parts of East Africa go to Lamu for the celebrations of the birth of the Prophet Mohammed, *Maulidi*. In a tourism sense, however, Lamu is an outpost of Malindi and Mombasa. One day excursionists fly to Lamu to enjoy its varied attractions (Musyoki, 1994). Although Lamu has several tourist attractions including dhow trips, small islands, mangrove swamps, plenty of sea life, and a myriad historical sites and monuments, its tourism facilities are relatively undeveloped.

As a centre of Islamic culture at the coast, Lamu betrays little evidence of overt prostitution:

> Women stay in their homes as much as possible, but when they do emerge into public view, especially in the evenings, they stroll shyly through the streets, covered from top to toe in the traditional black robes or *buibui* ... Lamu women dress in colourful Middle Eastern and Asian clothes concealed by the *buibui* (Musyoki 1994: 12).

And as Françoise le Guennec-Coppens (1984) confirmed after five years of research in Lamu, women's behaviour is still little affected by the increasing numbers of tourists each year. This behaviour and manner of Muslim women are very different from what is seen among the immigrant women at Mombasa and Malindi-Watamu. This latter group puts on unmistakable behaviour as to its intention through dress and its suggestive manner.

Since Lamu does not attract mass tourism, prostitution is less evident. Also, it appears that the Islamic prohibition of alcohol "is still strictly applied in Lamu restaurants, even against European tourists trying to by-pass the order" (Musyoki, 1994: 21). It is not clear who gave the "order" but Musyoki further claims that Lamu successfully fought against indecent dressing, homosexuality involving young boys, and drug consumption by white travellers in the 1970s. These actions of the Lamu community against some of the negative cultural effects of tourism reflect Lamu's standing as a citadel of Islamic scholarship and conservatism on the East African coast.

Areas of most prostitution

The areas of most prostitution in Mombasa and Malindi-Watamu are also associated with other vices such as violence, robbery, drug peddling, and alcoholism (Beckerleg, 1995; Migot-Adholla *et al.*, 1982: 36). Mombasa and Malindi-Watamu are the centres for mass tourism and this may explain the relatively high levels of female prostitution; some of the tourists tend to interact with local people at destination areas through commercial sex (Bachmann, 1988: 207; Ryan and Kinder, 1996). Also, Mombasa attracts many different groups of tourists. In turn, the presence of these tourists has encouraged large numbers of immigrant female sex workers. In a sense, tourism encourages overt prostitution. Among the tourists are long-haul air passengers who go for their holidays, shipping crews and passengers, long-distance truck drivers from other countries in East and Central Africa, and domestic tourists. Tourists are much sought after by Mombasa prostitutes. It is not uncommon, for example, to see prostitutes in Mombasa hotels reading shipping supplements in national newspapers and checking on expected ships at the port. Once a ship has docked at harbour, hordes of prostitutes emerge conspicuously along Kilindini Road and Moi Avenue to target their prey.

The immigrant population forms the core of Mombasa's female prostitutes. A study of prostitutes in Mombasa a few decades ago found the majority of the African prostitutes in the town to be Ugandans followed by groups from Kenya's interior (Wilson, 1980: 132). However, a 1969 study covering Mombasa bar-girls revealed that 58 percent (N=50) were Kikuyu and Kamba (Rutasitara, 1980: 153). And in Watamu village, where there is high level prostitution, 80 percent of the village population was made up of up-country immigrants (Migot-Adholla *et al.*, 1982: 36). Recent reports suggest that prostitution continues to be high at Watamu and Malindi and that up-country women form the largest proportion (Mwakisha, 1995; Beckerleg, 1995).

As noted above, younger prostitutes, especially those in their teenage years, are most sought after and attract higher payments from male clients. This is not to say that the older and experienced prostitutes quit the scene. Rather, they turn into female pimps to manage and promote the younger prostitutes. In this role, the older prostitutes recruit younger girls, usually from their home villages thereby assuring their income. As pimps, the older women also provide security to the younger ones in the new, often rough terrain of female prostitution.

Emergence of the landscape of AIDS

In the 1980s the AIDS pandemic emerged at the Kenya coast. This was probably associated with the presence of thousands of prostitutes who were attracted to the coast by tourism. AIDS was first identified in Kenya in 1984. The question of the origins of AIDS is steeped in controversy. Was HIV present in some part of Africa before the 1980s? What appears to be clear is that the emergence of the AIDS pandemic in tropical

Africa and almost simultaneously elsewhere in the world "was definitely a new and fast moving epidemic" (Caldwell and Caldwell, 1994: 197).

By August 1993, some 39,000 cases had been diagnosed with full-blown AIDS in Kenya, (Kenya 1994c: 261). This figure rose to 63,000 in 1995 indicating an alarming expansion of the pandemic (Kenya, 1997: 156). However, the total number of AIDS cases was believed to be three times as high because of the difficulties of reporting and diagnosis in the country. By 1993, 841,700 people were estimated to be HIV-positive, out of whom 30,000 were children. The HIV positive population was expected to rise from 448,000 in 1990 to one million in 1995 (Kenya, 1997: 156). In the absence of a comprehensive intervention programme, the current prevalence rate of 7 percent will rise to 10 percent by 2000 (Kenya, 1997: 156).

The Kenya coast which is a popular tourism destination also has the largest concentration of the AIDS cases. Of the 1995 cases, 27.2 percent were from Coast Province (Kenya, 1995b). Some 75 percent of the HIV/AIDS is transmitted through sex between males and females (Kenya 1994c: 262) and female prostitutes and their clients are the largest pool of HIV infection (Bwayo *et al.*, 1991b). Prostitution is central in sustaining a core of people with HIV (Caldwell and Caldwell, 1994: 205). As noted, the Kenya coast and Nairobi attract many tourists as well. The convergence of sex tourism and female prostitution results into sexually transmitted diseases.

A special category of tourists to the Kenya coast concern truck drivers operating from the neighbouring countries of Uganda, Sudan, Congo (Kishasa), Rwanda and Burundi. Truck drivers are a highly mobile group; in addition, they spend many days away from their families and have multiple sex partners along their routes of operation (Bwayo *et al*, 1991b). In a study of truck drivers in transit from Mombasa to destinations within east and central Africa, 61 percent admitted to visiting prostitutes (Bwayo *et al.*, 1991a). However, only one-third of this group "had ever used condoms with less than one percent who always used condoms with other sex partners" (p. 717). In yet another study of long distance truck drivers and their assistants, 26 percent were HIV-positive (N=276) (Mbugua *et al*, 1995). All the study subjects were sexually active with no reported cases of homosexuality and intravenous drug use. These truck drivers may be one of the groups contributing to increasing HIV infection rates in rural areas.

Disaggregated data on AIDS in the coast also show that the incidence of the disease varies within the province. The preponderant number of the cases are in Mombasa, which is also a centre for mass tourists, truck drivers and female prostitutes. This conjunction could lead to the expansion of HIV/AIDS. The next ranking in the number of cases are Taita Taveta and Kilifi Districts, both of which are tourist destinations. Malindi-Watamu is in Kilifi whereas Tsavo National Park traverses Taita Taveta. Predictably, Lamu and Kwale have comparatively fewer cases of AIDS. Both have a very strong Islamic culture and relatively small numbers of up-country immigrants who ordinarily provide the pool of female prostitutes at the coast. The exclusive Diani Beach hotels are in Kwale.

The presence of large numbers of people with risky behaviour towards HIV/AIDS (prostitutes, tourists and truck drivers) at the coast could further increase the probability of high prevalence rates of the disease in the general population. This could lead to a high infant and child mortality rate, and reduce life expectancy significantly, thereby threatening the labour force base of the country. According to Beckerleg (1995: 26), the AIDS pandemic at the coast appears to have had "little impact on either the supply or demand side of the tourist-led sex industry", especially at Watamu. A number of prostitutes have died of AIDS and blood tests on patients in Kilifi show a 5 to 10 percent HIV positive rate in the district (Beckerleg, 1995).

Conclusions

This section has shown that the locales of mass tourism at the coast, that is Mombasa Island and Malindi-Watamu are areas of high levels of prostitution. Most of the commercial sex workers are women from up-country seeking to make money from tourists. Most of the AIDS cases have been diagnosed in Mombasa District. Here, Western tourists, sailors, occasional American and British soldiers, truck drivers, and city workers converge. It is clear that the high population of prostitutes which is attracted to Mombasa by the presence of tourists provides a large reservoir for the HIV/AIDS virus.

There is demand for commercial sex among most groups of tourists and the urban population. This demand encourages the circulation of women from other regions. Although it is generally agreed that poverty sends women to prostitution, some scholars see it as an alternative economic strategy for higher earnings and a better standard of living (Pickering and Wilkins, 1993). This appears to be the case with coast prostitutes. Despite the knowledge that female prostitutes are a high risk group for AIDS transmission there appears to be no policy to deal with the matter. However the Kenya government recognizes that AIDS is more than a health problem and has economic, social and cultural elements (Kenya, 1997: 156). Interventions focused on groups such as commercial sex workers are more likely to be effective in AIDS prevention (Sindiga and Lukhando, 1993).

This concluding section raises a number of unanswered questions on the issue of tourism and prostitution at the Kenya coast. As such, an agenda and proposals for further research are provided. First, empirical data are required on the extent and magnitude of female prostitution at the coast. This will add detail to the picture painted in the present study of areas of most and least prostitution. Second, data are needed on the profiles of the female prostitutes. This study has established that the majority of the prostitutes are not natives of the coast. However, there is little knowledge on what motivates them to take up commercial sex work. Do they see it as a viable economic alternative or are they pushed into it by poverty in rural Kenya? Besides, it is necessary to find out the personal characteristics of the prostitutes — education, age, religion, family background and so on. Third, data are required on the categories of prostitutes and how they are organized including sexual networking, and self- and group-preservation. For example, commercial sex workers in Nairobi have already demanded that their trade be legalised and accepted in society although this has received some opposition from members of the public (Ngesa and Wachie, 1996: 7). However, obtaining field data on prostitution is not always an easy task. Prostitutes come in all categories; there are those who openly sell sex to any man who can pay a prescribed price, others sell sex selectively to influential men in society, still others periodically sell sex privately, yet there are those who complement petty trade with prostitution and so on (Pickering and Wilkins, 1993: 17-18 citing Comhaire-Sylvain, 1968). Nevertheless, careful fieldwork involving survey strategies and in-depth interviews could yield data on this subject. Fourth, there is need to determine the demand for commercial sex by different groups of tourists at the Kenya coast. Fifth, the impact of tourism on the level of prostitution and vice versa requires further inquiry. This is because prostitution as a source of income offers a very unstable livelihood and a myriad risks (Leheny, 1995). And now, more than ever before, prostitution provides grave risks through the AIDS pandemic. This is likely to affect the relationship and interaction between sex-seeking tourists and their hosts in the future. Sixth, the lacuna both in ordinary and legal definition on what constitutes prostitution or commercial sex should be investigated with a view to policy reform. This uncertainty must be clarified, especially because of the medical association of prostitution with HIV/AIDS. Finally, it may be emphasized that prostitution at the coast did not start with tourism. However, open competition for clients and suggestive dressing are associated with tourism. Also, it is clear that most prostitutes specifically target white tourists because they are believed to pay handsomely for sexual services.

References

ACHEBE, CHINUA (1984),*The Trouble with Nigeria*. Nairobi: Heinemann Kenya

ADAMS, W.M. (1996), Irrigation, Erosion and Famine: Visions of Environmental Change in Marakwet, Kenya. *The Lie of the Land: Challenging Received Wisdom on the African Environment*. Edited by Melissa Leach and Robin Mearns. London: International African Institute, 155-167.

AFRICA WATCH (1991), *Kenya: Taking Liberties*. New York: Africa Watch.

AKAMA, JOHN SORANA (1996), Western Environmental Values and Nature-Based Tourism in Kenya. *Tourism Management*, Vol. 17 No. 8: 567-574

AKAMA, JOHN SORANA (n.d.), *Wildlife Conservation in Kenya: A Political-Ecological Analysis of Nairobi and Tsavo-Regions*. Washington D.C.: African Development Foundation.

AKAMA, JOHN S., CHRISTOPHER L. LANT AND G. WESLEY BURNETT (1995), Conflicting Attitudes Towards State Wildlife Conservation Programs in Kenya. *Society and Natural Resources*, Vol. 8: 133-144.

ANARFI, JOHN K (1993), Sexuality, Migration and AIDS in Ghana — A Socio-behavioural Study. *Health Transition Review*, Vol. 3 Supplement Issue: 45-67.

ANDERSON, DAVID AND RICHARD GROVE (1987), The Scramble for Eden: Past, Present and Future in African Conservation. *Conservation in Africa: People, Policies and Practice*. Edited by David Anderson and Richard Grove. Cambridge: Cambridge University Press, 1-12.

ANKOMAH, PAUL K. (1991), Tourism Skilled Labor: The Case of Sub-Saharan Africa. *Annals of Tourism Research*, Vol. 18: 433-442.

ARCHAVANITKUL, KRITAYA AND PHILIP GUEST (1994), Migration and the Commercial Sex Sector in Thailand. *Health Transition Review*, Supplement to Vol. 4: 273-295.

ASANTE, S.K.B. (1990), Regional Economic Cooperation and Integration: The Experience of ECOWAS. *Regional Integration in Africa: Unfinished Agenda*. Edited by Anyang' Nyong'o. Nairobi: Academy Science Publishers, 99-138.

ASHLEY, CAROLINE (1995), Tourism, Communities, and the Potential Impacts on Local Incomes and Conservation. Research Discussion Paper No. 10. Windhoek: Directorate of Environmental Affairs, Ministry of Environment and Tourism.

ASHLEY, CAROLINE AND ELIZABETH GARLAND (1994), Promoting Community-Based Development: Why, What and How? Research Discussion Paper No. 4. Windhoek: Directorate of Environmental Affairs, Ministry of Environment and Tourism.

ASMAH, GEORGE FRANK (1997), Ghana Goes for the Afro Tourists. *New African*, No. 351 (April), p.33.

AUSTRALIA, COMMONWEALTH OF (1994), *National Ecotourism Strategy*. Canberra: Commonwealth Department of Tourism.

BACHMANN, PHILIPP (1988), *Tourism in Kenya: A Basic Need for Whom?* European University Studies Vol. 10. Berne: Peter Lang.

BAKWESEGHA, CHRISTOPHER J. (1982), *Profiles of Urban Prostitution: A Case Study from Uganda*. Nairobi: Kenya Literature Bureau.

BECKERLEG, SUSAN (1995), 'Brown Sugar' or Friday Prayers: Youth Choices and Community Building in Coastal Kenya. *African Affairs*, Vol. 94 No. 374: 23-38.

BERGER, DHYANI J. (1993), *Wildlife Extension: Participatory Conservation by the Maasai of Kenya*. Nairobi: Acts Press.

BISLETH, OLE AND LINE HOLST JENSEN (1995), Green Qualifications and Responsible Tourism. Copenhagen: Folkelight Oplysnings Forbund, Landorganisationen.

BOO, ELIZABETH (1990), *Ecotourism: The Potentials and Pitfalls Volume 1*. Washington D.C.: World Wildlife Fund.

BOYD, J. BARRON, JR. (1985), A subsystemic Analysis of the Southern African Development Coordination Conference. *African Studies Review*, Vol. 28 No. 4: 46-61.

BRADSHAW, YORK W., PAUL J. KAISER AND STEPHEN N. NDEGWA (1995), Rethinking Theoretical and Methodological Approaches to the Study of African Development. *African Studies Review*, Vol. 38 No. 2: 39-65.

BRETT, E.A. (1973), *Colonialism and Underdevelopment in East Africa*. London: Heinemann.

BRETT, E.A. (1996), The Participatory Principle in Development Projects: The Costs and Benefits of Cooperation. *Public Administration and Development*, Vol. 16 No. 1: 5-19.

BRITTON, STEPHEN G. (1982), The Political Economy of Tourism in the Third World. *Annals of Tourism Research*, Vol. 9: 331-358.

BROHMAN, JOHN (1996), New Directions in Tourism for Third World Development. *Annals of Tourism Research*, Vol. 23 No. 1: 48-70.

BRULE, CHRISTIAN (1988), Drugs and Drug Addiction in Africa. *Courier*, No. 112: 12-13.

BRUNER, EDWARD M. AND BARBARA KIRSHENBLATT-GIMBLETT (1994), Maasai on the Lawn: Tourist Realism in East Africa. *Cultural Anthropology*, Vol. 9 No. 4: 435-470.

BURNETT, G. WESLEY AND R. CONOVER (1989), The Efficacy of Africa's National Parks: An Evaluation of Julius Nyerere's Arusha Manifesto of 1961. *Society and Natural Resources*, Vol. 2: 251-260.

BUTLER, RICHARD (1992), Alternative Tourism: The Thin Edge of the Wedge. *Tourism Alternatives: Potentials and Problems in the Development of Tourism*. Edited by Valene L. Smith and William R. Eadington. Philadelphia: University of Pennsylvania Press, 31-46.

BWAYO, J.J., A.N. MUTERE, M.A OMARI, J.K. KREISS, W. JAOKO, C. SOKKADE-KIGONDU AND F.A. PLUMMER (1991a), Long Distance Truck Drivers 2: Knowledge and Attitudes Concerning Sexually Transmitted Diseases and Sexual Behaviour. *East African Medical Journal*, Vol. 68 No. 9: 714-719.

BWAYO, J.J., A.M. OMARI, A.N. MUTERE, W. JAOKO, C. SEKKADE-KIGONDU, J. KREISS AND F.A. PLUMMER (1991b), Long Distance Truck Drivers 1: Prevalence of Sexually Transmitted Diseases (STDs). *East African Medical Journal*, Vol. 68 No. 6: 425-429.

CALDWELL, JOHN C. AND PAT CALDWELL (1994), The Nature and Limits of the Sub-Saharan African AIDS Epidemic: Evidence from Geographic and other Patterns. *Sexual Networking and AIDS in Sub-Saharan Africa: Behavioural Research and the Social Context*. Edited by I. O. Orubuloye, J.C. Caldwell, P. Caldwell and G. Santow. Canberra: Australian National University, 195-216.

CAMPBELL, T. LEANNE. (1990), The Gambian Experience. *Ghana Tourism: Prospects and Possibilities*. Edited by Robert W. Wyllie. Accra: Akan-Torede, 31-52.

CATER, ERLET A. (1987), Tourism in the Least Developed Countries. *Annals of Tourism Research*, Vol. 14: 202-226.

CATER, ERLET (1994), Ecotourism in the Third World-Problems and Prospects for Sustainablity. *Ecotourism: A Sustainable Option?* Edited by E. Cater and G. Lowman. West Sussex: John Wiley and Sons Ltd., 69-86.

CHEGE, MICHAEL (1997), Paradigms of Doom and the Development Management Crisis in Kenya. *Journal of Development Studies*, Vol. 33 No. 4: 552-567.

CHRISTIAN AID (1995), *An Abuse of Innocence: Tourism and Child Prostitution in the Third World*. London: Christian Aid.

COOPER, FREDERICK (1991), Africa and the World Economy. *African Studies Review*, Vol. XXIV Nos 2/3: 1-86.

COPPOCK, J.T. (1977), Tourism as a Tool for Regional Development. Tourism: A Tool for Regional Development. Proceedings of the Leisure Studies Association Conference held in Edinburgh 1977. Edited by Brian S. Duffield. Eastbourne: University of Brighton, 1-13.

COURIER, THE (1988), *The Courier*, No. 112 (November-December 1988).

CROZE, HARVEY AND D.M. MBUVI (1981), Wildlife in the Development of Dry Lands. The Development of Kenya's Semi-Arid Lands. Edited by D. J. Campbell and S.E. Migot-Adholla, IDS Occasional Papers No. 36. Nairobi: Institute for Development Studies, University of Nairobi, 186-200.

CRUSH, JONATHAN, AND PAUL WELLINGS (1983), The Southern African Pleasure Periphery, 1966-83. *Journal of Modern African Studies*, Vol. 21 No. 4: 673-698.

CURRY, STEVE (1982), The Terms of Trade and Real Import Capacity of the Tourism Sector in Tanzania. *Journal of Development Studies*, Vol. 18 No. 4: 479-496.

CURRY, STEVE (1990), Tourism Development in Tanzania. *Annals of Tourism Research*, Vol. 17: 133-149.

DARTNALL, JEAN AND RON STORE (1990), The Literature of Tourism. *Journal of Tourism Studies*, Vol. 1 No. 1: 49-53.

DE KADT, EMANUEL, ed. (1979), Tourism: Passport to Development? *Perspectives on the Social and Cultural Effects of Tourism in Developing Countries*. New York: Oxford University Press.

DE SOUZA, ANTHONY R. AND PHILIP W. PORTER (1974), *The Underdevelopment and Modernization of the Third World*. Commission on College Geography Resource Paper No. 28. Washington D.C.: Association of American Geographers.

DIEKE, PETER U.C. (1991), Policies for Tourism Development in Kenya. *Annals of Tourism Research*, Vol. 18: 260-294.

DIEKE, PETER U.C. (1993a), Tourism and Development Policy in the Gambia. *Annals of Tourism Research*, Vol. 20 No. 3: 423-449.

DIEKE, PETER U.C. (1993b), Tourism Policy and Employment in the Gambia. Employee Relations, Vol. 15: 71-80.

DIEKE, PETER U.C. (1993c), Cross-National Comparison of Tourism Development: Lessons from Kenya and the Gambia. *Journal of Tourism Studies*, Vol. 4 No. 1:2-18.

DIEKE, PETER U.C. (1994), The Political Economy of Tourism in the Gambia. *Review of African Political Economy,* Vol. 21 No. 62: 611-627.

DIEKE, PETER U.C. (1995), Tourism and Structural Adjustment Programmes in the African Economy. *Tourism Economics*, Vol. 1 No. 1: 71-93.

DIEKE, PETER U.C. (1997), Overview of Tourism in Africa. OAU/AEC 7th All-Africa Trade and Tourism Fair-Conference on Promotion of Tourism in Africa, April 3, 1997, Kaduna, Nigeria. Glasgow: The Scottish Hotel School.

DIEKE, PETER U.C. (1998), Regional Tourism in Africa: Scope and Critical Issues. *Embracing and Managing Change in Tourism: International Case Studies*. Edited by E.Laws, B. Faulkner and G. Moscardo. London and New York: Routledge, 29-48.

DIETVORST, A.G.J. AND G.J. ASHWORTH (1995), Tourism Transformations: An Introduction. *Tourism and Spatial Transformations*. Edited by G.J. Ashworth and A.G.J. Dietvorst. Wallingford: CAB International, 1-12.

DOUGHERTY, N. (1994), Meru National Park: A True Wilderness. *Swara*, Vol. 17 No. 4: 17-19.

EADINGTON, WILLIAM R. AND VALENE L. SMITH (1992), Introduction: The Emergence of Alternative Forms of Tourism. *Tourism Alternatives: Potentials and Problems in the Development of Tourism*. Edited by Valene L. Smith and William R. Eadington. Philadelphia: University of Pennsylvania Press, 1.12.

EAST AFRICAN (1998), The East African Community: Draft Treaty. *East African*, June 1-7, 1998, pp.12, 14-17.

EAST AFRICAN STANDARD (1998), Tourism Earnings Fall: Board Blames Coast Violence. *East African Standard Business and Finance*, January 6, 1998, p.7.

EASTMAN C.M. (1995), Tourism in Kenya and the Marginalization of Swahili. *Annals of Tourism Research*, Vol. 22 No. 1: 172-185.

ECONOMIST INTELLIGENCE UNIT (1991), EIU International Tourism Reports No. 2: Kenya. London: EIU.

EDWARDS, K.A. (1981), Soil and Water Conservation in Semi-Arid Areas. The Development of Kenya's Semi-Arid Lands. Edited by David J. Campbell and S.E. Migot-Adholla. IDS Occasional Papers No. 36. Nairobi: Institute for Development Studies, University of Nairobi, 84-101.

ELIOT, C. (1966), *The East Africa Protectorate*. London: Frank Cass (First Published in 1905).

ELKAN, WALTER (1975), The Relation Between Tourism and Employment in Kenya and Tanzania. *Journal of Development Studies*, Vol. 11 No. 2: 123-130.

ELLIS, STEPHEN AND JANET MACGAFFEY (1996), Research on Sub-Saharan Africa's Unrecorded International Trade: Some Methodological and Conceptual Problems. *African Studies Review*, Vol. 39 No. 2: 19-41.

FAIR, DENIS (1996), East African Tourist Trends. *Africa Insight*, Vol. 26 No. 2: 156-161.

FARVER, JO ANN (1984), Tourism and Employment in the Gambia. *Annals of Tourism Research*, Vol. 11: 249-265.

FRIEDMANN, JOHN (1992), *Empowerment: The Politics of Alternative Development*. Cambridge, Massachusetts: Blackwell.

GACHAMBA, CHEGE WA. (1994), Bomas is Slowly Dancing to a Halt. *Daily Nation* (Nairobi), July 8, Weekender Magazine.

GAKAHU, C.G. ED. (1992), *Tourist Attitudes and Use Impacts in Maasai Mara National Reserve*. Nairobi: Wildlife Conservation International.

GAKAHU, CHRIS G. (1992), Participation of Local Communities in Ecotourism: Rights, Roles and Socio-Economic Benefits. *Ecotourism and Sustainable Development in Kenya*. Edited by C.G. Gakahu and B.E. Goode, Nairobi: Wildlife Conservation International, 117-123.

GAKAHU, C.G. AND B.E. GOODE. EDS. (1992), *Ecotourism and Sustainable Development in Kenya*. Nairobi: Wildlife Conservation International.

GAMBLE, W.P. (1989), *Tourism and Development in Africa*. London: John Murray.

GANT, ROBERT AND JOSE SMITH (1992), Tourism and National Development Planning in Tunisia. *Tourism Management*, Vol. 13 No. 3: 331-336.

GARDNER R. AND R. BLACKBURN (1996), People Who Move: New Reproductive Health Focus. *Population Reports* series J, No.45. Baltimore: Johns Hopkins School of Public Health, Population Information Programme.

GAYE, ADAMA (1998), What African Renaissance? *Newsweek*, Vol. CXXXI No. 24. June 15, 1998, p. 2.

GRABURN, NELSON H.H. (1977), Tourism: The Sacred Journey. *Hosts and Guests: The Anthropology of Tourism*. Edited by Valene L. Smith. Philadelphia: University of Pennsylvania Press, 17-31.

GREEN, REGINALD HERBOLD (1979), Toward Planning Tourism in African Countries. *Tourism: Passport to Development?* Edited by Emanuel de Kadt. New York: Oxford, 79-100.

GREEN, REGINALD HERBOLD (1994), Foreword. *Economic Cooperation in Africa: In Search of Direction* by Ahmad A.H.M. Aly. Boulder and London: Lynne Rienner Publishers, viii-xii.

GUENNEC-COPPENS, FRANÇOISE LE (1984), The Feminine Society in Lamu. *Bulletin de Liaison*, Issue 13: 13-37.

GUNN, CLARE A. (1988), *Tourism Planning*. New York: Taylor and Francis.

HALL, DEREK R. (1992), Tourism Development in Cuba. *Tourism and the Less Developed Countries*. Edited by David Harrison. London: Belhaven Press, 102-120.

HARRELL-BOND, B.E. AND D.L.HARRELL-BOND. (1979), Tourism in the Gambia. *Review of African Political Economy* No.14: 78-90.

HARRIS.ROB AND NEIL LEIPER.EDS. (1995), *Sustainable Tourism: An Australian Perspective*. Chatswood: Butterworth-Heinemann Australia.

HARRIS, ROB AND ALISON WALSHAW (1995), Club Mediterranee Lindeman Island. *Sustainable Tourism: Australian Perspective*. Edited by Rob Harris and Neil Leiper. Chatswood: Butterworth-Heinemann Australia, 89-99.

HARRISON, DAVID .ED. (1992a), *Tourism and the Less Developed Countries*. Edited by David Harrison. London:Belhaven Press.

HARRISON, DAVID (1992b), Tourism to Less Developed Countries: The Social Consequences. *Tourism and the Less Developed Countries*. Edited by David Harrison. London: Belhaven Press, 19-34.

HARRISON, DAVID (1994), Tourism and Prostitution: Sleeping with the Enemy? The Case of Swaziland. *Tourism Management,* Vol.15 No.6: 45-443.

HAZLEWOOD, ARTHUR (1979), *The Economy of Kenya: The Kenyatta Era.* New York: Oxford University Press.

HENRY, WESLEY R. (1992), Carrying Capacity, Ecological Impacts and Visitor Attitudes: Applying Research to Park Planning and Management. *Ecotourism and Sustainable Development in Kenya.* Edited by C.G. Gakahu and B.E. Goode. Nairobi: Wildlife Conservation International, 49-61.

HENRY, W.,J. WAITHAKA AND C.G.GAKAHU (1992), Visitor Attitudes, Perceptions, Norms and Use Patterns Influencing Visitor Carrying Capacity. *Tourist Attitudes and Use Impacts in Maasai Mara National Reserve.* Edited by C.G.Gakahu. Nairobi: Wildlife Conservation International, 39-61.

HIGGINS, BRYAN R. (1996), The Global Structure of the Nature Tourism Industry: Ecotourists, Tour Operators, and Local Businesses. *Journal of Travel Research,* Vol. XXXV No. 2:11-18.

HILL,KEVIN A. (1996), Zimbabwe's Wildlife Utilization Programs: Democracy or an Extension of State Power? *African Studies Review,* Vol. 39 No.1: 103-121.

HOFMEIER,ROLF (1988), Regional Cooperation in Crisis or Crisis in Regional Groupings? *Courier,* No.112: 54-57.

HOMEWOOD, K.M.AND W.A. RODGERS (1991), *Maasailand Ecology: Pastoralist Development and Wildlife Conservation in Ngorongoro, Tanzania,* Cambridge: Cambridge University Press.

HORNER, ALICE E. (1993), Tourist Arts in Africa Before Tourism. *Annals of Tourism Research,* Vol. 20 No. 1: 52-63.

HVENEGAARD, GLEN T. (1994), Ecotourism: A Status Report and Conceptual Framework. *Journal of Tourism Studies,* Vol.5 No.2: 24-35.

HYDEN, GORAN (1996), African Studies in the Mid-1990s: Between Afro-Pessimism and Amero-Skepticism. *African Studies Review,* Vol. 39 No.2: 1-17.

INSKEEP, EDWARD (1991), *Tourism Planning: An Integrated and Sustainable Development Approach.* New York: Van Nostrand Reinhold.

INSKEEP, EDWARD (1994), *National and Regional Tourism Planning:m Methodologies and Case Studies.* WTO Publication.London and New York: Routledge.

INTERNATIONAL BANK FOR RECONSTRUCTION AND DEVELOPMENT (1963), *The Economic Development of Kenya.* Baltimore: Johns Hopkins University Press.

INTERNATIONAL LABOUR OFFICE (1972), *Employment, Incomes and Equality: A Strategy for Increasing Productive Employment in Kenya.* Geneva: ILO.

JACKSON, R.T. (1973), Problems of Tourist Industry Development on the Kenyan Coast. *Geography,* Vol. 58: 62-65.

JAETZOLD, RALPH AND HELMUT SCHMIDT, eds. (1982), *Farm Management Handbook of Kenya-Natural Conditions and Farm Management Information-Vol.II/B West Kenya (Nyanza and Western Provinces).* Nairobi: Ministry of Agriculture, Kenya and German Agency for Technical Cooperation.

JAETZOLD RALPH AND HELMUT SCHMIDT, eds. (1983a), *Farm Management Handbook of Kenya Volume II-Natural Conditions and Farm Management Information — Vol. II/B Central Kenya (Rift Valley and Central Provinces).* Nairobi: Ministry of Agriculture, Kenya and German Agency for Technical Cooperation.

JAETZOLD, RALPH AND HELMUT SCHMIDT, eds. (1983b), *Farm Management Handbook of Kenya. Natural Conditions and Farm Management Information Part C East Kenya (Eastern and Coast Provinces).* Nairobi: Ministry of Agriculture, Kenya and Germany Agency for Technical Cooperation.

JAFARI, JAFAR (1990), Research and Scholarship: The Basis of Tourism Education. *Journal of Tourism Studies,* Vol. 1. No. 1: 33-41.

JAPANESE INTERNATIONAL COOPERATION AGENCY AND REPUBLIC OF KENYA (1995a), The Study on the National Tourism Master Plan in the Republic of Kenya: National Tourism Development Master Plan-Draft Final Report Vol.1.Nairobi: Pacific Consultants International.

JAPANESE INTERNATIONAL COOPERATION AGENCY AND REPUBLIC OF KENYA (1995b), The Study on the National Tourism Master Plan in the Republic of Kenya-Priority Tourism Region Development Master Plan-Draft Report Volume 2. Nairobi: Pacific consultants International.

JAPANESE INTERNATIONAL COOPERATION AGENCY AND REPUBLIC OF KENYA. (1995c), The Study on the National Tourism Master Plan in the Republic of Kenya: Environmental Conservation and Management Plan-Draft Final Report Volume 3. Nairobi: Pacific Consultants International.

JAPANESE INTERNATIONAL COOPERATION AGENCY AND REPUBLIC OF KENYA. (1995d), The Study on the National Tourism Master Plan in the Republic of Kenya-Supporting Documents-Draft Final Report Volume 4. Nairobi: Pacific Consultants International.

JOHNSON, PETER AND BARRY THOMAS (1992), Tourism Research and Policy: An Overview. *Perspectives on Tourism Policy*. Edited by Peter Johnson and Barry Thomas. New York: Mansell Publishing Ltd, 1-13.

JOMMO, ROSEMARY BEREWA (1987), *Indigenous Enterprise in Kenya's Tourism Industry*. Itinéraires Etudes du Développement No. 3. Geneva: Institute Universitaire d'Etudes Du Développement.

KAHAMA, C.G. (*Tanzania into the 21st Century*. Dar es Salaam: Tema Publishers.

KANTAI, B.K. OLE (1971), Forward. In S.S. Sankan. *The Maasai*. Nairobi: East African Literature Bureau.

KENYA HUMAN RIGHTS COMMISSION (1997), *Kayas of Deprivation, Kaya of Blood: Violence, Ethnicity and the State in Coastal Kenya*. Nairobi: KHRC

KENYA, REPUBLIC OF (1966a), *Development Plan for the Period 1966-1970*. Nairobi: Government Printer.

KENYA, REPUBLIC OF (1966b), *Economic Survey 1966*. Statistics Division, Ministry of Economic Planning and Development. Nairobi: Government Printer.

KENYA REPUBLIC OF (1970), *Development Plan for the Period 1970-1974*. Nairobi: Government Printer.

KENYA REPUBLIC OF (1971a), Proposed Tourism Resort on the Kenya Coast: Report of the Government Working Party. Town Planning Department. Nairobi: Ministry of Lands and Settlement.

KENYA REPUBLIC OF (1971b),*Economic Survey 1971*. Statistics Division, Ministry of Finance and Economic Planning. Nairobi: Government Printer.

KENYA REPUBLIC OF (1974),*Development Plan for the Period 1974-1978*. Nairobi: Government Printer.

KENYA REPUBLIC OF (1975),*Sessional Paper No. 3 of 1975: Statement on Future Wildlife Management Policy in Kenya*. Nairobi: Government Printer.

KENYA REPUBLIC OF (1979), *Development Plan for the Period 1979-1983*. Nairobi: Government Printer.

KENYA REPUBLIC OF (1980), *Economic Survey 1980*. Nairobi: Government Printer

KENYA REPUBLIC OF (1983), *Report of the Presidential Committee on Unemployment 1982/83*. (Chairman: Maina Wanjigi). Nairobi: Government Printer.

KENYA REPUBLIC OF (1984a), *Development Plan for the Period 1984-1988*. Nairobi: Government Printer.

KENYA REPUBLIC OF (1984b), *Economic Survey 1984*. Nairobi: Government Printer.

KENYA REPUBLIC OF (1985a), *The Wildlife (Conservation and Management)* Act. Chapter 376 Laws of Kenya. Nairobi: Government Printer.

KENYA REPUBLIC OF (1985b), *The Wildlife (Conservation and Management) Amendment Act 1989*. Kenya Gazette Supplement No. 95 (Acts No. 9). Nairobi: Government Printer.

KENYA REPUBLIC OF (1985c), Kwale District Environmental Assessment Report. Nairobi: National Environment Secretariat.

KENYA REPUBLIC OF (1989), *Development Plan for the Period 1989-1993*. Nairobi: Government Printer.

KENYA REPUBLIC OF (1991a), *Development and Employment in Kenya: A Strategy for the Transformation of the Economy-Report of the Presidential Committee on Employment.* Nairobi: Government Printer.

KENYA REPUBLIC OF (1991b), *Economic Survey 1991.* Nairobi: Government Printer.

KENYA REPUBLIC OF (1992), *Report of the Parliamentary Select Committee to Investigate Ethnic Clashes in Western and other Parts of Kenya 1992.* Nairobi: The National Assembly.

KENYA REPUBLIC OF (1993), *Economic survey 1993.* Nairobi: Government Printer.

KENYA REPUBLIC OF (1994a), *Kenya Population Census 1989 Volume 1.* Nairobi: Central Bureau of Statistics, Office of the Vice-President and Ministry of Planning.

KENYA REPUBLIC OF (1994b), *Sessional Paper No. 1 of 1994 on Recovery and Sustainable Development to the Year 2010.* Nairobi: Government Printer.

KENYA REPUBLIC OF (1994c), *Development Plan for the Period 1994-1996.* Nairobi: Government Printer.

KENYA REPUBLIC OF (1994d), *Statistical Abstract 1994.* Nairobi: Government Printer.

KENYA REPUBLIC OF (1994e), *Kenya Population Census 1989 Volume II.* Nairobi: Government Printer.

KENYA REPUBLIC OF (1994f), *Economic Survey 1994.* Nairobi: Government Printer

KENYA REPUBLIC OF (1994g), *Kenya Forestry Beyond 2000: An Overview of the Kenya Forestry Master Plan.* Nairobi: Ministry of Environment and Natural Resources.

KENYA REPUBLIC OF (1994h), *Mombasa District Development Plan 1994-1996.* Nairobi: Office of the Vice-President and Ministry of Planning and National Development.

KENYA REPUBLIC OF (1994i), *Kisii District Development Plan 1994-1996.* Nairobi: Office of the Vice-President and Ministry of Planning and National Development.

KENYA REPUBLIC OF (1995), *Economic Survey 1995.* Nairobi: Government Printer.

KENYA REPUBLIC OF (1995b), *AIDS Cases by District of Reporting Site.* Nairobi: Kenya National AIDS Control Programme. Mimeographed.

KENYA REPUBLIC OF (1996a), *Economic Survey 1996.* Nairobi: Government Printer.

KENYA REPUBLIC OF (1996b), *Kenya Economic Reforms for 1996-1998: The Policy Framework Paper.* Nairobi: Government of Kenya, International Monetary Fund and the World Bank.

KENYA REPUBLIC OF (1997), *The Eighth National Development Plan for the Period 1997 to 2001.* Nairobi: Government Printer.

KENYA REPUBLIC OF (1997b), *Economic Survey 1997.* Nairobi: Government Printer.

KENYA REPUBLIC OF (1998a), *Economic Survey 1998.* Nairobi: Government Printer.

KENYA REPUBLIC OF (1998b), *Budget Speech for the Fiscal Year 1998/99 (1st July — 30th June)* by Simeon Nyachae, Minister for Finance. Nairobi: Government Printer.

KENYA REPUBLIC OF (1998c), *Kenya Gazette,* Vol. C No. 36 (July 1st 1998). Nairobi: Government Printer.

KENYA TIMES (1998), Media Support Vital for Development of Tourism, Editorial, *Kenya Times,* June 16, 1998, p. 6.

KENYA UTALII COLLEGE (1991), General Information on Kenya Utalii College. Nairobi: Kenya Utalii College.

KENYA WILDLIFE SERVICE (1990), A Policy Framework and Development Programme 1991-96. Nairobi: Kenya Wildlife Service.

KENYA WILDLIFE SERVICE (1994), Wildlife-Human Conflicts in Kenya. Report of the Five-Person Review Group 19 December 1994. Nairobi: Kenya Wildlife Service.

KENYA WILDLIFE SERVICE (1996), *Tourism in Kenya: A New Perspective.* Notes prepared by the Kenya Wildlife Service, Tourism Division and Presented by Ms. Isabella Ocholla-Wilson at the Moi University Department of Tourism Staff/Dutch Counterparts Workshop at Kericho on 6 May 1996. Nairobi: Kenya Wildlife Service.

KENYA WILDLIFE SERVICE (n.d.), *Kenya National Parks and Reserves Tour Planner*. Nairobi: Kenya Wildlife Service.

KIHORO, WANYIRI (1998), *Never Say Die: The Chronicle of a Political Prisoner*. Nairobi: East African Educational Publishers.

KILLICK, TONY (1992), *Explaining Africa's Post-Independence Development Experiences*. Working Paper No. 60. London: Overseas Development Institute.

KINYATTI, MAINA WA (1996), *Kenya: A Prison Notebook*. London: Vita Books.

KIPKORIR, B.E., R.C. SOPER AND J.W. SSENYONGA, eds. (1981), *Kerio Valley, Past, Present, and Future*. Proceedings of a Seminar held in Nairobi at the Institute of African Studies, University of Nairobi: Nairobi: University of Nairobi.

KISS, AGNES, ed. (1990), *Living with Wildlife: Wildlife Resource Management with Local Participation in Africa*. World Bank Technical Paper No. 130. Washington D.C.: World Bank.

KLUMPP, DONNA AND CORINNE KRATZ (1993), Aesthetics, Expertise and Ethnicity: Okiek and Maasai Perspectives on Personal Ornament. *Being Maasai: Ethnicity and Identity in East Africa*. Edited by Thomas Spear and Richard Waller. London: James Currey, 195-221.

KNOWLES, JOAN N. AND D.P. COLLETT (1989), Nature as Myth, Symbol and Action: Notes Towards a Historical Understanding of Development and Conservation in Kenyan Maasailand. *Africa*, 59 No. 4: 433-460.

KOIKAI, M.K. (1992), Why Maasai Mara is the Most Visited Reserve in East Africa. *Tourist Attitudes and Use Impacts in Maasai Mara National Reserve*. Edited by C.G. Gakahu. Nairobi: Wildlife Conservation International, 6-10.

KRHODA, GEORGE A. (1994a), Economic Planning Through Drainage Basins in Kenya. *Eastern and Southern Africa Geographical Journal*, Vol. 5 No. 1: 44-55.

KRHODA, GEORGE A. (1994b), The Impact of Water Resources Utilization on Land Use in a Semi-Arid Environment of Amboseli Area in Kenya. *Eastern and Southern Africa Geographical Journal*, Vol. 5 No. 1: 62-67.

KRHODA, GEORGE, O. (f.c.), Water resources development. In Jan Hoorweg, Dick Foeken & R.A.Obudho, eds., *The Kenya Coast Handbook*. Hamburg: Lit Verlag (forthcoming).

LAMB, DAVID (1982), *The Africans*. New York: Random House.

LAMPREY, H.F. (1969), Wild Life as a Natural Resource. *East Africa: Its Peoples and Resources*. Edited by W.T.W. Morgan: Nairobi: Oxford University Press, 141-151.

LANGDON, STEVEN W. (1981), *Multinational Corporations in the Political Economy of Kenya*. London and Basingstoke: Macmillan Press.

LEA, JOHN P. (1981), Changing Approaches Towards Tourism in Africa: Planning and Research Perspectives. *Journal of Contemporary African Studies*, Vol. 1 No. 1: 19-40.

LEA, JOHN P. (1993), *Tourism and Development in the Third World*. London and New York: Routledge.

LEHENY, DAVID (1995), A Political Economy of Asian Sex Tourism. *Annals of Tourism Research*, Vol. 22 No. 2: 267-284.

LEYS, COLIN (1975), *Underdevelopment in Kenya: The Political Economy of Neocoloniaslism 1964-1971*. London: Heinemann.

LINDBERG, KREG, JEREMY ENRIQUEZ AND KEITH SPROULE (1996), Ecotourism Questioned: Case Studies from Belize. *Annals of Tourism Research*, Vol. 23 No. 3: 543-562.

LINDBERG, KREG AND DONALD E. HAWKINS .EDS. (1993), *Ecotourism for Planners and Managers*. North Bennington, Vermont: Ecotourism Society.

LOTODO, F.P.L. (1996), Statement on Child Prostitution in Kenya. *Daily Nation*, August 23, 1996, p. 20.

LUSIOLA, GRACE J. (1992), The Role of the Cobra Project in Economic Development of Local Communities. *Ecotourism and Sustainable Development in Kenya*. Edited by C.G. Gakahu and B.E. Goode Nairobi: Wildlife Conservation International, 125-131.

MAAS, MARIA (1991), Women's Social and Economic Projects: Experiences from Coast Province. Food and Nutrition Studies Programme Report No. 37. Nairobi and Leiden: Ministry of Planning and National Development and African Studies Centre.

MCCARTHY, COLIN (1996), Regional Integration: Part of the Solution or Part of the Problem? *Africa Now: People, Policies and Institutions*. Edited by Stephen Ellis. The Hague, London and Portsmouth: Ministry of Foreign Affairs (DGIS), James Currey and Heinemann, 211-231.

MCKERCHER, BOB (1996), Differences Between Tourism and Recreation in Parks. *Annals of Tourism Research*, Vol. 23 No. 3: 563-575.

MCNEELEY, JEFFREY A. (1995), Economic Incentives for Conserving Biodiversity: Lessons from Africa. *Conservation of Biodiversity in Africa: Local Initiatives and Institutional Roles*. Edited by L.A. Bennun, R.A. Aman and S.A. Crafter. Nairobi: National Museums of Kenya, 199-215.

MAGOME, HECTOR (1996), Land Use Conflicts and Wildlife Management. *Rural Development and Conservation in Africa: Studies in Community Resource Management*. Edited by Paula Hirschoff, Simon Metcalfe, Liz Rihoy and Eren Zink. Harare: Africa Resources Trust, 10-14.

MANDAZA, IBBO (1990), SADCC: Problems of Regional Political and Economic Cooperation in Southern Africa: An Overview. *Regional Integration in Africa: Unfinished Agenda*. Edited by Anyang' Nyong'o. Nairobi: African Academy of Sciences, 141-155.

MARTIN, ESMOND BRADLEY (1973), *The History of Malindi: A Geographical Analysis of an East African Coastal Town from the Portuguese Period to the Present*. Nairobi: East African Literature Bureau.

MARTIN, GUY (1990), The Preferential Trade Area (PTA) for Eastern and Southern Africa: Achievements, Problems and Prospects. *Regional Integration in Africa: Unfinished Agenda*. Edited by Anyang' Nyong'o. Nairobi: African Academy of Sciences, 157-179.

MASCAREHHAS, ADOLFO (1971), Agricultural Vermin in Tanzania. *Studies in East African Geography and Development*. Edited by S.H. Ominde. London: Heinemann, 259-267.

MATHIESON, ALISTER AND GEOFFREY WALL (1982), *Tourism: Economic, Physical and Social Impacts*. Harlow, Essex: Longman Scientific and Technical.

MATZKE, GORDON EDWIN AND NONTOKOZO NABENE (1996), Outcomes of a Community Controlled Wildlife Utilization Program in Zambezi Valley Community. *Human Ecology*, Vol. 24 No. 1: 65-85.

MBOVA, S.M. (1996), Paper presented by the Permanent Secretary, Ministry of Tourism and Wildlife During the Moi University Department of Tourism Staff/Dutch Counterparts Workshop held at Kericho on May 6, 1996. Nairobi; Ministry of Tourism and Wildlife.

MBUGUA, G.G., L.N. MUTHAMI, C.W. MUTURA, S.A. OOGO, P.G. WAIYAKI, C.P. LINDAN AND N. HEARST (1995), Epidemiology of HIV Infection Among Long Distance Truck Drivers, Kenya. *East African Medical Journal*, Vol. 72 No. 8: 515-518.

MEMON, P.A. AND E.B. MARTIN (1976), The Kenya Coast: An Anomaly in the Development of an "Ideal Type" Colonial Spatial System. *Kenya Historical Review* Vol. 4 No. 2: 187-206.

MIDDLETON, JOHN (1992), *The World of the Swahili: An African Mercantile Civilization*. New Haven and London: Yale University Press.

MIDDDLETON, VICTOR T.C. (1977), Some Implications of Overseas Tourism for Regional Development. *Tourism: A Tool for Regional Development*. Edited by Brian S. Duffield. Eastbourne: University of Brighton, 99-107.

MIGOT-ADHOLLA, S.E., KATAMA G.C. MKANGI, JOSEPH MBINDYO, JOHN K. MULAA AND N.O. OPINYA (1982), Study of Tourism in Kenya with Emphasis on the Attitudes of Residents of the Kenya Coast. IDS Consultancy Reports No. 7. Nairobi: University of Nairobi, Institute for Development Studies.

MITCHELL, FRANK (1970), The Value of Tourism in East Africa. *Eastern Africa Economic Review*, Vol. 2 No.1: 1-21.

MITCHELL, LISLE S. AND RICHARD V. SMITH (1989), The Geography of Recreation, Tourism and Sport. *Geography in America*. Edited by Gary L. Gaile and Cort J. Willmott. Columbus, Ohio: Merrill Publishing Co., pp. 387-408.

MORLEY, CLIVE L. (1990), What is Tourism? Definitions, Concepts and Characteristics. *Journal of Tourism Studies*, Vol. 1 No. 1: 3-8.

MUCHIRI, MUCAI (1995), The Potential for Recreational Fisheries in Kenya's Tourism Industry. Department of Tourism Staff Seminar Paper MUDOT8/1994/95. Eldoret: Moi University.

MUGA ERASTO, ed. (1980), *Studies in Prostitution (East, West and South Africa, Zaire and Nevada)*. Nairobi: Kenya Literature Bureau.

MUNYORI, N.K. (1992), Information, Education and Training Needs for Sustaining Tourism. *Ecotourism and Sustainable Development in Kenya*. Edited by C.G. Gakahu and B.E. Goode. Nairobi: Wildlife Conservation International, 109 — 115.

MURINDAGOMO, FELIX (1990), Zimbabwe: WINDFALL and CAMPFIRE. *Living with Wildlife: Wildlife Resource Management with Local Participation*. Edited by Agnes Kiss. World Bank Technical Paper No. 130. Washington D.C.: World Bank, 123-139.

MURPHY, PETER E. (1985), *Tourism: A Community Approach*. New York and London: Routledge.

MUSUVA, J.K. (1992), Present and Future Railway Transport in Africa: The Example of Kenya. *Symposium on Transport and Communication in Africa (Brussels, 27-29 November 1991): Proceedings*. Edited by J.J. Symoens. Brussels: Royal Academy of Overseas Sciences, 263-283.

MUSYOKI, B.M. (1992), Marine National Parks and Reserves of Kenya. *A Proposal for the Establishment of the Mafia Island Marine Park, Tanzania Part II: Proceedings of the Planning Workshop 20th-24th October 1991*. Edited by C.J. Mayers and C.K. Rumisha. Dar es Salaam: World Wide Fund for Nature.

MUSYOKI, BENJAMIN. (1994), *Lamu: The Last Tourist Resort of the Kenya Coast*. Department of Tourism Staff Seminar Paper No. 8/1993/94. Eldoret: Moi University. Mimeographed.

MUTHEE, L.W. (1992), Ecological Impacts of Tourists Use on Habitats and Pressure-Point Animal Species. *Tourist Attitudes and Use Impacts in Maasai Mara National Reserve*. Edited by C.G. Gakahu. Nairobi: Wildlife Conservation International, 18-38.

MUTUA-KIHU (1984), Kenya National Report. *Socio-Economic Activities That May Have an Impact on the Marine and Coastal Environment of the East African Region: National Reports*. UNEP Regional Seas Reports and Studies No. 51. Nairobi: United Nations Environmental Programme, 127-150.

MWAKISHA, JEMIMAH (1995), Trade in the Flesh: The Kenya Link. *Daily Nation* (Nairobi), April 21, 1995.

MWANGI, WANJIKU (1995), Ban Homosexuality. *East African Standard*, August 25, 1995.

NAITORE, JANE (1995), Boom Turned Ruin for Maasai Women. *East African Standard*, August 25, 1995.

NAMIBIA, REPUBLIC OF (1995), Wildlife Management, Utilisation and Tourism in Communal Areas: Policy Document. Windhoek: Ministry of Environment and Tourism.

NAMIBIA, REPUBLIC OF (n.d.), *First National Development Plan (NDPI) Volume 1: 1995/1996-1999/2000*. Windhoek: National Planning Commission.

NATIONAL CHRISTIAN COUNCIL OF KENYA (1968), *Who Controls Industry in Kenya?* Nairobi: East African Publishing House.

NATION, THE DAILY (1995), This Sex Trade is Everyone's Shame, Editorial. *Daily Nation* (Nairobi), October 25,1995, p.6.

NATION, THE DAILY (1996), Tourism Board unveils mission. *Daily Nation*, July 2, 1996, p. BW9.

NATION, THE DAILY (1998), Bed Occupancy Falls. *Daily Nation*, May 15, 1998, p. 5.

NATIONAL ELECTION MONITORING UNIT (1993), Courting Disaster: A Report on the Continuing Terror, Violence and Destruction in the Rift Valley, Nyanza and Western Provinces of Kenya. Nairobi: NEMU.

NDIAYE, B. (1990), Prospects for Economic Integration in Africa. *Regional Integration in Africa: Unfinished Agenda*. Edited by Anyang' Nyong'o. Nairobi: Academy Science Publishers, 35-41.

NELSON, J.G. AND R.W. BUTLER (1974), Recreation and the Environment. *Perspectives on Environment*. Edited by Ian R. Manners and Marvin W. Mikesell. Washington D.C.: Association of American Geographers, 290-310.

NGESA, MILDRED AND JENNIFER WACHIE (1996), It's No to Making 'Sex Work'. *East African Standard*, August 30, 1996.

NGETICH, HENRY (1996), Address to Moi University Department of Tourism Staff and Dutch Counterparts, Kericho, May 6, 1996. Nairobi: Kenya Tourist Development Corporation.

NGUGI, ELIZABETH N. (1995), Sexually Transmitted Diseases (STDs): The Importance of Early Diagnosis and Treatment — A Focus on Women. *A Healthy Balance?* Edited by Elizabeth Hayle. Amsterdam: Women's Health Action Foundation.

NYAMORA, PIUS (1982), The Dehorning of an Editor. *Daily Nation*, July 24, 1982, p. 6.

NYEKI, DANIEL MUSILI (1982), *Wildlife Conservation and Tourism in Kenya*. Nairobi: Jacaranda Designs.

NYONG'O ANYANG', ed. (1990), *Regional Integration in Africa: Unfinished Agenda*. Nairobi: Academy Science Publishers.

OBUDHO, R.A. AND G.O. ADUWO (1990), Small Urban Centres and the Spatial Planning of Kenya. *Small Town Africa: Studies in Rural-Urban Interaction*. Edited by Jonathan Baker. Uppsala: Scandinavian Institute of African Studies.

ODAK, O. (1986), Material Culture of Narok District. Narok District Socio-cultural Profile Draft Report. Edited by G.S. Were, C. Wanjala and J. Olenja. Nairobi: Ministry of Planning and National Development and Institute of African Studies, University of Nairobi, 216-241.

OGOT, BETHWELL A. (1974), Kenya Under the British, 1895 to 1963. *Zamani: A Survey of East African History*. Edited by B.A. Ogot. Nairobi: East African Publishing House and Longman, 249-294.

OGOT, BETHWELL A. (1981), *Historical Dictionary of Kenya*. Metuchen, New Jersey and London: Scarecrow Press.

OJANY, FRANCIS F. (1971), Drainage Evolution in Kenya. *Studies in East African Geography and Development*. Edited by S.H. Ominde. London: Heinemann, 137-145.

OJANY, FRANCIS F. AND REUBEN B. OGENDO (1973), *Kenya: A Study in Physical and Human Geography*. Nairobi: Longman Kenya Ltd.

OJWANG, J.B. (1990), *Constitutional Development in Kenya: Institutional Adaptation and Social Change*. Nairobi: Acts Press.

OLINDO, PEREZ (1991), The Old Man of Nature Tourism: Kenya. *Nature Tourism: Managing for the Environment*. Edited by Tensie Whelan. Washington D.C.: Island Press, 23-38.

OLTHOF, WIM (1995), Wildlife Resources and Local Development: Experiences from Zimbabwe's CAMPFIRE Programme. *Local Resource Management in Africa*. Edited by J.P.M. van den Breemer, C.A. Drijver and L.B. Venema. West Sussex: John Wiley and Sons Ltd, 111-128.

ONDIMU, KENNEDY I. (in prep. *Planning for Tourism in Urban Areas: A Case Study of the Kenya Coast*. Ph.D. Dissertation. Wageningen Agricultural University.

ONGARO, STEPHEN AMBROSE LULALIRE (1995), *Transportation as a Medium for Spatial Interaction: A Case Study of Kenya's Railway Network*. Masters Thesis in Geography. Nairobi: University of Nairobi.

ONGARO, STEPHEN AMBROSE (1996), *Commercial Air Transportation in Kenya: A Geographical Study of Some Aspects of Domestic Flights*. Department of Tourism Staff Seminar MUDOT/10/1995/96. Eldoret: Moi University.

OTIENO, BARRACK (1998), Two Challengers for Kenya Airways. *New African*, No. 366, September 1998, p.31.

OUMA, JOSEPH P.M.B. (1970), *Evolution of Tourism in East Africa (1900-2000)*. Nairobi: Kenya Literature Bureau.

PEAKE, ROBERT (1989), Swahili Stratification and Tourism in Malindi Old Town, Kenya. *Africa* Vol. 59 No. 2: 209-220.

PEARCE, DOUGLAS (1989), *Tourist Development*, 2nd ed. Harlow, Essex: Longman Scientific and Technical.

PERRAULT, KEVIN (1990), Finding the Afro-American *Tourists. Ghana Tourism: Prospects and Possibilities*. Edited by Robert W. Wyllie. Accra: Akan-Torede, 53-72.

PHILIPPI, BRUNO, KAREN R. POLENSKE, EVERETT J. SANTOS AND CLIFFORD WINSTON (1994), Critical Issues in Infrastructure in Developing Countries. *Proceedings of the World Bank Annual Conference on Development Economics 1993*. Edited by Michael Bruno and Boris Pleskovic. Washington D.C.: World Bank, 473-489.

PICKERING H. AND H.A. WILKINS (1993), Do Unmarried Women in African Towns Have to Sell Sex, or is it a matter of Choice? *Health Transition Review*, Supplement to Vol 3: 17-27.

PODHISITA, CHAI, A. PRAMUALRATANA, U. KANUNGSUKKASEM, M.J. WAWER AND R. MCNAMARA (1994), Scio-Cultural Context of Commercial Sex Workers in Thailand: An Analysis of Their Family, Employer, and Client Relations. *Health Transition Review*, Supplement to Vol. 4: 297-320.

POIRIER, ROBERT A. AND STEPHEN WRIGHT (1993), The Political Economy of Tourism in Tunisia. *Journal of Modern African Studies*, Vol. 31 No. 1: 149-162.

POOLE, J.H. (1992), Kenya's Elephants. *Swara*, Vol. 15 No. 1: 29-31.

POPOVIC, VOJISLAV (1972), *Tourism in Eastern Africa*. Munich: Weltforum Verlag.

PRENTICE, RICHARD (1993), *Tourism and Heritage Attractions*. London and New York: Routledge.

PROTHERO, R. MANSELL (1961), Population Movements and Problems of Malaria Eradication in Africa. *Bulletin of World Health Organization*, 24: 405-425.

PRUITT, DEBORAH AND SUZANNE LA FONT (1995), For Love and Money: Romance Tourism in Jamaica. *Annals of Tourism Research*, Vol. 22 No. 2: 422-440.

RAJOTTE, F. (1983), The Potential for Further Tourism Development in Kenya's Arid Lands. *Kenyan Geographer*, Vol. 5 Nos. 1 and 2: 133-144.

REID, DONALD G. (1995), *Work and Leisure in the 21st Century: From Production to Citizenship*. Toronto: Wall and Emerson.

REID, DONALD G., I. SINDIGA, N. EVANS AND S. ONGARO (1998), *Community Participation in Tourism in Kenya*. Report of a Study Supported by CIDA and submitted to the Environmental Capacity Enhancement Project. Guelph: University of Guelph, School for Rural Planning and Development.

RICHTER, LINDA K. (1992), Political Instability and Tourism in the Third World. *Tourism and the Less Developed Countries*. Edited by David Harrison. London: Belhaven Press, 35-46.

RIGBY, PETER (1996), *African Images: Racism and the End of Anthropology*. Oxford and Washington D.C.: Berg.

RODNEY, WALTER (1974), *How Europe Underdeveloped Africa*. Dar es Salaam: Tanzania Publishing House.

ROGGE, JOHN (1993), The Internally Displaced Population in Kenya, Western and Rift Valley Provinces: A Need Assessment and A Programme Proposal for Rehabilitation. Final Report to the UNDP. Nairobi: UNDP.

RUTASITARA, W.K. (1980) Mombasa Bar Girls. *Studies in Prostitution (East, West and South Africa, Zaire and Nevada)*. Edited by E. Muga. Nairobi: Kenya Literature Bureau: 142-182.

RYAN, CHRIS AND RACHEL KINDER (1996), Sex, Tourism and Sex Tourism: Fulfilling Similar Needs? *Tourism Management*, Vol. 17 No. 7: 507-518.

RWEYEMAMU, JUSTINIAN (1973), *Underdevelopment and Industrialization in Tanzania: A Study of Perverse Capitalist Industrial Development*. Nairobi: Oxford University Press.

SAITOTI, TEPILIT OLE (1978), A Maasai Looks at the Ecology of Maasailand. *Munger African Library Notes*. Issue No. 42: 1-24.

SALIM, A.I. (1973), *Swahili-speaking Peoples of Kenya's Coast 1895-1965*. Nairobi: East African Publishing House.

SALIM, A.I. (1992), East Africa: The Coast. *General History of Africa Volume V: Africa from the Sixteenth to the Eighteenth Century*. Edited by B.A. Ogot. Oxford, Berkeley and Paris: Heinemann, California and UNESCO, 750-775.

SCHADLER, KARL FERDINAND (1979), African Arts and Crafts in a World of Changing Values. *Tourism: Passport to Development?* Edited by Emanuael de Kadt. New York: Oxford, 146-156.

SCHOORL, JAAP AND NICO VISSER (1991), Towards Sustainable Coastal Tourism: Environmental Impacts of Tourism on the Kenyan Coast. Discussion Paper. Nairobi: Netherlands Ministry of Agriculture, Nature Management and Fisheries.

SCHWEIKERT, RAINER (1996), Regional Integration in Eastern and Southern Africa. *Africa Insight*, Vol. 26 No. 1: 48-56.

SEAL, J. (1997), Take a Walk on the Wild Side. *The Times* (London), April 19, 1997, Travel Section, p. 19.

SHARPLEY, RICHARD; JULIA SHARPLEY AND JOHN ADAMS (1996), Travel Advice or Trade Embargo? The impacts and Implications of Official Travel Advice. *Tourism Management* Vol. 17 No. 1: 1-7.

SHAW, G. AND A.M. WILLIAMS (1994), *Critical Issues in Tourism: A Geographical Perspective*. Oxford: Blackwell.

SHELDON, PAULINE J. (1990), Journals in Tourism and Hospitality: the Perceptions of Publishing Faculty. *Journal of Tourism Studies*, Vol. 1 No. 1: 42-48.

SHERMAN, PAUL B. AND JOHN A. DIXON (1991), The Economics of Nature Tourism: Determining if it Pays. *Nature Tourism: Managing for the Environment*. Edited by Tensie Whelan. Washington D.C.: Island Press, 89-131.

SHIVJI, I.G, ed. (1975), *Tourism and Socialist Development*. Dar es Salaam: Tanzania Publishing House.

SINCLAIR, M. THEA (1990), *Tourism Development in Kenya*. Consultancy Report. Nairobi: World Bank.

SINCLAIR, M.THEA (1992), Tour Operators in Kenya. *Annals of Tourism Research*, 19: 555-561.

SINCLAIR, M. THEA, PARVIN ALIZADEH AND ELIZABETH ATIENO ADERO ONUNGA (1992), The Structure of International Tourism and Tourism Development in Kenya. *Tourism and the Less Developed Countries*. Edited by David Harrison. London: Belhaven Press, 47-63.

SINCLAIR, M. THEA AND ASRAT TSEGAYE (1990), International Tourism and Export Instability. *Journal of Development Studies*, Vol. 26 No. 3: 487-504.

SINDIGA, ISAAC (1984), Land and Population Problems in Kajiado and Narok, Kenya. *African Studies Review*, 27 No. 1: 23-39.

SINDIGA, ISAAC (1994), Employment and Training in Tourism in Kenya. *Journal of Tourism Studies*, Vol. 5 No. 2: 45-52.

SINDIGA, ISAAC (1995), Wildlife-based Tourism in Kenya: Land Use Conflicts and Government Compensation Policies over Protected Areas. *Journal of Tourism Studies*, Vol. 6 No. 2: 45-55.

SINDIGA, ISAAC (1996a), Domestic Tourism in Kenya. *Annals of Tourism Research*, Vol. 23 No. 1: 19-31.

SINDIGA, ISAAC (1996b), International Tourism in Kenya and the Marginalization of the Waswahili. *Tourism Management*, Vol. 17 No. 6: 425-432.

SINDIGA, ISAAC (1996c), Tourism Education in Kenya. *Annals of Tourism Research*, Vol. 23 No. 3: 698-701.

SINDIGA, ISAAC (f.c.), Tourism. In Jan Hoorweg, Dick Foeken & R.A.Obudho, eds., *The Kenya Coast Handbook*. Hamburg: Lit Verlag (forthcoming).

SINDIGA, ISAAC AND G. WESLEY BURNETT (1988), Geography and Development in Kenya. *Professional Geographer*, Vol. 40 No. 2: 232-237.

SINDIGA, ISAAC AND MARY KANUNAH (1998), Unplanned Tourism in Sub-Saharan Africa with Special Reference to Kenya. *Journal of Tourism Studies* (forthcoming).

SINDIGA, I. AND M. LUKHANDO. (1993), Kenyan University Students' Views on AIDS. *East African Medical Journal*, Vol. 70 No. 11: 713-716.

SINDIYO, J. (1992), Management Proposal for the Mara Dispersal Area. *Tourist Attitudes and Use Impacts in Maasai Mara National Reserve*. Edited by C.G. Gakahu. Nairobi: Wildlife Conservation International, 76-78.

SINDIYO, D.M. AND F.N. PERTET (1984), Tourism and its Impact on Wildlife Conservation in Kenya. *Swara*, Vol. 7 No. 6: 13-17.

SMITH, DAVID LOVATT (1995), *Amboseli: Nothing Short of a Miracle*. Nairobi: Kenway Publications.

SMITH, STEPHEN L.J. (1993), *Tourism Analysis: A Handbook*. Harlow, Essex: Longman Scientific and Technical.

SMITH, VALENE L. (1977), Introduction. *Hosts and Guests: The Anthropology of Tourism*. Edited by Valene L. Smith. Philadelphia: University of Pennsylvania Press, 1-14.

SNELSON, DEBORAH AND PETER LEMBUYA (1990), Protected Areas: Neighbours as Partners Program. *Living with Wildlife: Wildlife Resource Management with Local Participation*. Edited by Agnes Kiss. World Bank Technical Paper Number 130, Africa Technical Department Series. Washington D.C.: World Bank, 103-110.

SOJA, EDWARD W. (1968), *The Geography of Modernization in Kenya: A Spatial Analysis of Social, Economic, and Political Change*. Syracuse: Syracuse University Press.

SOJA, EDWARD W (1979), The Geography of Modernization — A Radical Reappraisal. *The Spatial Structure of Development: A Study of Kenya*. Edited by R.A. Obudho and D.R.F. Taylor. Boulder: Westview Press, 28-45.

SOMBROEK, W.G., H.M.H. BRAUN AND B.J.A. VAN DER POUW (1982), *Exploratory Soil Map and Agro-Climatic Zone Map of Kenya 1980*. Exploratory Soil Survey Report No. E1. Nairobi: Kenya Soil Survey.

SOMMER, AGNES (no date *Retour Nairobi*. Amsterdam: Babylon-De Geus.

SONYIKA, WOLE (1985), The Arts in Africa During the Period of Colonial Rule. *Africa under Colonial Domination 1880-1935*. Unesco General History of Africa VII. Edited by A. Adu Boahen. Paris: UNESCO.

SPEAR, THOMAS (1993), Introduction. *Being Maasai: Ethnicity and Identity in East Africa*. Edited by T. Spear and R. Walter. London: James Currey, 1-18.

SPENCER, PAUL (1988), *The Maasai of Matapato: A Study of Rituals of Rebellion*. Manchester: Manchester University Press.

STANDARD, THE (1982), Detention Without Trial. *The Standard*, July 20, 1982, p. 4.

SUMMARY, REBECCA M. (1987), Tourism's Contribution to the Economy of Kenya. *Annals of Tourism Research*, Vol. 14: 531-540.

SUTTON, J.E.G. (1976), The Kalenjin. *Kenya Before 1900: Eight Regional Studies*. Edited by B.A. Ogot. Nairobi: East African Publishing House, 21-52.

SWAINSON, NICOLA (1980), *The Development of Corporate Capitalism in Kenya 1918-77*. London: Heinemann Educational Books.

TAGAMA, HERALD (1998), Bombs Hit East African Tourism. *New African*, No. 367 (October 1998), p. 31.

TALBOT L. AND P. OLINDO (1990), The Maasai Mara and Amboseli Reserves. *Living with Wildlife: Wildlife Resource Management with Local Participation in Africa*. Edited by Agnes Kiss. World Bank Technical Paper No. 130. Washington D.C.: World Bank, 67-74.

TAYLOR, D.R.F. (1992), Development from Within and Survival in Rural Africa: A Synthesis of Theory and Practice. *Development from Within: Survival in Rural Africa.* Edited by D.R.F. Taylor and Fiona Mackenzie. London and New York: Routledge, 214-258.

TEYE, VICTOR B. (1986), Liberation Wars and Tourism Development in Africa: The Case of Zambia. *Annals of Tourism Research* Vol. 13: 589-608.

TEYE, VICTOR B. (1988), Coups d'etat and African Tourism: A Study of Ghana. *Annals of Tourism Research*, Vol. 15: 329-356.

TEYE, VICTOR B. (1991), Prospects for Regional Tourism Cooperation in Africa. *Managing Tourism.* Edited by S. Medlik. Oxford Butterworth-Heinemann, 286-296.

THIONG'O NGUGI WA (1977), *Petals of Blood.* London: Heinemann.

THIONG'O, NGUGI WA (1981), Detained: A Writer's Prison Diary. Nairobi: Heinemann Educational Books.

THIONG'O, NGUGI WA (1983), *Moving the Centre: The Struggle for Cultural Freedoms.* Nairobi: East African Educational Publishers.

TIBAZARWA, C.M. (1988), The East African Community — A Tragedy in Regional Cooperation. *Courier* No. 112: 48-50.

TOLE, MWAKIO P. (f.c.), Environmental Problems. In Jan Hoorweg, Dick Foeken & R.A.Obudho, eds., *The Kenya Coast Handbook.* Hamburg: Lit Verlag (forthcoming).

TOSUN, CEVAT AND C.L. JENKINS (1996), Regional Planning Approaches to Tourism Development: The Case of Turkey. *Tourism Management* Vol. 17 No. 7: 519-531.

TURTON, B.J. AND C.C. MUTAMBIRWA (1996), Air Transport Services and the Expansion of International Tourism in Zimbabwe. *Tourism Management,* Vol. 17 No. 6: 453-462.

TUYA, S. OLE (1992), Keynote Speech. *Tourist Attitudes and Use Impacts in Maasai Mara National Reserve:* Proceedings of a Workshop Organized by Wildlife Conservation International at Maasai Mara National Reserve, March 1991. Edited by C.G. Gakahu. Nairobi: Wildlife Conservation International, 3-5.

UBWANI, ZEPHANIA (1998), Tourist Gate Dispute in Focus. *East African,* May 18-24: 18.

UNDP AND WTO (1993), National Tourism Development Planning Programme for Kenya. Nairobi: United Nations Development Programme and World Tourism Organization.

UNECA (1989), *African Alternative Framework to Structural Adjustment Programmes for Socio-Economic Recovery and Transformation.* Addis Ababa: United Nations Economic Commission for Africa.

URRY, JOHN (1991), *The Tourist Gaze: Leisure and Travel in Contemporary Societies.* London: Sage Publications.

VILLIERS, JOHN DE (1994), *Day of the Broadbill.* Nairobi and London: Equatorial Books.

VIRANI, M. (1995), The Sokoke Scops Owl Project: Who gives a Hoot? *Swara,* Vol. 18 No. 1: 24-27.

VISSER, N. AND A. KOYO (1992), Coastal Tourism: Impacts and Linkages with Inland Destinations and Amenities. *Ecotourism and Sustainable Development in Kenya.* Edited by C.G. Gakahu, and B.C. Goode. Nairobi: Wildlife Conservation International, 63-98.

VISSER, N. AND S. NJUGUNA (1992), Environmental Impacts of Tourism on the Kenya Coast. *UNEP Industry and Environment,* Vol. 15 No. 3-4: 42-52.

WALL, GEOFFREY (1996), Rethinking Impacts of Tourism. *Progress in Tourism and Hospitality Research,* Vol. 2: 207-215.

WASS, P. (1994), A Forest with A Future? The Challenge of Conserving the Arabuko-Sokoke Forest. *Swara,* Vol. 17 No. 3: 8-11.

WEEKLY REVIEW (1998), The Tourist Industry on the Mend. *Weekly Review,* May 22, 1998, pp. 17-18.

WEILER, BETTY (1995), Ecotourism Association of Australia. *Sustainable Tourism: An Australian Perspective.* Edited by Rob Harris and Neil Leiper. Chatswood: Butterworth-Heinemann Australia, 63-68.

WESTERN, DAVID (1982a), Amboseli National Park: Enlisting Landowners to Conserve Migratory Wildlife. *Ambio*, Vol. 11 No. 5: 302-308.

WESTERN, DAVID (1982b), Amboseli. *Swara* Vol. 5 No. 4: 8-14.

WESTERN, DAVID (1992a), Taking Stock of the Ivory Ban. *Swara*, Vol. 15 No. 1: 21-23.

WESTERN, DAVID (1992b), Ecotourism: The Kenya Challenge. *Ecotourism and Sustainable Development in Kenya*. Edited by C.G. Gakahu and B.E. Goode. Nairobi: Wildlife Conservation International.

WESTERN, DAVID (1992c), Planning and Management for Optimal Visitor Capacity. *Tourist Attitudes and Use Impacts in Maasai Mara National Reserve*. Edited by C.G. Gakahu. Nairobi: Wildlife Conservation International, 66-75.

WESTERN, DAVID (1993), Defining Ecotourism. *Ecotourism: A Guide for Planners and Managers*. Edited by Kreg Lindberg and Donald E. Hawkins. North Bennington, Vermont: Ecotourism Society, 7-11.

WESTERN, DAVID AND R. MICHAEL WRIGHT (1994), The Background to Community-Based Conservation. *Natural Connections: Perspectives in Community-Based Conservation*. Edited by David Western and R. Michael Wright. Washington D.C.: Island Press, 1-12.

WHELAN, TENSIE (1991), Ecotourism and its Role in Sustainable Development. *Nature Tourism: Managing for the Environment:* Edited by Tensie Whelan. Washington D.C.: Island Press, 3-22.

WILLIAMS, ANTHONY V. (1976), Tourism. *Contemporary Africa: Geography and Change*. Edited by C. Gregory Knight and James L. Newman. Englewood Cliffs, New Jersey: Prentice Hall, 457-465.

WILSON, G.M. (1980), A Study of Prostitution in Mombasa. *Studies in Prostitution (East, West and South Africa, Zaire and Nevada)*. Edited by E. Muga. Nairobi: Kenya Literature Bureau: 130-141.

WORLD BANK (1989), *Sub-Saharan Africa: From Crisis to Sustainable Growth — A Long-Term Perspective Study*. Washington D.C.: World Bank.

WORLD BANK (1991), *World Development Report 1991*: The Challenge of Development. New York: Oxford University Press.

WORLD BANK (1994), *World Development Report 1994: Infrastructure for Development:* New York: Oxford University Press.

WORLD BANK (1995), *African Development Indicators* 1994-95. Washington D.C.: World Bank.

WTO (1997), Personal Communication, 28 February 1997.

WTO (1997), Personal Communication, 2 April 1997.

WTO (1998), Personal communication, 1 June, 1998.

WRIGHT, STEPHEN AND ROBERT A. POIRIER (1991), Tourism and Economic Development in Africa. *TransAfrica Forum*, Vol. 8 No. 1: 13-27.

ZARWAN, JOHN (1975), The Social and Economic Network of an Indian Family Business in Kenya, 1920-1970. *Kroniek van Afrika*, 1975/3 New Series No. 6: 219-236.

ZEHENDER, WOLFGANG (1988), Regional Cooperation in Perspective — Some Experiences in Sub-Saharan Africa. *Courier*, No. 112: 51-53.

ZWANENBERG, R.M.A. VAN, WITH ANNE KING (1975), *An Economic History of Kenya and Uganda 1800-1970*. London: Macmillan Press.

Research Series of the African Studies Centre, Leiden, The Netherlands

1. Dick Foeken & Nina Tellegen
   1994
   Tied to the land. Living conditions of labourers on large farms in Trans Nzoia District, Kenya

2. Tom Kuhlman
   1994
   Asylum or Aid? The economic integration of Ethiopian and Eritrean refugees in the Sudan

3. Kees Schilder
   1994
   Quest for self-esteem. State, Islam and Mundang ethnicity in Northern Cameroon

4. Johan A. van Dijk
   1995
   Taking the waters. Soil and water conservation among settling Beja nomads in Eastern Sudan

5. Piet Konings
   1995
   Gender and class in the tea estates of Cameroon

6. Thera Rasing
   1995
   Passing on the rites of passage. Girls' initiation rites in the context of an urban Roman Catholic community on the Zambian Copperbelt

7. Jan Hoorweg, Dick Foeken & Wijnand Klaver
   1995
   Seasons and nutrition at the Kenya coast

8. John A. Houtkamp
   1996
   Tropical Africa's emergence as a banana supplier in the inter-war period

9. Victor Azarya
   1996
   Nomads and the state in Africa: the political roots of marginality

10. Deborah Bryceson & Vali Jamal, eds.
    1997
    Farewell to farms. De-agrarianization and employment in Africa

11. Tjalling Dijkstra
    1997
    Trading the fruits of the land: horticultural marketing channels in Kenya

12. Nina Tellegen
    1997
    Rural enterprises in Malawi: necessity or opportunity?

13. Klaas van Walraven
    1999
    Dreams of power. The role of the organization of African Unity in the politics of Africa 1963 - 1993

14. Isaac Sindiga
    Tourism and African development. Change and challenge of tourism in Kenya

Copies can be ordered at: Ashgate Publishing Ltd.
Gower House
Croft Road
Aldershot
Hampshire GU11 3HR
England